THE OLDEST

THE OLDEST

IN CELEBRATION OF BRITAIN'S LIVING HISTORY

JULIAN CALDER & ALASTAIR BRUCE

CASSELL ILLUSTRATED

CONTENTS

FOREWORD

previous pages
page 1 The oldest sweet shop, Pateley Bridge, Yorkshire, see page 140.
page 2 The oldest stone-built castle, Chepstow, see page 130.
page 4 The oldest fair, Goose Fair, Nottingham, see page 100.

right
Britain's oldest native mammal, an Exmoor pony, on Winsford Hill.

STORIES FROM HISTORY and lavish period dramas have given us a romantic view of the past. I was curious and excited when I set off on the task of photographing my list of oldest subjects. I did most of my intial research on the internet, which Alastair then followed up with his own at archives and libraries. In many cases, I had no vision of what I was going to photograph until I saw it myself. I drove around the country for a month, meeting people and looking at subjects before I even began to take any pictures, and in a lot of cases I had to return several times. It soon became apparent that many of the oldest things are very ordinary but this is precisely why they have survived. They are off the beaten track and if you were not looking for them, you could easily miss them. In many cases time has passed them by, but other subjects – businesses, some institutions and sports – have evolved and kept going by adapting to the demands of the time. There are many family businesses that are over 300 years old. Other subjects have recently been rediscovered and revived by people fired up with enthusiasm by the quirkiness of our history

I covered 22,000 miles around Ireland and the British Isles while taking photographs, meeting many people on the way who were passionate about their involvement in their particular 'oldest' subject, which always compensated for bad weather or my initial disappointment that the subject was not as beautiful or as photogenic as I had imagined.

It is interesting to view old Britain, by looking at maps, and to speculate why certain areas were so important. Why were Zennor, the Dingle Peninsula and the Orkneys so significant 3500 years ago? Why have so many old shops survived in London's St. James's?

The selection of subjects in the book is completely subjective. They are
my choice and I make no apologies for those I have had to leave out. These
are, purely and simply, the collection that appealed to me. I do apologise
if others can claim to be older than any I have chosen. We have done our best
to verify the claims of those in the book but we cannot claim that we have got
everything 100 per cent right. Above all, we hope we have proved that history
is a living subject.

JULIAN CALDER

INTRODUCTION

THE DESCRIPTION, 'OLDEST' is often more difficult to prove than others – such as newest, longest, shortest, biggest, smallest, highest, lowest, cheapest and most expensive. However, in gathering together some of the oldest things in the British Isles, which can not be placed in a museum, this book hopes to find out how and why each came into existence, what it tells us about the people of these islands and what enabled each to survive. In many cases, a respected authority associated with each subject has been called upon to adjudicate between competing claims for antiquity and, as none of us lived to see the first pub open or watch the first castle built, the choice is arguably neither empiric nor assailable.

These islands have a national history that is probably better known than most in the world because of the influence of imperial education and the recent popularisation of British history through film, both in America and Britain. Icons, such as Henry VIII, King Arthur and William Wallace inspire recognition further afield than Belfast, London, Edinburgh, Dublin and Cardiff. Standing before the tomb of Edward the Confessor in Westminster, the Stone of Destiny in Edinburgh, the ancient parliament on Tynwald Hill in the Isle of Man there is a sense of destiny reached.

Compared to many civilisations in the world, British and Irish culture is not that ancient. Others that predate our own have scattered the Mediterranean, the Nile river and the former imperial cities across the world with ancient monuments, waterways and earthworks. Each was testament to a people's greatness, ingenuity and need. Most are now in ruin, the unfortunate victims of the vicissitudes of politics, war and neglect. The few that stand, known and unknown, conjure fascination. Tourists and academics alike stand in awe of the men and women whose minds and hands fashioned these objects from the past. They stare and try to imagine the lives lived by the craftsmen and labourers. What was life actually like for these people? Their imaginations may struggle to reach beyond the comforts of this century, to grasp a mind gripped by the simplicities of subsistence, love, death and God.

All these unanswerable questions fill the minds of travellers in the British Isles too. Why did our ancestors drag vast menhirs from the coast of Wales to an apparent waste ground in Wiltshire? By comparison, the oldest orchestra in these islands is not difficult to comprehend. However, discovering how the orchestra came into existence tells us an enormous amount about the evolution of music as a language – itself one of the oldest forms of communication known to Man. The oldest regiment can breathe tangible reality into the understanding of the very real chaos of insecurity that existed in these islands for centuries and may, in one sphere, only now be closing on peace. Leaving the motorway, a road stretches before us, sometimes as straight as any soldier's crease. Littered with road sign warnings of hidden dips, we see the design fault of the Roman builders who thought 30 miles per day quite fast enough, let alone 30 miles an hour, along the oldest roadways of the kingdom.

Age is not an attribute in itself, as those who suffer its tribulations will explain, but it brings with it the dignity of provenance, of knowledge and, occasionally, of wisdom. The oldest person, along with all living fauna, is not included in this book, but, just as time spent in the company of the oldest in our family or community is seldom wasted, neither is discovering the oldest objects that these lands have gathered as treasure. Their survival is also their vulnerability. We can see how ideology can damage the, mostly inanimate, oldest things in our care. The Dissolution and Reformation destroyed swathes of architecture and art in a few decades leaving headless saints to remind us of the innate human cruelty that can come to the surface in ideological violence. How many people lost their heads in the same way as these old statues? What a fascinating story these twice martyred symbols now represent.

Oldest either is or isn't. And that is what makes travelling these islands in search of the oldest example of everything so intrinsically special. Reaching the oldest thing, feeling its value to us all and trying to capture its story in words and pictures is what this book is about.

ALASTAIR BRUCE

Authors note: Throughout this book, the terms Britain/British have been used in their loosest possible geographical sense to refer to not only England, Scotland and Wales, but also the Channel Islands and the Isle of Man. On occasion, 'British Isles' has also been used to refer to the UK and Ireland.

NATURE

HUMANITIES REFERENCE

LANDSCAPE

previous pages

A rainbow fills the sky over the Caledonian Forest, the oldest forest (see page 34).

right

The lighthouse standing on the ancient rocks at the Butt of Lewis is battered by a storm force gale in November. The Hebrides are thought to have been created as a result of a rise in sea level at the end of the Ice Age, about 8000 years ago.

OLDEST ROCK FORMATION

Along the shoreline of Lewis, an island just off Scotland's West Coast, much of the sturdy stone underfoot is part of the oldest rock formation in Britain. In this wild place, where the sea fingers its way into the deep loch inlets, two great powers are evident. First, the speed and danger of the tide, as the sea rushes to keep pace with lunar demands, and also the ferocious geological tumult that must have caused this tortured but beautiful landscape.

All around are the gnarled rock formations thrust up from the seabed by millions of years of geological change. Below the sea's surface these cliffs and ravines plunge into the deep apex of their conflict between the mainland and its continental shelf. Apparently all is benign now, but among the smooth worn stones and limpet covered rocks are veins of quartz, feldspar, hornblende and mica. It is estimated that this bonded coarse mix was forged and crystallised about 3000 million years ago, some 25 miles below the Earth's surface, at temperatures and under pressures that only prolonged nuclear explosion might be able to imitate today. The fold of what is called Lewisian Gneiss forms part of the backbone for the Hebrides archipelago. Much else was carried here in the midst of a cooling and shifting world but no coagulum of rock has so ancient a story to share.

Brilliant white features of quartz, sometimes carrying within them both deep pink-red or green tinctures, appear wherever you tread along the West Coast of Scotland, fooling children into thinking that they have discovered precious marble. The mica from this ancient geological battle was a favoured raw material in the furnaces of industrial Britain and played its part in the armament production of the First World War. However, even the madness of human conflict could not compare with the violent foundry where this raw material was forged.

OLDEST LAND MANAGEMENT

Marking out territory is an instinct, and flight and an aerial perspective have enabled scientists to look more thoroughly at the way our ancestors farmed their landscape. Evidence of Neolithic agriculture at Zennor in Cornwall is provided by unmistakable physical remains of some of the oldest boundaries created by man.

On the uplands of the Penwith peninsular, towards the tip of Britain at Lands End, are the oldest granite 'hedges' that have been discovered. These hedges are not just lines of bushes but carefully constructed walls built either side of a core of earth. The oldest are just a line of substantial boulders, called grounders, which have been dragged into line. Many consist of both the grounders as a core and the walls either side, with the gaps filled with earth. The best place to see these granite hedges in around the village of Zennor, which is just north from Treen and takes its name from the female 11th century saint called St Sinar.

Looking north across Tremedda near the Cornish village of Zennor. The fields are enclosed by stone boundaries which are amongst the world's oldest artefacts still in use. The average field size is about 3 acres.

But Neolithic Man lived in other parts of Britain too, and to find traces of this ancient culture elsewhere, ecologists have looked for similarities in hedgerows across the southern lowlands. The signature of design that denotes the granite hedges and banking is called co-axial. This means that while there are two parallel sides to a Neolithic field enclosure, the top and bottom are almost always set at an angle and these are often randomly different. Placing this criterion on the landscape, various areas have a similar signature.

OLDEST HEDGEROWS

Clues about the evolution of the human species can be seen everywhere, and few features of landscape provide more tangible signs of the earliest human cultivation of the British Isles than the field boundaries on Devon's Exmoor. The oldest of these are simple banks that date from the Bronze Age, over 3,000 years ago. The construction of the banks has altered over the centuries because this area remained useful to succeeding generations, who used their own techniques and skills to reinforce them. Evidence of Saxons usage is also visible, as construction in this period used trees that bordered a fresh clearing, turning the banks into hedges. During the middle ages, some of the banks were further reinforced using stones that had been lifted from the field they enclosed. The banks were built up into walls and covered with earth so that hedges could grow on top to strengthen the boundary. The result was sturdy, and the trees and hedges enclosed the animals and gave them shelter. Sadly, damage has been done to these ancient boundaries in recent years because changes in farming practices have favoured larger fields and boundaries that are cheaper to maintain. Although efforts have been made to protect the banks and hedges, the work of maintaining and 'banking up' is both time consuming and labour intensive: this in itself is a clue to the intensely manual life that our ancestors led.

The banking near Weddon Cross on Exmoor. The National Parks are renovating and maintaining the hedges. Although labour intensive, this keeps alive century-old skills.

Wheel Stones seen from White Tor on Derwent Edge. There are walks of every type in the national park, from a gentle Sunday stroll along Derwent Resevoir to an 8-hour trek over Kinder Scout requiring stamina and full foul weather kit as conditions can change for the worse.

Looking more closely from the ground and bearing in mind the other evidence that has been found, there are three places in England that are thought to have the oldest ordinary hedgerows, which were probably laid out in the Neolithic Bronze or Iron Age. The first of these is near the village of Diss, on the Norfolk border with Suffolk, where early settlers were attracted to farming the boulder clay lowlands. Second, there are traces of co-axial hedgerows at Dengie in Essex, and, finally, there is evidence of hedgerows at the foot of the Chiltern Hills in Hertfordshire. Jon Stokes, who is Director of Community Projects for The Tree Council says, 'Looking at these sites you get a sensation of stepping back into the past, into the peace and quiet. It is like finding a slice of the past written into the fields and nobody realises what they are looking at when they walk past these hedges'.

OLDEST NATIONAL PARK

The modern world places a heavy burden upon the natural environment. This increases every year with exponential speed. In most peoples' lifetime their towns and cities have expanded noticeably. Juxtaposing this growth against the finite resources available and the speed of change, it was perhaps just in time that the Labour Government passed legislation to protect areas of countryside and to declare them as National Parks.

This decision was provoked by direct action. In 1932 hundreds of walkers engaged in a 'mass trespass' of Kinder Scout, one of the most prominent peaks. Legislation followed the American example, where national parks had been established to protect beautiful areas from development. In 1951, the Peak District was designated Britain's first National Park and it is therefore

until the 20th century, the challenge came from both industrialisation and taxation. The latter increased, after the People's Budget in 1911, and hitherto philanthropic land owners looked to exploit their assets for financial survival. They did this by selling land for development. This was facilitated by society's growing need for housing and its infrastructure.

Vast populations around its boundary can now enjoy the Peak District, treading in the steps of our earliest ancestors. The tradition for protection continues (as does development) and recently the New Forest was added to the list of National Parks.

OLDEST NATIONAL TRUST PROPERTY

Before persuading a friend to give some land, called Dinas Oleu, to the National Trust in 1895, Miss Octavia Hill had learnt a thing or two about life. She was a granddaughter of Doctor Southwood Smith, the pioneer of sanitary reform, and she followed his example by establishing homes for the poor in London's Marylebone district. She helped them in every way possible, even providing a room in her own house where they could come for advice. To be sure of their wellbeing she insisted on visiting each tenant every week and collecting the rents herself. Octavia and her sister Miranda were philanthropists. They were not wealthy but they tried to ease the plight of many caught in the industrialisation of inner cities. They led a movement to bring beauty into the homes of the poor and it was this eccentric activity that led them to see how access to open spaces would ease the privations of 19th

Just a short walk up the hill behind Barmouth is Dinas Oleu with spectacular views of the miles of sand that edge Cardigan Bay.

the oldest. Ironically, it also encompasses some of the oldest clues to the nation's earliest civilisations. Mesolithic hunter-gatherers scoured these hills for boar and wolves, scattering the archaeological footprint of flint axes in the peat. The Nine Ladies stone circle on Stanton Moor poses more questions than it answers about the Beaker people of the Bronze Age, who had some purpose for these menhirs. The Roman fort at Navio, near Brough, may be the finest site of its kind in the park. The Normans were quick to declare the area subject to Forest Law and here kings and their tenants-in-chief enjoyed the Royal Forest, its trees and deer – which they called vert and venison.

Since feudal times the responsibility for land management had been left to manors and their owners. The Peak District was divided into administrative structures answerable to shire authorities. Protected in this way

century poverty. Two months after the National Trust was established, Octavia persuaded her friend, Mrs Fanny Talbot, to make over 4.5 acres of Welsh coastline in trust for the nation. The land, called Dinas Oleu, which means Fortress of Light, is the oldest possession among the trust's growing chest of riches. There are now 600 miles of British coastline protected by the National Trust's Neptune Coastline Campaign. Each of these sites is protected from development, which was the reason Octavia stepped in to help in 1895. Thus the threat of development was sensed even before the 20th century dawned. The National Trust and its voluntary gifts and contributions embrace an enormous scope of national nature and culture, bringing beauty into the lives of us all.

OLDEST LONDON PARK

It is always surprising to find enclosed green spaces in the midst of urban developments. London is fortunate, by comparison with most European capitals, in that its sprawling growth has hardly touched the many Royal Parks that monarchs have established over time to improve their sport, leisure and larders. The first of these enclosures was laid out in 1433 at Greenwich, just south of the River Thames and to the east of the City of London. Today, the oldest Royal Park still consists of 186 acres within walls and Royal gates, and is just 14 acres short of the land Henry VI originally granted to Humphrey, Duke of Gloucester. Then, as now, the instinct of power and wealth was to secure territory around a residence as a luxury – in those days it was also to keep disease at bay. Within these parks deer were bred and sport could be pursued without the danger of poachers; strict laws enforced the owner's whim. When Humphrey died in 1447, Henry VI took Greenwich for his new wife, Margaret of Anjou. No children survived to succeed this hapless king but Greenwich was to be the nursery of many monarchs. Henry VIII grew up here and developed his love of ships by the river, while his two daughters, Mary and Elizabeth, were born here. Their respective lives were to divide the nation. Now the world is divided by the Meridian line, which passes through the Royal Observatory located here, symbolising how man has

The boathouse on the lake at Birkenhead Park on the Wirrall. The Park has benefitted from Heritage Lottery money to bring the Grade 1 listed landscape back to its former glory. It is also the oldest publicly-funded park.

sought to understand and master the world. While Royal Astrologers scrutinised the heavens from its telescopes the park's seasons have brought sap and life into the landscape of Greenwich since the 15th century.

Outside London, Henry II built a palace complete with park at Woodstock in the 12th century, where he wooed his mistress, the Fair Rosamund. This park is now part of the grounds of Blenheim Palace, and a well remains that is named after the 12th century beauty – Rosamund's Well.

OLDEST NATURE RESERVE

Charles Darwin went to Cambridge as a student in the 1820s to become a clergyman, but he was fascinated by entomology. When possible, he travelled to Wicken Fen, 12 miles north, to explore the wetlands and search for beetles. These specimens formed the foundation for a career that changed the scientific understanding of life. However, as his lessons were being absorbed the Fens themselves came under threat. Their existence resulted from human cultivation and shaping of the marsh (peat was dug up for fuel and sedge was cut to cover roofs), but

towards the end of the 19th century these practices fell into decline as other materials were cheaper and the Fens were gradually drained for other cultivation or were taken over by encroaching scrub. The key to their survival was work by Frederick Bond in the 1850s. He documented the plethora of moth and butterflies that thrived in this declining habitat. Popularity with lepidopterists raised the profile of Wicken Fen's plight. Though it was not possible to employ the large number of people needed to work the Fen properly, the National Trust bought parts of the area in 1899. The reserve is now over 800 acres in size. Work is done by a small number of dedicated wardens, with the assistance of volunteers. These were originally press ganged from the Royal Navy's training base in Ipswich, but now the work is supported by holidaymakers dedicated to the lessons that scientists like Darwin inspired.

OLDEST MUNICIPAL PARK

Britain's national conscience awoke to reform in the 1830s. The Great Reform Act changed the social balance of power, slavery was abolished and, in the lee of the Industrial Revolution, it was time to improve the conditions of working families. Birkenhead was a quiet market town on the Wirral peninsular, separated from the extreme industrialisation of Liverpool by the narrow river Mersey. However, the arrival of a steam ferry changed the town into a dormitory of the city overnight. Action was taken with an Act of Parliament to improve the town. To provide the growing population with leisure facilities, land was bought for development into a public park that would mimic the space and virtues of the gardens of a stately home. In 1843, the committee developing this public space engaged Joseph Paxton's magical skills as a landscape gardener. He built a scale model of the existing topography and then worked out his vistas, lakes and banks. He tried each plan in a sandpit, training his eye at the height of the people who would experience the completed park. When Lord Morpeth opened the Park in 1847 it coincided with the opening of Birkenhead's new docks, from which much of the stone used to build the fine lodges and pavilions that punctuate the vistas was cut. The oldest Municipal Park was a complete success and still serves the people of Birkenhead well. It inspired the Parks Movement in the United Kingdom, which campaigned for public spaces in other cities and towns. It also prompted the fathers of New York to grasp the basalt heart of Manhattan Island and create Central Park, probably the most well known municipal park in the world.

OLDEST BOTANIC GARDENS

The Oxford Botanical Garden may have inspired Lewis Carroll to develop the imaginary world of *Alice in Wonderland* and JRR Tolkein to conjure up Middle Earth

The walled garden is the oldest part of Oxford's Botanical Garden, where it stretches towards the church tower of Magdalene College. The gardens contain over 7000 species of plants.

for the *Lord of the Rings,* but it was created in 1621 to harbour and nurture the properties of plants that world exploration had discovered.

Trade across Asia and Africa had introduced exotic plants and spices into Europe. With them came stories of hidden, almost magical, healing properties which became absorbed into the crude medical mantra of the Middle Ages. Mastery of the seas in the 16th century brought life-changing plants to Britain, including the potato, the tomato and tobacco. However, many other species had been found and science sought to learn from them. Thus in 1621, Henry Danvers, who was Earl of Danby, founded the nation's first Physic Garden, now called the Botanic Garden, on the site of a Jewish cemetery next to Magdalen College in Oxford. He built a high wall to protect the tropical plants from wind and encourage growth. Ever since then, the garden has given science a growing array of opportunities to study species, their habitats and properties. One famous plant brought here in 1728 from the slopes of Mount Etna escaped: the yellow Oxford ragwort is now the scourge of Britain's countryside.

Covent Garden in London is still dominated by St. Paul's Church, which is called the Actors' Church. Little else remains of the original square but it continues to be the cosmopolitan centre of the vibrant West End.

OLDEST HEDGE MAZE

After the Glorious Revolution in 1688, two Protestant monarchs, William III and Mary II were offered joint sovereignty by Parliament. For them it must have been confusing to succeed in a time of constitutional chaos. However, the pair came to Hampton Court – which had been home and palace to Cardinal Wolsey and monarchs since Henry VIII – and engaged Christopher Wren to rebuild its state apartments. Outside, the vast garden was ordered into broad radiating avenues. Perhaps to mirror the state of Britain they inherited from the exiled James II, part of this design involved a Wilderness Garden. One of its most famous surviving features is the oldest maze in Britain. It was planted in 1691, the year after William's critical defeat of James at the Battle of the Boyne. There was much to celebrate and this distraction, originally planted with hornbeam, covered 1,350 square metres and enclosed half a mile of confusing paths. Over time, the hornbeam was re-planted with yew. There is a trick to finding the correct path, but for three centuries this has been one of the chief attractions of one of Britain's most magnificent Palaces.

Sid Fuller has tended his allotment, in Nottingham's Hunger Hill allotment garden, for 18 years. Amongst other things, he grows red beans and cabbages, the food he missed when he came to Britain from the West Indies.

OLDEST SQUARE

The first square to be laid out in London was at Covent Garden in the 1630s. The scheme was a shock to Londoners, who had never seen Italian-style piazzas surrounded by houses and were used to winding streets and avenues. The Earl of Bedford was persuaded to construct the first British square by his architect, Inigo Jones, who was also the King's Surveyor of Works. The land at Covent Garden had been in his family's hands since the Reformation, before which it had been part of the Convent connected to Westminster Abbey. Inigo Jones had studied the architectural style developed in Padua, by Palladio, and wanted to try it out in London. It became a sought-after residential area until more fashionable properties were built to the west, the houses fell into disrepair, a fruit and flower market moved in, and prostitution, Turkish baths and playhouses proliferated. Today, just the church remains, as all the houses were gradually replaced. The oldest surviving square in London was inspired by Covent Garden but built by another aristocrat, the Earl of Southampton, soon after the Restoration in 1660. Lessees of land around the central square were instructed to build according to strict style and form. The result was so popular that visiting princes came to view the 'Little Towne', as this fashionable suburb was

called. Now known as Bloomsbury Square, it had everything, including a small market where Barter Street now stands. Most building schemes since the pioneering import of continental piazzas in the 17th century have included squares and gardens. This was repeated in towns and cities throughout the United Kingdom.

OLDEST ALLOTMENT

Allotments for the needy folk of Nottingham have a tradition that echoes the city's place in English folklore. The city was the stronghold that suppressed Robin Hood and his merry men in the 13th century. From its battlements the wealthy and wicked sheriff extorted taxes from the poorest in society. The sheriff's eventual overthrow by the infamous outlaws perhaps set a precedent for the innovation at St Anne's, close to Nottingham's city centre before 1834.

The precise date is difficult to surmise but the provision of allotments to the poor on Hunger Hill had been made by the time cartographers mapped the area the following year. It was possibly due to the collapse of the knitting trade and to avoid the rigours of the Poor Laws that this means of subsistence appeared.

Hunger Hill had been marked as common ground as far back as 1609, when a map showed the 40 plots granted to

The Queen Anne's Gate entrance to St James' Park. The flower beds are constantly changed throughout the summer so it is always a mass of colour. Besides the gardeners, who also look after the gardens in front of Buckingham Palace, there is an officially appointed person to care for the birds. During the weekends in the summer bands play in the bandstand.

burgesses of the town four years before. The 1830s built on this tradition and the allotments enabled artisans to cultivate nature for a harvest they could eat or sell. The idea caught on, and in towns and cities throughout the country, organisations responded to the hardships of the poor by setting aside land, often ground that had formerly been used as communal gardens, and provided plots at reasonable rents. The existence of these toast-racked gardens, their modern-day solace and changing purpose was dramatised in the BBC series, 'Eastenders'. But it was in a time of need that this tradition began, at Nottingham's St Anne's, where the oldest allotments in Britain still boast a society of gardeners with stories to share and produce to trade.

OLDEST INNER LONDON PARK

In the past, leprosy had no cure and was deeply feared in Britain. But in one of the ironies of history, the oldest Royal Park in London and the principal royal palace in Britain were both built over the remains of a women's leprosy hospital that was dedicated to St James. It was Henry VIII who chose to construct himself a residence on this site, just a short distance from his Palaces of Westminster and Whitehall. In 1531, he bought the surrounding land, which surprisingly belonged to far away Eton College. This land had been used by the leper women for grazing hogs – Henry wanted it for hunting and taking exercise. The terrain was marshy, so Henry drained and levelled it to

make way for a tilt yard for jousting, which is now where Horse Guards Parade Square stands. His palace and park were named after the old hospital and became St James's Palace and St James's Park. He acquired more land, so that the hunting ground reached out to the villages of Islington, Marylebone and Hampstead. James I developed a physic garden and put in aviaries, where Birdcage Walk is now located; his son Charles I walked through the park to his execution. During Charles II's reign the park was improved with a long avenue. This was added to provide an elegant walkway but also to replace the nearby area for playing the Italian game *pallo a maglio*, which was called Pall Mall'. The new avenue for the game, which was played with

wooden mallets rather like croquet, became known as the Mall. When the Duke of Buckingham built his new house in the park (Buckingham House), he placed it perpendicular to this Mall. George III later bought the house and it became Buckingham Palace. Those who think that the Mall was laid out for the palace are wrong; it was the inspiration for the palace's location. For many years St James's Park was a haunt for prostitutes and hotbed of crime, but this was tidied up in the middle of the 18th century. Perhaps the magnificence of St James's Park, surrounded by palaces and London's greatest landmarks is the best possible memorial to the many leper women who died and were buried in pits, which are still carefully left undisturbed.

ANIMALS

OLDEST NATIVE MAMMAL

The Exmoor Pony could be the oldest native mammal in Britain. As with all the truly ancient questions concerning provenance, it is difficult to be certain, but the evidence suggests that the endangered few surviving ponies of this breed probably descend from predecessors that walked to Britain from the Continent before the land separated. The breed is recognised internationally as endangered and efforts are taken to monitor the number of foals each year without unduly interfering with the habitat or freedom of the ponies. It is not the first time that these mammals have been so vulnerable to extinction.

It is possible that the first wild ponies ventured into Britain as long as 200,000 years ago. They would have been able to roam from Siberia to Wales across one great landmass. The other fauna of the time included mammoths, bears and sabre-toothed tigers. As prey for these animals, the ponies would have developed speed and resilience. They would have been in danger from humans too. Hunters would have preyed upon the wild ponies in the earliest days of human settlement. The English

Exmoor Ponies on a cold February day, on Winsford Hill. The Exmoor Pony Society select the pure bred foals, around 130 a year, which are branded with an individual and a herd number. There is a small herd on Scoraig in Scotland.

Channel developed between five and eight thousand years ago, which would have confirmed the breed's gene pool and its fate in Britain. It is possible that centuries of hunting may have reduced the numbers of ponies so much that the Celts had to import more from the continent in order to maintain the breed.

As farming developed elsewhere and the population increased, Royal Hunting Forests ensured a protected wild habitat for the ponies. However, in 1818, the Crown sold Exmoor for £50,000 to an industrialist called John Knight, who had plans to enclose and cultivate the wilderness for profit. Fortunately some ponies were kept separate because the development did a great deal of damage;

not least when John crossed Exmoor ponies with other breeds. The knowing farmers of the region waited until the opportunity was right and, after Lord Fortescue bought Exmoor in 1879, they revived the breed from the few that had been kept separate. These surviving ponies were called the 'Anchor'. The Second World War brought a further danger to the breed as military manoeuvres across Exmoor did terrible damage to the habitat, the enclosures and to the horses, some of which were felled by stray or aimed bullets.

It is still not possible to take the survival of the Exmoor Pony for granted. Its distinctive features are reminiscent of the cartoons drawn by the artist Thelwell.

They are a dark shade of brown with almost jet-black legs and some fawn highlights around the girth. The ponies do not lack for supporters. There are many societies that do whatever is possible to increase the annual birth rate and help these ancient mammals to feel safe in the land they adopted before Man.

OLDEST BREED OF HORSE

When Caesar came to Britain in the first century before Christ he admired the Essedarii, who were Celtic and Briton warriors who handled their horse-drawn war chariots with ferocious skill. Their horses may well have been the ancestors of the Thoroughbred, or 'blood horse',

A Cleveland Bay mare and foals on the hills bordering the Yorkshire Dales. In the 16th century, monks in the many local monasteries took a great interest in breeding horses and evidence of this remains today. There are racecourses and trainers all over Yorkshire and many pubs are called 'The Bay' or 'The Cleveland Bay'.

Bullocks of the 125 year old Achnacloich herd of West Highland cattle near Oban. The Victorians thought the golden-brown cattle looked so good in a landscape that they bred them selectively. They were very popular subjects of paintings of the time and remain one of the traditional postcard images of Scotland.

as it was known, because of its pure line of descent from the wild horses that roamed Europe before the Aryan dispersion. Horses of the Roman cavalry were crossed with native breeds and when William the Conqueror landed riding a Spanish horse, his Norman mounts added to this mix. Both the feudal system of tenants and the similar needs of the monasteries nurtured horses for work. Following the decline of both feudalism and the monasteries, horses became more generally utilised. In the north-east of England in the 17th century a new breed was created that claims to be Britain's oldest – the Cleveland Bay. It was bred from one of the monastic strains, which were called 'Chapmen' after the itinerant workers that used them to peddle their trade. They were crossed with the

'Barb' breed, which was imported to Whitby at this time and the result was a powerful workhorse. Over time, the breed was refined and the elegant Cleveland Bay carriage horse emerged. Purists demand the pure bay colour is interrupted only by dark legs for the horse to be perfect. Cleveland Bays are still used by the Royal Mews to draw the Queen's carriages.

OLDEST CATTLE

The West Highland cow is probably the oldest type of cattle in Britain. It is certainly the most picturesque, with its shaggy coat and floppy fringe falling either side of two impressive and majestic curvy horns: it is affectionately referred to as the 'Highland Coo'. There are other ancient

cattle in the country, like those that evolved from the old roaming forest herds and the Longhorn, which may have evolved from the Aurochs of ancient cave paintings, but the advantage for the Highland is that it is almost certainly still pure. This is because it was never crossed with other strains due to its remote habitat. In feudal times wealth was simple to measure, what mattered most was the number of cattle you owned. In England, William the Conqueror directed a survey of the nation's possessions in 1086, called the Domesday Book. It describes the possessions held at each manor and hamlet. The Latin word capitale was used to define movable possessions, which generally meant livestock. The word cattle derives from this practice, just as the word chattel is the legal term for possessions today. Equally, the word pecuniary derives from the Greek word pecus, meaning cattle and it shows the close link between money and livestock. Both of these etymological facts emphasise the role that these beasts have played in the evolution of human civilisation.

Evidence has been uncovered to show that Highland cows were in Scotland from the 6th century, and erhaps this proves the theory that the Vikings introduced the breed into what were their southern territories. The breed has remained almost unaltered because of its isolated location in the north-west highlands of Scotland, where it was ideally suited to the wild climate and was able to survive in the rugged land-scape. The Victorian discipline of establishing and keeping pedigrees documented the wide range of breeds that now thrive in the country. The Highland Cattle Herd Book was opened in 1885, and written records exist that go back further to the 17th century. The book lists every new fold, which is how each new herd of Highlands are known. Some folds were gathered for export to colonies where their attributes would be well suited and now the Highland cow can be found in New Zealand, Australia and North America. No cow in Britain carries the same cultural heritage as the Highland Cow.

OLDEST PEDIGREE CATTLE

In the north of England the Romans are said to have found Celts looking after small herds of short-horned oxen. The Shorthorn, which is the oldest pedigree breed in England, owes its history to the northern counties and, in particular, to the agricultural heartland of the Tees River valley. If the Roman reports are correct then these animals would have bred with imported cattle that arrived with the Angles and Vikings when they made this area part of their domain.

During the Middle Ages the great landlords in the north were the Earls of Northumberland, who held the precarious borders with Scotland. In the 1580s, the Earls boasted a large breed of Shorthorns, although this did not benefit did the 7th Earl who was executed by Elizabeth I for branding her a heretic. These cattle varied in hue from deep red to light roan and some were patchy, probably due to imported influence from the continent. They fed well and produced good milk, while the bullocks put on weight to deliver a fine carcass for the table. In 1726, an agriculturalist called Robert Bakewell was born, and despite being considered completely mad by many peo-ple, he became known as the 'Father of Animal Breeding' because he encouraged farmers to change their habits and breed closely related animals rather than keep trying to find variety. This practice was combined with ruthless culling of animals with undesirable characteristics. Gradually, the pure characteristics of the original strain re-emerged with strength. In 1822 the pedigree breed of the Shorthorn was established. A breed starts when its pedigree becomes a matter of record, and this was the year when the English Herd Book for the breed was opened; its discipline has ensured that the breed has continued to survive ever since.

OLDEST HERD OF ABERDEEN ANGUS

Sir George Macpherson-Grant of Ballindalloch was just 21 years old when he became laird of his estate in 1850, but he and two other enthusiasts established a herd that is now recognised as the oldest Aberdeen Angus herd in Britain. The animal is the careful unification of two native types that had lived on the fertile east coast of Scotland for many centuries. The source of each is not clear but the

An Iron Age sow at the Cotswold Farm Park, Britain's oldest farm park and home of many rare breeds. They have fewer, larger piglets than their domesticated cousins and they make very good sausages.

Hummlies of Aberdeenshire's agricultural Buchan district and the Doddies of Angus – the county to the south – were brought together and the strengths of both were combined to form one of the great British breeds. Supporting George in his quest was both Hugh Watson of Keillor, from Angus, and also William McCombie of Tillyfour, in Aberdeenshire. The intention was that a Scottish breed would both challenge and outperform the established breeds in England. George had learned a great deal about agriculture while he studied at Balliol College in Oxford, and he was keen to make a difference at Ballindalloch. He inherited what was even then considered to be the oldest polled herd in Scotland. His programme of improvement was marked by the purchase of Erica, a cow he bought from another east of Scotland landowner, the Earl of Southesk. The bloodline that Erica mothered is now one of the most famous of the breed. Perhaps the great realisation of success in this endeavour was reached in 1878 when a Ballindalloch bull called

Judge won first prize at the Paris Exhibition. A year later, once his herd had been established, George was elected Member of Parliament for Elgin and Nairn. Heading for Westminster he left the herd grazing in the Cow Haugh beside the 16th century castle, just as cattle had done since the 12th century.

OLDEST PIG BREED

All pigs can probably trace a lineal descent to the same creature and so establishing the oldest breed in Britain is difficult. Where better to take a lead than from the British Pig Association. The purest and least interfered with animal was one that was most ignored in the 18th century when human demands led to scientific crossing of types. The pig that was left alone was the Tamworth. It is probable then, that this animal directly descends from the Old English Forest Pig, which in turn evolved from the Wild Boar that once roamed freely in the wilderness of the country.

Another breed, the Berkshire pig, was recorded by Cromwell's troops when they were resting up at Reading, which is in the centre of the county. But however old this breed and its record might be, the animal was crossed with both Chinese and Siamese animals at some point in its history, which has altered their appearance. They are no longer as large and have lost their dark and sandy-red colouring. Now they are black with white noses and feet.

The Tamworth remains the most unaltered breed because it was considered unfashionable. This has also, however, put it at risk because the breed has not coped well with modern farming practices. The number of Tamworths in Britain dropped to a critically low level and it was with good fortune that Tamworths were also located in Australia. These animals descended from pigs taken to the country to help establish the colony and, in recent years, have been crossed with the British Tamworths in order to enrich the stock and increase numbers. The Tamworth's reddish-gold hair, simple appearance, long uppish snout and pointy ears give us the best link to the pigs of medieval Britain, and it is therefore probably the purest and oldest breed in the nation. It is also possibly one of the most at risk of extinction.

(NEWEST) OLDEST PIG

The oldest pigs in Britain disappeared because other breeds were crossed with them in order to develop a more useful animal. This process took place gradually over the last three centuries. The original strain was called the Iron Age pig, which gives a clear indication of its ancestry and provenance.

This line was revived during the early 1970s, in order to provide authentic animals for an Iron Age project at Butser Hill in Hampshire. It was a remarkable scientific experiment that has almost turned the evolutionary clock back. The aim was to place all the natural animals from the period in a replica Iron Age village, called Little Butser. Of course, the pigs of Britain had long since lost their ancient identity to the strong influence of imported Chinese breeds, but Cotswold Farm Park, which was the first Rare Breeds Survival Centre, set about reviving the past by taking the two most pure and ancient breeds and crossing them together. They took a Wild Boar from London Zoo and crossed it with a Tamworth sow. As described above, the Tamworth is the purest strain left in Britain and is

regarded by many as the oldest breed. The intention was to breed an animal that most closely resembled the remains of the last known Iron Age pig. The piglets that were born to this match looked much like a throw back to the original Iron Age pig; they had similar features and were ginger in colour with thick black stripes running across their backs. Gradually, as these piglets grew and bred themselves, the Cotswold Farm Park kept a vigilant eye on the characteristics of the revived breed. Any sign of wildness was culled, and the result has been the successful return of a tame breed of Iron Age pigs to forage the British countryside, just as their ancestors had done for millennia.

Soay sheep (see page 33) have no natural predator, and still retain instincts which are not apparent in domesticated sheep. They moult naturally, the lambs are on their feet and running within minutes of birth and they scatter rather than flock when worked with a sheep dog. A low maintenance breed, they look attractive in parkland and are often used for conservation grazing.

Six year-old Jack (Davy's Delight to use his kennel name) has twice been champion in the Welsh Terrier class at Cruft's, and best in show at many other shows.

OLDEST SHEEP BREED

Something of the mystery of mankind was lost when the archipelago of St Kilda was evacuated of its human population in 1930. Probably since Neolithic times, there had been a small population living on these islands, which sit in the Atlantic west of the Outer Hebrides. However, what they left behind was a breed of sheep, which is the oldest in Britain.

Taking their name from one of the islands, Soay sheep are thought to be similar to the Neolithic domestic animal and may well have been introduced at that time. The islands are so remote that the growing burden of responsibility for the population during the 20th century, gave mainlanders sufficient concern to force the evacuation. It was not popular and it uprooted the small population into a world that was alien. For generations St Kildans had supported themselves by eating puffins, fulmar petrels, guillemots and razor birds. They supplemented this with Manx shearwaters and solan geese. In the dangerous waters of the Atlantic, fishing was largely ignored but the Soay sheep provided wool for rough tweed, from which clothing and blankets were made. The wool was not cut from the sheep, it was plucked as the season turned from winter to spring.

When the islands were left to the forces of nature, the sheep were brought onto Kirta, the largest of the islands, whose Gaelic name means 'the Western land'. They have been left to survive with only occasional checks being made by scientists. Some Soay sheep have been taken and introduced onto the mainland; they differ hugely from other breeds. Firstly, they differ in size and appearance but more significantly, they seem to resist many of the prevalent ailments. Left to survive, the Soay sheep sometimes shock their monitors by dying in large numbers one year and then breeding back to a sustainable population quite quickly.

OLDEST DOG BREED

Apart from the wolf packs that stalk the fences of Safari Parks, there are no free-roaming descendants of the ancient wild animals left. The dog family embraces lineal links to the wolf but only distant kin to the jackal and fox; the latter being an ancient native inhabitant. The *cannis familiaris*, or domesticated dog, evolved from wolves; a process that some estimate to have started about 12,000 years ago. Remains of a dog found in Yorkshire have been dated as more than 9,500 years old.

The Greek historian and geographer, Strabo, refers to hunting dogs being exported from Britain in the century before Christ and perhaps the most significant European dog to be recorded was the hound bred to honour St Hubert in the 8th century. From this animal descend bloodhounds and other hunting hounds. Little other facts about the antiquity of the dog in Britain are known, though the Romans introduced collies into many parts of the empire. Some dogs were domesticated but in medieval villages packs of undomesticated dogs roamed scavenging, which is why stones cover most early graves.

Perhaps the strongest hint for an ancient domestic breed in Britain comes in the 2nd century when Oppian, the Greek poet, refers to the *agassaeus*, which is probably the terrier. The Welsh Terrier may therefore be the oldest dog that is native to these islands. It gained the name in 1885, having been called the Tan, or English, Terrier until then; it was a time when a profusion of dog competitions overtook the British race. The breed has strong hunting instincts and will chase a fox to ground, perhaps a link from its wild ancestors.

OLDEST CAT BREED

Purring on laps around Britain are some of the nation's most popular animals, the wide range of domestic cats. These tame creatures are descended from the wild cats that once stalked Europe. In some remote parts of the Scottish highlands, they still patrol the forests looking for prey. These rarely sighted wild cats are the oldest cats in Britain. However, part of the blotchiness of their coat comes from the mating between the native *felis catus*, or wild cat, and the domestic animals that were imported by the Romans more than 2,000 years ago.

Tame cats were used by the Romans to protect their granaries from mice, and cat remains were found when Roman villas in Silchester and Dursley were excavated. The cats that the Romans imported probably descended from Egyptian domesticated cats, which were all of the short-haired variety. The first reference to the species existence in Britain comes in a law enacted by Hywel Dda, Prince of South Wales, in the year 936AD, which protected them from abuse. The oldest domestic breed of cat is the British Shorthair, which is probably most closely linked to the Roman imports. It has what is described as a blue coat but looks more grey, and gold- or copper-coloured eyes. It is often referred to as the 'British Blue'.

TREES

Remains of the ancient Caledonian Forest in Glen Affric, the largest and least disturbed forest in Scotland. The Forestry Commission and volunteer organisations are working to re-create the original forest – a long-term goal that will take 200 years.

OLDEST FOREST

The Caledonian Forest, which once covered most of central Scotland, is arguably the oldest British forest but it only survives in small patches that bear little resemblance to its former proliferation. The word 'forest' may now describe many forms of agricultural planting but it originally described the wild evolution of vegetation across the temperate world – an ecosystem that provided nature's lungs – consisting of trees, shrubs and open meadow.

Prior to the Bronze Age, the Caledonian Forest was part of the conifer belt that circled the Earth. Its decline since then has been gradual. Climate change has always been the principal influence upon this environment but time and fauna have also played a role – most particularly Man and Red Deer.

Destructive Viking raids, when areas were laid waste to fire, coupled with man's need to clear land for cultivation and gather fuel, reduced the dwindling resource. The relatively recent 'Little Ice Age', from 1320–1750 killed off the trees, and peaty moors developed in their stead. Evidence of the ancient forest can be found by trudging the mossy bog-ridden moors, where stumps and petrified roots emerge, like bleached bones, from the peat.

Surviving patches of the Caledonian Forest exist in remote places, like Glen Affric, or on the islands of Lochs Maree and Morar. Bear and wolves once prowled these forests, but their place has been taken by Red Deer. The warming climate enables this breed to flourish and the effect of large numbers of deer foraging among the saplings has severely stunted regeneration. Close to extinction, the Caledonian Forest has been identified for investment and it is now part of European policy to revive the forest.

OLDEST WOOD

The whole of Britain was once covered in forest, which was unenclosed and uncultivated natural growth. The relentless drive to develop and exploit the natural landscape has meant that in almost every part of the

British Isles this ancient natural growth has given way to human intervention. A few areas of woodland survive that some claim have never been interfered with. It is difficult to decide which is the oldest because they must be equally old. Many are in the middle of private land and are kept discreetly out of public awareness, in order to better protect their survival.

However, in Dartmoor, there is an area of upland oakwood which is described as Britain's oldest wood. It is called Wistmans Wood and sits above the West Dart River in the valley of the Devonport Leat. This is a National Nature Reserve and it attracts an enormous number of visitors that seek its magical wilderness and imagine truth behind the inevitable ghostly stories that have become associated with the very ancient trees. There is a remarkable beauty in the sessile dwarf oak trees that are wrapped in the most prolific mosses. Looking at this beauty and comparing it with a cultivated landscape it is easy to feel nostalgic for the untouched innocence of our prehistoric flora. Through this sort of webbed and entangled wilderness our ancestors felt their way to develop communities, lines of communication and food throughout these islands. The remnants of this uncultivated chaos have been constantly under threat, and it is a powerful thought that Wistmans Wood is both incredibly old and terribly fragile.

OLDEST ROYAL HUNTING FOREST

At Savernake in Wiltshire, just 4,500 acres remain of what was once an enormous expanse of wild primeval forest. The rise in population during the Roman occupation of England opened large parts of the country to trade and communication, and as a result, de-forestation of the island began. The Anglo-Saxons that filled the vacuum left by the collapse of Rome's administration developed a Heptarchy of English kingdoms, which staked out their territory. Forests had a part to play in this cultivated environment, the fruits of which sustained life for all. King Athelstan passed by 'Savernoc' in 934AD and a Royal Hunting Forest was established, under the wardenship of Aluric, in 1050. The Normans imposed Forest law on the new feudal landscape after the conquest. Savernake's records date from about 1086 and show the manner in which the forest was managed and the interest of monarchs protected. The forest is now a private possession, though traditional links to the Crown survive through an ancient Wardenship. Perhaps,

Savernake Forest is criss-crossed with very good roads that were laid down in the Second World War when the forest was used to hide transport being prepared for the D-Day landings. The Earls of Cardigan ensure it remains in private possession by closing it to the public on one day each year.

by comparison, the oldest forest to remain continually in royal hands is at Windsor, where the Crown has directly controlled its management since Saxon times.

OLDEST ASH TREE

There are two ash trees in the British Isles that appear to be more than 400 years old. One is in Northern Ireland at Ballintray House in County Waterford and the other is near

Crewkerne in England's Somerset. The ash tree is one of the few species that are native to the province. In a private garden near Crewkerne is the oldest ash tree in Britain. It was analysed by the enthusiast and expert, Alan Mitchell. The buttresses it has sprouted now support the tree, which makes the traditional method of aging, by measuring its girth, more difficult. The common ash, or *fraxinus exceisior*, likes a good loamy soil and to be relatively protected. It tends to send out large numbers of roots horizontally but at a shallow depth and perhaps the one by Crewkerne has lived so long because its roots have embedded deeper than normally would be the case. The timber from an ash tree is the next most valuable wood for building after oak in Britain. Its chief use for many centuries was for making the spokes of coach wheels, where strength, reliability and the minimum of distortion were essential.

OLDEST OAKS

There are a few oak trees that claim to be the oldest in Britain. Unfortunately, it is difficult to be accurate as the usual process of counting rings requires the trees' trunks to be complete. One of the characteristics of aged oaks is that the centre of the tree rots away, leaving the outer bark to support the remaining branches. The result is haphazard and beautiful; more of a circle of individual trees than one single growth. This book calibrates the claims of the Bowthorpe Oak, Marton Oak and the Sessile Oak at Cowdray Park, known as the Queen Elizabeth Oak because the great Tudor queen visited the tree in 1591. British oak was the only indigenous species of *Quercus* to grow on the British Isles before others were imported – it has a firm place in the nation's history and legend. Originally oaks were spread in large forests across Britain until farming cut back their number. The suitability of oak's hard wood to working and building made it the staple to Saxon builders, and the ability of the wood to adapt to both dry and wet conditions made it the ideal raw material for boat building. Both the security of the island and the development of an empire – not least the extensive discoveries in far off parts of the globe – owe everything to the oak. For this reason it is venerated in the State's semiotics and oak leaves and acorns still entwine the symbols of national office and the Crown itself: admirals are identified by the oak leaves upon their uniform in salute to the crop that won Trafalgar.

Bowthorpe Oak

Just to the south of Bourne, in Lincolnshire, close to the village of Manthorpe is where Bowthorpe Park Farm's wizened oak tree stands with its crown held together by chains. This is perhaps the oldest British oak tree. Its girth is the largest of any other aged oak, at just short of 40 feet and therefore it is not surprising that in the past the centre of the tree was used as a home. In 1768, the centre was fitted out with seats and a door was added, and there was a pigeon house built in the crown of the tree. It sometimes served as a convenient enclosure to feed cattle and it was often used as a perfect location for parties and gatherings. Inside the trunk there are some graffiti inscriptions that give clues to the people who have used this tree in different ways. It is estimated to be over 1,000 years old but exact dating is impossible and there may never be a chance to prove how this aged tree ranks with other oaks.

The Bowthorpe Oak at Bourne in Lincolnshire. Over the years, this hollow oak has been used as a pigeon house, a dining room for 20 and now a cosy home for neighbouring sheep and chickens. As it took around 3500 mature trees to build one Man o'War, it is a wonder any oaks survive.

There are oak trees growing everywhere in this corner of Cheshire. Experts say this tree at Marton could be 1200 years old and, like the Bowthorpe, it has been put to practical use. Acorns from the tree are sold to help conserve the local church which is the oldest timber-framed building (page 126).

Marton Oak

Another decaying oak tree that is said to be over 1,000 years old is the oak at Marton in Cheshire. It is probably better known for having once claimed to be the largest girthed tree in Britain. It hardly deserves this title now that its centre, which was once used as a pigsty, has completely disappeared and only three separate parts of the trunk are left standing, with their remaining wispy branches aloft. It still comes into leaf, however, and each autumn, when the acorns drop, local children come and gather them to sell to raise funds for the local church, which is also no ordinary building. Built in the 14th century on a small tumulus, it is believed to be the oldest half-timbered church in Europe that is still in use today.

Queen Elizabeth Oak

The third of the oaks is found in Sussex, at Cowdray Park, beside a public footpath. In 1591, Queen Elizabeth came here to spend the week hunting. It is said that she killed three or four deer before coming to a great oak. She marvelled at the size of the tree and rested a while beneath its broad boughs. The tree is now said to be over 1,000 years old and therefore one of the oldest oaks in Britain. When the first Queen Elizabeth stopped to gaze at it the oak was already about 500 years old and it has been named after the Tudor monarch ever since. Today, the tree is hollow like the others of this age and yet supports a healthy growth of branches from its trunk. Elizabeth II often visited the park to watch Prince Philip play polo nearby, an interesting link between the two Elizabethan queens.

OLDEST YEW

If the estimated age of Fortingall's yew tree is ever proved then this is not just the oldest yew in Britain, it is possibly the oldest living tree in Europe. Its age is estimated to be more than 5,000 years old.

The small village of Fortingall, north of Scotland's Loch Tay, has recognised the antiquity of this tree for many centuries, which has been both to its advantage and disadvantage. When the centre of the yew was completely eaten away, it left an arch-like route through which funeral processions would pass. But this supersti-tious respect was not at the expense of potential profit. Some villagers made an industry of removing chunks in order to fashion cups and boxes for sale to any prepared to pay a good price, while others just hacked away for their own souvenirs. Recently a wall has been built in order to protect the yew's growth. In 1769, its circum-ference measured 52 feet and in 1833, there were still strong branches issuing from parts of the circular shell of the original tree. Today, it survives although few would dare to estimate how long it will continue to occupy this highland meadow after a presence of so many thousand years.

OLDEST DOUGLAS FIR

Empiric evidence can date the oldest Douglas Fir in Britain to the one standing in the grounds of Scone Palace, north of Perth. It was grown from a seed brought back to the place of his birth by the famous Scottish botanist, David Douglas. He was the son of the Earl of Mansfield's stone-mason, and played truant from school before apprenticing as a gardener at Scone. His obsession for horticulture earned him a commission to explore north-western America in 1823, and his discoveries along the Columbia River, inland from Fort Vancouver, produced specimens of plants, birds and mammals that amazed European scientists. Some of the fir trees he brought home to Scotland were to transform the British timber industry and, in time, to carpet the scenery of Scotland with fast-growing harvestable conifers. Douglas returned to the Columbia River in 1830. After four years his exploration in the Pacific took him to Hawaii, but on 12 July 1834 he fell into a cattle trap and was gored by a wild bull. It was an extraordinary end to a young but brilliant career. Buried in Honolulu, his life is commemorated by the tree that bears his name in Britain, the first of which dominates part of the park he helped to tend in the gardens of Scone Palace.

The Fortingall yew may not look like the oldest living thing in Britain, until you look over the wall and see how big the girth used to be. Yew trees constantly regenerate themselves and grew near places of worship long before Christianity. There are many theories that attempt to explain this connection, the most probable being that as they are evergreen they are a symbol of immortality.

'Of vast circumference and gloom profound
This solitary tree! A living thing
Produced too slowly ever to decay;
Of form and aspect too magnificent
To be destroyed.'

WILLIAM WORDSWORTH

The Winter Pearmain, thought to be the oldest English apple, is one of hundreds of varieties in the National Fruit Collection at Brogdale in Faversham. The Court Pendu Plat from France and the Decio from Italy are also very old. In his *Natural History* written in 1st century AD, Pliny mentions 20 different varieties of apple grown in Rome. It is not known which variety grew in the Garden of Eden!

OLDEST APPLE

There is evidence that since the earliest times apples have been part of the human diet. Around the Swiss and Italian lakes, prehistoric and carbonised apple pips have been found, which confirms their popularity. The wild apple variety called *malus silvestris* grew in Britain in Neolithic times, and evidence for this has been found on Windmill Hill in Wiltshire. The druids planted apple trees near groves of oak, probably to encourage the growth of mistletoe but it was really the Roman policy of encouraging its retiring centurions to settle in areas such as Doncaster that saw the apple take hold in the diet of Britain.

Christianity was also a catalyst for orchards because apples were used for food and cider in the monasteries. The latter required Pearmains and these are probably the oldest apples to have a recorded provenance. In 1204 the Old English Pearmain is referred to in the Exchequer rolls because the Manor of Runham, near Great Yarmouth in Norfolk, had to pay four hogsheads of cider made from Pearmains and also a further 200 fruits. By this time, apple cultivation would have been widespread and the three types of usage were becoming clear. There were dessert apples, those for cooking and others for making cider. The monks steadily developed a skill for grafting the strains and evolving better varieties. In 1296, there is a record of 100 Costard apples being bought for a Shilling in England – the same year king Edward I invaded Scotland to strip the king of a throne. Apples have become perhaps the most prolific fruit to grow in England and there are few country gardens that do not have a tree or orchard from which to draw fruits for healthy eating.

OLDEST LIME TREE

Before Christ walked the Earth a small-leaved lime tree germinated and sprouted at Westonbirt, in Gloucestershire. This tree was coppiced over the centuries, and the discovery of its age was a surprise when, in the 1970s, DNA tests proved that all the individual limes were in fact rising from the 52 foot stool of one original tree. The age was estimated in excess of 2,000 years. Hitherto the curator of this wood had thought little of the unkempt growth of limes. This overlooked treasure had rooted itself in land that became an arboretum as recently as the 1960s.

Since 1829, the Holford family who lived at Westonbirt, had gathered together species of trees in and around what they called Silk Wood, but the family was forced to surrender this land to the Government in lieu of death duties when a relation, the 4th Earl of Morley, died in 1951. As yet no other similarly camouflaged lime has been proved to be older than this extraordinary witness to time.

OLDEST CEDAR OF LEBANON

In the peaceful garden of the Old Rectory in Berkshire's village of Childrey, stands the oldest Cedar of Lebanon in Britain. The Reverend Doctor Edward Pococke, who lived here in the 17th century, is believed to have planted it when he was rector between 1642 and 1660. He probably introduced the species to England when he came back from his time in the Levant. A brilliant Arabist, he had spent much of the 1630s studying manuscripts, language and religions at Aleppo before returning to England to be Archbishop Laud's first professor of Arabic in Oxford. He had been born, educated and ordained in the city and would lecture here until he died in 1691. 'We think he planted the tree in 1646, or possibly earlier', explains the present owner of the rectory, Nicholas Burton, who describes himself and his wife not as owners but as caretakers for a brief chapter in the tree's life. 'It has great presence, standing some distance from the house with its huge energy and massive trunk'. The years have taken their toll; perhaps particularly in 1893 when the incumbent

Although it continues to suffer from wind and snow damage and a fallen bough lies to the right of the picture, the oldest Cedar of Lebanon still looks magnificent.

The fig tree in the garden of Lambeth Palace, home for centuries of Archbishops of Canterbury. Legend has it that Judas hanged himself from a fig tree.

wrote in his diary about thirteen limbs falling that Boxing Day under the sheer weight of snow. Another branch fell recently but every effort is made to keep the tree in good order. Planted at a time of great tumult in society, the species, called *cedrus libani* became one of the favourite additions to the gardens of great houses in the years after the Restoration – in particular those laid out by 'Capability' Brown. Dr Pococke also planted other special trees, including a fig tree at Christ Church where he ended his days.

OLDEST FIG TREE

In the Bible, St Luke's Gospel (22: 29–1) describes how Jesus Christ used a fig tree coming into fruit as an example of the coming Kingdom of God. In the garden of Lambeth Palace, which has been the official residence of the Archbishops of Canterbury since 1190, there are some fig trees that are probably the oldest in Britain. The story goes that they sprouted from originals planted by Cardinal Reginald Pole, who lived here after his predecessor Archbishop Thomas Cranmer was burnt at the stake. Pole had argued with Henry VIII, left the country and nearly

became Pope in 1549. He returned to forgive Queen Mary's England for its schism five years later. But Pope Paul IV turned against him and, though Mary protected him from the inquisition, Pole's health declined and he died the same day as his Queen in 1558. Perhaps he planted the first fig tree at Lambeth following Christ's inspiration. Pole prayed that the Roman Catholic kingdom of God would thrive and keep Protestant heresy at bay. If this was his prayer it did not succeed. He was England's last Catholic Archbishop of Canterbury.

OLDEST MULBERRY

In every generation luxury is sought and valued. At Charlton House in Greenwich, in the east of London, there is a Mulberry tree that is living evidence of a king's aspiration to bring a new luxury industry to Britain. When Scotland's King James came to inherit the English throne on Elizabeth's death in 1603, he united both countries and sought to build upon this peace. One economic venture he championed was to establish a silk industry in England. To this end, he gave mulberry seeds to anyone prepared to cultivate trees for the leaves that silkworms ate. One recipient was Adam Newton, the tutor to Prince Henry, the prince of Wales. Newton lived at Charlton House and planted seeds in his garden at his master's command in 1608. His tree has survived to be the oldest mulberry in England but, unfortunately, as a foundation of the silk industry it was hopeless. Silkworms eat leaves of the white and not the black mulberry and James had promoted the latter. Ironically, Buckingham Palace now stands on the grounds of the Mulberry Garden James established as part of his fledgling industry. For Newton, it was not just his mulberry tree that would prove useless. His charge, Prince Henry, died leaving the weaker brother Charles to fatally inherit his father's divine interpretation of kingship.

OLDEST ARBORETUM

An arboretum is a place set aside for the nurture and display of trees. A grieving Princess of Wales founded Britain's oldest arboretum at Kew Gardens in 1759. Her husband Frederick, who was the son of George II, had died eight years before, having already invested his love for the arts and gardening in the landscape around their home here. Augusta, Princess of Wales, was just 32 when she became a widow and she was a brilliant and determined

woman. Her best friend – he was probably more than that – Lord Bute became her guide, and together they established a 9-acre botanical garden into which they planted specimen trees, such as *ginkgo biloba, saphora japonica* and *Robinia pseudoacacia*.

Two years before, the area had been re-landscaped by William Chambers following bold plans that included a tall pagoda which still dominates the horizon today. George III ascended the throne when his grandfather died in 1760. When his mother, Augusta died 12 years later, her son took charge of the improvements and development of the arboretum. Known as 'Farmer George', he was fascinated by the flora of the world. It was a time of great discovery and one of the boldest botanists, Sir Joseph Banks, who had travelled as a young man with Captain Cook to Australasia became a friend of the king.

After both men had died, the arboretum and botanical garden fell into disorder until, in 1840, the Government assumed control and William Hooker took the arboretum in hand. A little before this, another arboretum had taken root. In 1830 Edward Vernon-Harcourt inherited the fine property of Nuneham Courtenay near Oxford. It was a significant inheritance for a man who had been in the clergy most of his life and Archbishop of York for 23 years.

The mulberry tree in the grounds of Charlton House in Greenwich, behind a disused public lavatory. If you weren't looking for it you would never know it was there.

The Preston Twins, the two oldest elm trees, stand in Preston Park Brighton. Constable's landscapes of Suffolk show how England looked when elm trees were a more common sight. Efforts are still being made to develop a parasite-resistant tree so that the species can be widely reintroduced .

Five years after taking possession, Archbishop Edward commissioned an arboretum of trees from the western side of North America. William Gilpin laid out the plan and as a specifically appointed arboretum, it too claims to be Britain's oldest.

OLDEST ELM TREES

The 'Preston Twins' and one tree in the garden of the Prince Regent's Royal Pavilion, all in Brighton, are probably the oldest elms left in Britain. The English countryside suffered a catastrophe in the 1970s, when blight infected elm trees and spread with furious speed across the nation. Ancient elms that had punctuated the landscape for centuries quickly withered when the Elm Tree Beetle carried the crippling wilt fungus, called *ophiostoma ulmi*, from tree to tree. There was nothing that could be done to stop the spread and elm felling became the only response as the 3mm beetles were carried by the wind to unaffected trees. Brighton has been unaffected so far because there were no elm trees on the surrounding hills for the beetles to use in their progress. Recent research suggests that all British elms evolved from a single tree imported by the Romans more than 2000 years ago. The Atinian elm, which was used for vine cultivation in the Roman Empire, is apparently identical to the strain found striving to survive in England.

OLDEST VINE

The Great Vine at Hampton Court Palace is not only the oldest in Britain but also probably the oldest in the world. It still yields nearly 700 pounds (315 kilos) of grapes each year, which, considering it was planted in 1768, is testament to its designer, the landscape-gardener Lancelot Brown. The Hampton Court commission came at the height of Brown's career. He had gained a reputation for enormous vision and creating an entirely English garden style for the great houses of England. He earned the nickname 'Capability Brown' because he always told clients that their gardens and parks had great 'capabilities'. Brown planted the Great Vine with Black Hamburgh, which is particularly suited to the English climate and high yielding, as the annual crop of grapes today still demonstrates. This fertility was exactly what the great farmer king, George III, appreciated most – the Great Vine was possibly planted to celebrate the birth of the king's second daughter and sixth child, Princess Augusta: eventually King George would father fifteen legitimate children.

SOCIETY

PEOPLE

OLDEST PEOPLE

In the counties of Connaught and Munster, which are on Ireland's west coast, can be found a family with the oldest traceable and undiluted Y-chromosome in the British Isles. In the mid-19th century, Charles Darwin finally destroyed the Biblical view that God created human beings on the fifth day of the World's creation. The Bible's first chapter, from the book of Genesis, was a cornerstone of the Christian faith but Darwin's discoveries forced the re-evaluation of this theology, just as it gave scientists renewed confidence to question evolution itself. It was soon understood that human beings evolved from apes through the gradual modification of their hips and lower limbs, enabling them to stand on two legs and have their hands free to grasp and manipulate. The history of Homo Sapiens begins when tools and implements were first formed. The discovery of DNA has opened new research into the origin of people. It is now possible to detect the unique signature of the Y-chromosome, which is passed unaltered down the male line, as it is relayed through successive generations. This can answer questions about migration patterns through history, showing where people have come from and who they relate to and provide final pieces of evidence to assessments of history.

Location is the reason that Connaught and Munster hold this particular unbroken link with prehistoric times. The area is one of the farthest points from the centre of Europe and therefore since the first settlers established themselves, few of the major migrations into the British Isles have reached as far. Recent research led by Doctor Daniel Bradley of the Department of Genetics at Trinity College in Dublin has made some significant discoveries. First it would seem that the Celts who settled the coastline of Connaught and Munster came from the Basque area of Spain: the population at both places share the same Y-chromosome signature, which is one of the oldest types on the Atlantic coastline of Europe. More significant though, are the results of some research performed on the Y-chromosomes of 221 Irish males. Although much of this work has yet to be published, it was announced that one surname showed a particular trend. This is because in the

British Isles the surname tends to follow the Y-chromosome and therefore it is easy to plot the link. The research established that 94.6 per cent of the O'Sullivans checked in the Munster area carried a variant that in their chromosome comes directly from Neolithic hunters. These were the first to establish themselves in pre-agricultural times on the Irish coast. O'Sullivan is the anglicised version of O'Suileabhain, which means descendants of the dark-eyed one. Whoever the dark eyed one was, his descendants were left virtually undisturbed in Connaught until the 1850s. This was after the peril of the potato blight, when cultural opportunities to travel emerged, leading O'Sullivans and many other similarly unique Y-chromosone carriers to mix more with the population who carried variants from other ancient roots, like the Vikings, the Britons, the Normans and the Romans. The 21st century has further increased this opportunity for interrelationship, and Y-chromosomes from the Far East, Africa, Australasia and elsewhere are more readily available to the variant mix. For the moment, however, although all people share the same origins, the O'Sullivans arguably carry the oldest type of unaltered Atlantic Façade Y-Chromosome in the British Isles.

OLDEST TITLE

The island of Lismore, which sits at the entrance of Loch Linnhe and at the head of the Firth of Lorne is the romantic setting for a title that had its beginnings in the time of St Moluag. In 2004, what is probably the oldest barony in Britain was reaffirmed in the Matriculation of Arms granted to William Livingstone of Bachuil by Scotland's Lord Lyon King of Arms, on behalf of the Queen of Scots.

The title is known as the Baron of Bachuil 'by grace of God', and evolved from the original 'keepership' into a feudal barony, which the Scottish Parliament recognised in 1399. The Kings of Dalriada probably first created the appointment in the 6th century. The title originated from the responsibility of caring for the Bachuil Mor, or great staff of St Moluag.

This saint first came to the island in the year 562AD in a race. He competed against St Columba for ownership of the place, which was the sacred island of the western Picts. The two religious missionaries were possibly brothers and they agreed that the first boat to reach the shore would claim the island. As the coracles came close, St Moluag desperately chopped off his finger and threw it ashore in order to win. Moluag came from the ancient

Irish tribe called Dál nAraide, which systematically settled around what is now Argyll, creating one of the kingdoms that ultimately merged into a single Scotland. With them came Christianity. When Moluag died his descendants, known as Coarbs, became hereditary Abbots of Lismore and thereby keepers of the Bachuil Mor, or great staff of the saint. In the kingdom of Dalriada, the influence of the Coarbs was immense. The Bachuil Mor, which is still held by the Baron today, is supposed to have miraculous powers. It is rumoured to be able to protect men from the plague and ensure truth on the land while assuring safety at sea. Perhaps its most useful asset was that it could protect cattle from murrain. It is also supposed to have the power to find its way back to

Lismore. Legend has it that one Baron left it behind on the mainland; he realised the mistake as the boat pulled into Lismore and just as he did, he heard a sound in the air of something rushing past. The object landed in the seaweed and, as he stooped to investigate, he realised it was the Bachuil Mor.

The very presence of this simple stick had its effect on history. The great feudal lord of the area was the Earl of Argyll, but it was said that even he would bend his knee to the Baron of Bachuil, who was the descendant of St Moluag and the keeper of the holy crosier. In 1544, the Earl of Argyll, as Lord of Lorne, confirmed the privileges and title of the Baron. The present Baron is Chief of MacLea, possibly the oldest Irish tribal 'Mac' in Scotland.

Peter Maxwell, the 28th Baron de Ros, in his workshop in Strangford, Northern Ireland where he restores and makes Georgian Irish furniture. He built his house with his own hands. He appreciates and is proud of his heritage but for him it is a private matter and less important than the work he does.

He was born in Nyasaland and worked hard to prove the hereditary and ancient rights of his family to probably the oldest surviving title in Britain, other than the Sovereign.

OLDEST FORMAL TITLE

It will not be long before someone takes to the European Court of Human Rights a challenge to the custom that most British peerages may only pass through the male line. This rule seems to be unfair at a time when attitudes have changed and even the monarchy passes quite happily through the female line. Frequently titles become extinct when there are heirs living who descend from the original recipient of the title, but being female, they are not able to qualify.

The oldest peerage title in Britain is the Barony de Ros which was created in England on 14th December 1264. Oddly, the title was not granted by a grateful king Henry III. On the contrary, de Ros had been one of the Chief Barons fighting against the king under Simon de Montfort. The battle of Lewis had seen the monarch defeated by the baron's army, who had captured the king and his son Prince Edward. De Montfort and his followers were pursuing the essence of English liberty and the Provisions of Oxford, whereby the king had promised to rule through a council, or Parliament, but had reneged.

The line has survived because it is one of the few baronies that is permitted to pass through the female line. Had this not been the case, the title would have become extinct in the late 15th century, when the male line died out. The survival occured because the Barony de Ros was created by a writ of summons, which is nowadays used to call all peers and Members of Parliament to Westminster. In the 13th century, a peerage created by writ had the advantage that it could pass through the female line if there were no heirs. In addition, in a case where there were two or more daughters then it was for the Crown to decide which of the co-heiresses should inherit. As a result of this situation the Barony de Ros has frequently been temporarily in abeyance while a decision is taken about who should succeed.

Peter Maxwell is now the 28th Baron de Ros, having inherited the title through his mother, who had inherited it through hers as well. In this way, the family managed to outmanoeuvre the tragedy of Peter's uncle dying in the Second World War, the fate of many peerages that lost their male heirs during the First and Second World Wars. This means that the surname of the holders of this oldest of peerages is frequently changing. There are, however, other titles that can be inherited through the female line, particularly Scottish peerages because Scottish society was always more matriarchal than England's — where the inheritance of land was a masculine prerogative and it was not until the 20th century that women could play a part in politics or, indeed, Parliament.

OLDEST PEERAGES

The legislative powers of the Peerage may be almost defunct but it remains extant as a reminder of the way in which the country was feudally ruled through the monarch. There are five ranks in the peerage, which are called in ascending order: baronies, viscounties, earldoms, marquessates and dukedoms. There were more ancient systems of lordship, which predated the Norman Conquest and the establishment of Parliaments in Scotland and Ireland, but the Peerage as regulated by the Crown is the subject of this section. The oldest of all the titles is the Barony of de Ros, which is discussed above as 'Oldest Formal Title'.

The oldest viscounty is that of Hereford, which was given to Walter Devereux on 2nd February in either 1549 or 1550 by Edward VI. The Devereux family were given the lands of a former Earl of Hereford by Richard II in 1387. The oldest earldom was granted on 22nd May 1442 to Sir John Talbot. Shakespeare referred to him in his play *Henry VI*, 'But where's the great Alcides of the field, Valiant Lord Talbot, Earl of Shrewsbury'. The oldest marquessate is Winchester, granted to Sir William Paulet by Edward VI on 12th October 1551. Not only did Paulet gain sufficient trust of Henry VIII to act as his executor, he went on to serve three of his children, Edward VI, Mary and Elizabeth as Lord Treasurer. Asked how he managed to do this, the Marquess replied, 'By being a willow, not an oak'.

Lastly comes the oldest dukedom. Sir John Howard's mother was a Mowbray, which was one of the great families in the Yorkist camp during the Wars of the Roses. He was therefore in a good position to inherit the extinct titles of his forebears. On 28th June 1483, the moment came, and Howard was created Duke of Norfolk and much else besides. Today, the Duke of Norfolk has the oldest dukedom and is therefore the most senior peer of the United Kingdom.

OLDEST SCOTTISH CLAN

The ancient clans of Scotland have uncertain histories but a few have mythic claims to provenance that have been passed down by family poets and therefore carry credibility. Of these clans, the Robertsons of Struan claim a link to royal foundations in the Dark Ages.

The Scottish clan system was struck a severe blow during the Jacobite risings. After the defeat of Bonnie Prince Charlie, in 1746, the historic role of the clan, as a tribal and territorial unit, was over. Since that time, the clans, which were temporarily forbidden to maintain their customs, have re-emerged as romantic sources of genealogical association, following the emigration of Highlanders during the economic disasters of the late 18th century. Assessing the oldest clan is no easy matter and probably impossible to prove anyway. However, the Robertsons claim an ancient beginning in Ireland's Donegal on the 7th December 521AD, for this is when the prince who would become Saint Columba was born. He brought the Celtic Church to Scotland, establishing roots on the island of Iona. His 'kin', or those who were gathered close, were regarded as family and the Robertsons of Struan claim to evolve directly from this community. The exact evolution is hard to plot because Norsemen later threw out Columba's kin from the islands. Some settled around Dunkeld, where the abbots had carried the saint's relics, making this Scotland's capital city. Most members of the Clan claim descent from Grizzled Robert, the 4th Chief of Clan Donnachaidh and therefore from the sons of Robert, Robertson.

OLDEST SITE OF HUMAN EVIDENCE

It is often said that in life two things are certain: death and taxes. From the evidence at Britain's oldest archaeological sites there are two certainties in death; erosion and decay. Firstly, there is Kents Cavern, near Torquay, where discov-

Aveline's Hole in Burrington Coombe in the Mendip Hills, just off the B3134, is the site of the oldest burial ground. It was discovered in 1797 by boys chasing a rabbit down a hole.

eries have been made that date back 700,000 years to the Paeleolithic era. There is evidence of every age of man having lived there: *Homo erectus*, Neanderthals and modern man, and the caves were even in use during the Ice Age because Devon was never submerged in ice. Over time, similar discoveries may be made from this period to further unwrap the mysteries of Britain's earliest inhabitants.

Secondly, just outside Chichester, at Boxgrove, are eroded chalk cliffs that once faced the sea but now stand more than two miles away from the coast. Archaeologists carefully lifted away the gravel left on the chalk base by the receding sea during either the 'Great' or 'Anglian' Ice Age. In one part of the dig they discovered an old stream bed. Where it must have flowed into the sea, they unearthed evidence from 500,000 years ago. Most significantly, they found a tibia bone and two teeth of a man who lived over half a million years ago. The tibia had been gnawed off at both ends, probably by wolves, which preyed upon early human settlements. Close by there was other evidence; including the oval blade of a flint hand axe, skeletal parts of rodents and other animals. For the moment, these are the oldest evidence of human life in Britain.

OLDEST CEMETERY

The Roman word for burial ground was *necropolis*, or city of the dead, but belief in eternal life gave early Christian writers the inspiration for a new word. It came from a Greek root *koimeterion*, meaning place of sleep. Cemetery is therefore the gentle spin on Christian death.

More than 8,000 years before Christ, a cave called Aveline's Hole in Somerset's Mendip Hills was last used to bury human remains. It is Britain's oldest cemetery. These remains were discovered in 1797 and have been dated to be more than 10,400 years old. There were estimated to be nearly 100 skeletons, and because the cave had probably remained sealed since the last interment until the discovery, they were perfectly preserved. Many of the ancient remains were removed and put on display in Bristol, but were destroyed when bombs hit the university's speleological museum in the blitz of November 1940. They had represented the largest set of Mesolithic remains in Britain and Europe. The Mesolithic period is loosely described as the Middle Stone Age and humans then were hunter-gatherers. This immediately post-glacial, pre-agricultural period sits between the more ancient Palaeolithic age, when crude hand axes appeared, and the Neolithic age, when agricultural practices developed. Not all the skeletal remains were lost in 1940 but it is still tragic that so many were lost within 150 years of their discovery after lying intact and undisturbed for 10,200 years.

OLDEST 'TOURIST' ATTRACTION

According to legend, a thunder crack marked the birth of Ursula Sontheil in 1488, and the air filled with the noxious smell of sulphur. She was born in a cave close to Knaresborough and her mother, who was just 15 years old, was supposed to have slept with the devil. It was a story that gripped a confused England, which was emerging from civil war and facing religious overhaul. Her birthplace and its neighbouring magical well became an attraction for visitors, making it the oldest tourist attraction in Britain. Shakespeare's plays tell us a great deal about the beliefs and superstitions of this time and in *Macbeth* the play begins with three witches. The existence of supernatural powers was accepted and often feared; they were also confused with devil worship at a time of religious turmoil. Ursula became known by her married name, as Mother Shipton, but the truth of her life is clouded by rumours, imagination and myth. It is said that she foresaw the Spanish Armada, London's Great Fire and coming technology. She died in

The entrance to the oldest 'tourist' attraction, Mother Shipton's Cave in Knaresborough. Everyday objects are allegedly turned to stone in the petrifying well.

1561, and 70 years later the cave of her birth was opened to visitors. The cave remains a tourist attraction today, showing how fascination with the unbelievable still challenges and attracts humankind in the 21st century.

OLDEST VISITED SITE

The earth is still scarred by the drag marks made by the 45 tonne menhirs that were hauled 20 miles to the site of Stonehenge from the Marlborough Downs, 4,300 years ago, by our pre-historic ancestors. It is possible to under-estimate the feat of dragging the stones because of the mechanisation and power available today. This site still attracts the curious and the overwhelmed, just as it has always done. Roman centurions and 21st century travellers have been equally struck by this ethereal place in a way that no one can fully explain.

It is much less easy to comprehend the other scar on the Earth that these same ancestors caused 4,500 years ago and nearly 245 miles away. In the Prescelli Mountains of Pembrokeshire, on the western tip of Wales, they worked a quarry to cut rectangular bluestones, each weighing about five tonnes. Each of these was then heaved to the sea, probably in Milford Haven, and floated across the Bristol Channel on vast rafts before being brought up the River Avon and dragged the remaining distance over Salisbury Plain. Why? This has been the question since modern history began. The answer will never be known. In 1666, the antiquarian John Aubrey excavated a circular ditch dug with animal bones and 56 holes in which sat wooden poles. This was evidence of a structure that predated the stone circle by a further five and a half centuries. It means that whatever happened here was worthy of the greatest efforts man could make as long as 5,100 years ago.

OLDEST HILL FIGURE

We will never know for certain what actually motivated our forebears to carve the vast white horse into the hill south of Uffington, in Berkshire. It dominates the land-scape today as it must have done in ancient times, when unknown hands set about making this enormous symbolic gesture. Oxford academics date the carving to be over 3,000 years old, which makes it far and away the oldest hill figure in Britain. What no amount of research can ever confirm is whether this is representative of a deity, a tribe or just a symbol to celebrate some event that was once tremendously important. From forward hoof to tail the figure is 374 feet long and 110 feet tall. The white

incision in the hillside fluctuates from five to ten feet wide and these trenches have been filled with up to two feet of chalk, resting upon the natural chalk core of the hill. High on the escarpment it faces north-west across the valley and over Dragon Hill. The horse is first mentioned in 1190, though White Horse Hill was referred to more than a century before. Theories abound to explain its existence. Following the Oxford Archaeological Unit's assessment that this is three millennia old, it concurs with evidence that the horse was sacred to Iron Age man. Alternatively, if it is Celtic it could be Epona, the horse god. If later still, the Saxons may have portrayed the dragon supposedly slaughtered by St George or the horse he rode during the deed.

OLDEST BRITISH SAINT

It was probably just a decade before the Emperor of Rome, Constantine the Great, converted to Christianity that it is believed Britain's oldest saint was martyred for his faith. Constantine's conversion, in the year 313AD, changed the attitude of the Roman Empire and provided Christianity with the chance to flourish. Nothing helped the faith more than the example of belief up to death. The story goes that Alban was living in Verulamium, now the site of the city of St Albans, in the 3rd century and was an adherent to the worship of Roman gods. During one of the purges of Christians, a cleric sought refuge in Alban's house. After the danger had passed, Alban was converted by the cleric and was baptised a Christian. The centurions soon returned to search again and found Alban dressed as the cleric, in order to save him. Alban angered the judge by his deception and his new faith, and was sentenced to death. He was taken to a hill which, according to legend, meant crossing a river which miracu-lously dried up in order for them to cross. Then, on top of the hill, at the point of execution, a spring bubbled to the surface. The executioner lost confidence and refused to do his duty. The man who stepped forward to strike the fatal blow was miraculously blinded – some stories say that his eyes dropped out. Almost immediately after Alban's martyrdom, which was probably around the year 304, he became the subject of veneration. In about the year 760 a cathedral was built on the hill where Alban was killed, called a confession because it was built over the site of a martyrdom. The shrine has been ravaged by time but St Alban's Day is still observed on 22nd June each year in the cathedral and city that bear his name.

ARTS

Artistic Director Mark Baldwin with some of the artists from Rambert Dance company in theatrical moments from the 2004/5 season, including *A Tragedy of Fashion, Elsa Canasta, Linear Remains, a Song of A Wayfarer, Swamp* and *PreSentient*. Although based in Chiswick, the company spends a great deal of time touring the country.

OLDEST DANCE COMPANY

At the start of the 20th century it was said that the British could not dance. In 1926, Marie Rambert sought to change that by founding the Ballet Rambert, the first dance company in the United Kingdom. There had been ballets before in Britain but they tended to be hastily brought together for entertainment at State occasions. The precision and skills that are taught and performed in Britain today are a far cry from these early events, where actors and those who danced for pleasure provided the entertainment.

The art of dance was developed in Europe but perfected in France and Russia before being imported into the United Kingdom. In 1489, the first recorded ballet was performed at the wedding of the Duke of Milan, at Tortona in Italy. Dance evolved in France as an entertainment for the Royal Court and Catherine de Medici spent large sums providing distractions for her son, when he was king. In 1581, she commissioned the composer Baltasarini, who was known as Beaujoyeulx, to stage a performance called 'Ballet Comique de la Reyne'; this was probably the first time dance conveyed a story and ideas in its drama. Louis XIII and Louis XIV were passionate about dance, which filled the lazy days at Versailles, and frequently the Sun King danced in ballets himself, especially as a young man. Cardinal Richelieu recognised the power of this drama to influence the Court and instructed composers and choreographers to dramatise according to his instructions. It was gentle diplomatic influence at its most un-typical from this vigourous religious statesman.

Peter the Great toured Europe in what was called his 'Great Embassy'. Returning to Russia, he set about building a city from scratch that would mimic all that he had seen and admired. The city was to be the stage for opulent display and art, so it was not surprising that ballet was used to entertain the Tsars. The French dancer and choreographer Marius Petipa joined the Russian Imperial Ballet of St Petersburg, which became known as the Kirov Ballet. In a setting of crystal chandeliers and gold-leafed ceilings, Petipa's skills developed and Russia became the centre for ballet in the world.

In 1909, Sergei Diaghilev established a touring company in St Petersburg. It employed the greatest dancers of the city, among whom were Anna Pavlova and Vaslav Nijinski. Called the Ballets Russes, Diaghilev took them around Europe and over to the United States. These performers inspired countries that did not possess professional dancers to consider the role they could play in cultural life.

Britain was one of these countries. It had little dance culture to boast of. Dryden had referred to a 'Balette' once in 1667 and, in 1702, the first descriptive dance was performed at London's Drury Lane, called 'The Tavern Bilkers'. But it was an indifferent audience that came to watch Diaghilev's dancers perform at Covent Garden in 1911. The First World War destroyed Tsarist Russia and those dancers who were able to see the dangers fled St Petersburg before the Bolsheviks took control of the Imperial Ballet, which did not fit in with Marxist ideology. The dancers that escaped were quickly engaged in countries where there was a company with money to take them on. However, Britain still had no formal dance company.

One of Diaghilev's dancers, Marie Rambert, became the 'Midwife of British Ballet'. Born in Warsaw, in 1888, Marie worked closely on choreography with Nijinski, who was Diaghilev's lover. But when the two men broke up, this period came to an end and, with the outbreak of war in 1914, Marie left Russia and settled in England. She married a successful writer who had great financial success with a play in 1925. This gave them the chance to develop Marie's dream of a small ballet company. In 1926, she inspired Frederick Ashton to choreograph a short ballet, called 'A Tragedy of Fashion'. It was a British product, with British resident dancers and inspired by Marie's enthusiasm, and it marked the start of a British choreographic tradition and launched the ballet company. Marie's husband bought then her a hall in Notting Hill, which was transformed into the Mercury Theatre. Long closed down, this hall is still marked with a plaque to mark the birthplace of British ballet. From this small start developed a dance company that was first called the Marie Rambert Dancers, then the Ballet Club, and from 1935 until 1987, the Ballet Rambert. To reflect its spread into contemporary dance, it has changed its name once more to the Rambert Dance Company. Dame Marie Rambert died in 1982, at the age of 94.

OLDEST MUSIC HALL

In the middle of the 19th century, strict moral values were heavily promoted by a powerful Church, and society presented itself with an increasingly starched Victorian façade. Reality was not so perfect and, with these increasing pressures upon human expression, other outlets emerged for the stresses of industrial life and the working man. One of these was the bawdy entertainment of the music hall. In 1857, one of these halls was built above a warehouse in Glasgow's Trongate, called the Britannia Music Hall, or Panopticon, which means the place where everything is on view. Although the venue fell into disuse in 1938, it remains intact and has re-emerged into public consciousness as the oldest British music hall.

The Theatre Royal in Bristol was licensed by King George III. In 1946, a resident theatre company arrived from the Old Vic in London and the Theatre Royal in Bristol was renamed the Bristol Old Vic.

Among famous thespians who performed to the rowdy gatherings here was the future royal mistress, Marie Lloyd. She went on to become one of the fore-most singers in the business, but her brash and earthy femininity attracted Edward VII, when he was Prince of Wales. Later the Hall provided a setting for Trade Union meetings but did not last long after the depression of the early 1930s. With the approach of war and changing appetites, Music Hall was finished but revival may be in the air for this moth-balled heritage.

OLDEST THEATRE

In Bristol the Theatre Royal, or Old Vic, is the oldest theatrical building in Britain. Theatre in England had been restricted to religious, or miracle plays, up until the Reformation, when the Court of Queen Elizabeth patronised the celebration of literature for the stage. However, performance was restricted and seditious material was suppressed by a bill that effectively confined legitimate theatre to Westminster, or wherever the monarch happened to reside, and only allowed plays that met with the Lord Chamberlain's approval. From 1737 until 1843, legitimate drama could only be performed at the London theatres of Drury Lane or Covent Garden. However, in Bristol a number of lawyers, politicians and businessmen opened an illegal playhouse off King Street. Outrage followed because people of the town feared the influence it would have on morality and good order. In 1778, George III issued a Royal Licence to the Bristol playhouse. This licence made it a 'patent theatre' and others were granted to Bath and Liverpool. In due course, all legitimate theatres, which had licences, were called 'Theatre Royal' and while many survive around the country, the building in Bristol is the original.

OLDEST CINEMA

The Duke of York's Picture House in Brighton and the Phoenix in London's East Finchley claim to be Britain's oldest cinemas. Both were founded in 1910 and have been in continuous service ever since, managing to remain open during both World Wars.

Film emerged at the start of the 20th century and has become one of the foremost forms of entertainment in the world. In 1833, the zoetrope was invented, which was a hollow cylinder filled with drawings that rotated giving an observer the view of a moving horse. Forty-four years later, photographic images of a horse were used to achieve the

same effect. By the start of the 20th century, short black and white silent films lasting just a few minutes were being shown in music halls and at fairgrounds. In 1908, at London's Society of Arts, the first colour film was shown but showings were dangerous because of the frequent fires that started when celluloid was ignited by the bright lamps. Some dedicated pioneers opened picture houses just two years later. Of these, the Duke of York's in Brighton seated almost 330 people in old-fashioned comfort. The design was naturally similar to the theatres of the time, with balconies and boxes to provide privacy for those willing to pay the tariff. The Phoenix was opened as the East Finchley Picturedrome – it was one of the first cinemas to show 'talkies' in 1929. Its name changed to the Coliseum in 1938, and to the Rex following its refit in art deco style. The large corporation Granada bought the cinema in the 1970s but it later returned to private ownership, as it was from its foundation and still is today.

This Grade II listed cinema in Brighton has been showing films continuously since it was opened in 1910. The original feel of the auditorium has been retained and now it even has a licence for weddings. The legs on the roof come from a cinema in Oxford.

OLDEST ART GALLERY

How could a king of Poland possibly be the catalyst for Britain's oldest public art gallery, at Dulwich College in south London? It occurred at a time of enormous change in Europe. France was in torment after the French Revolution of 1789, where monarchy and aristocracy were overthrown ushering in a dark age. Monarchs across the Continent, along with their governing classes, watched the Terror and wondered where the sparks from this uprising might fall and whether the tinderbox of suppressed ambitions might explode into revolution elsewhere. For many artists, driven by a liberal loathing of power, this was an exciting time. For art dealers too, the harvest of the guillotine was a haemorrhage of art objects at meagre prices coming from one of the most elegant cultures in the world.

A Frenchman, Noel Desenfans, and his Swiss friend, Sir Francis Bourgeois, capitalised upon this situation and developed one of the most successful partnerships of the time in London. One year after the start of the revolution, in 1790, the King of Poland, Stanislas Poniatowski, placed an order for a Royal art collection. This was not a purchase of one or two paintings, this was the expectation of a complete collection – an inheritance – to form the nucleus of art and culture in Poland. The example of Peter the Great of Russia some years before stood as a template for how monarchs should ape the culture and niceties of western royalty.

At this time, Poland was struggling to reorganise its constitution along more liberal lines in the face of Russian disapproval. The period became known as the Polish Question. The new Polish Diet, or parliament, recognised the danger that Russia represented to its ambitious liberalism, especially while France was scaring Europe with its version of freedom. It therefore voted a huge sum of money to bolster the monarch and state. The money apportioned to the art purchase in London, however large the undertaking, was but a tiny part. A love affair made Poland's position even more precarious. The Russian Tsarina, Catherine the Great, had a new lover, Zubov, who was hungry for wealth and fortune in Poland. Playing the diplomatic game well, Catherine distracted Europe's attention by drawing it to France. Five years later, Poland had been swallowed up and its king pensioned off with barely enough to live on, let alone to underwrite the great gathering of art waiting for him in London.

The dealers Desenfans and Bourgeois tried to place the collection with a wealthy owner but there were few around who could take on such an investment. They contacted the new Tsar of Russia, Paul I, who refused. The British Museum was the only means through which the British Government could acquire the works, but the Prime Minister, William Pitt, saw no advantage in this investment while the country was struggling to arm itself against Napoleon. In 1807, Desenfans died leaving his partner with the whole collection. With nowhere else to take the 371 paintings, Sir Francis Bourgeois contacted the Trustees of Dulwich College. It was here that he had admired a collection gathered by the founder, Edward Alleyn, a notorious actor in the early 17th century.

The Enfilade is Sir John Soane's term for the central core of the Dulwich Art Gallery. The permanent collection is housed here and in the left-hand side rooms. Dulwich is a 'family' gallery. It has the largest organisation of friends in the country and retains strong links with both the local community in Dulwich and the international art world.

Immoral earnings are relative. Edward Alleyn was born an innkeeper's son but he rose to become a great performer hailed by Ben Jonson. This brought its reward: a wealth he supplemented by becoming James I's Master of the Royal Game of Bears, Bulls and Mastiff Dogs. He sold licences for bear baiting and dog fights, while running a baiting house himself. He had no children to inherit Dulwich Manor and so he left this fortune and the property to become Dulwich College; known as Alleyn's College of God's Gift.

In 1811, the vast collection gathered for the Polish king was added to the paintings Alleyn originally bequeathed in 1626. With the collection came £10,000 to maintain the collection and a further £2,000 for refitting the gallery to display the works. The Trustees went further, they built a new gallery and included in it a mausoleum for the two men who formed the collection. Sir John Soane designed the new building, which was completed in 1814. It was opened immediately to ticket bearing members of the public for one day a week, thus making this the oldest art gallery in Britain. Bombed in the Second World War, the gallery and mausoleum were restored by Arthur Davis and Edward Maude. Since 1953, the gallery's riches, including works by Rubens, Van Dyck, Cuyp, Gainsborough, Poussin, Rembrandt and Murillo, have been available for all to see, setting an example of freely available art, which is now part of the country's culture.

The musicians of the Royal Artillery Band are also members of the oldest orchestra founded in 1762, seen here playing during a formal lunch in the Officer's Mess of Woolwich Barracks in south-east London.

OLDEST MUSEUM

Elias Ashmole was an antiquary, a herald and scholar, who studied mathematics, astrology, alchemy and philosophy. He busied himself with books, while supporting the Royalist cause during the Civil War, but in 1677, he gave a large collection of rarities to Oxford University. They had come into his possession by chance. His friend, John Tradescant (the Younger), bequeathed the contents of his late father's museum to Ashmole during a drunken evening. The Museum Tradescantium, which Tradescant's father opened in Lambeth, had been the very first to admit the public. It was a collection that Tradescant had gathered travelling the world following John Tradescant (the Elder)'s appointment as gardener to Charles I.

Thus the first Ashmolean Museum opened its doors in the Old Ashmolean building in 1683. It moved to its present site in Beaumont Street in 1845, a few years after the British Museum had admitted the public to its new galleries in London. So Oxford's Ashmolean is the oldest public collection, but it lost the claim to be the oldest museum building by just a few years.

OLDEST ORCHESTRA

The name orchestra derives from the word given in Ancient Greek to the space between the stage and the audience in a theatre. It was here that choruses and instrumentalists gathered to provide the accompaniment to plays and other performances.

The orchestra that claims to be the oldest in Britain comes from the Armed Forces, where music was vital because in the days when mercenaries were employed, musical sounds were better than words for conveying

military commands. The Royal Artillery established the oldest orchestra in Britain in 1762 after the Battle of Minden. The Royal Artillery had been inspired by the drumme and phife since their use in 1557, and the idea for a band came from the example set by Frederick the Great of Prussia, who was a phenomenal soldier and an icon for a nation that prided itself on martial excellence. German military bands were developed to boost morale and strike a clear lead on parade and manoeuvres, and After the guns fell silent and the smoke cleared from the battlefield at Minden, the articles of agreement for a British military band were drawn up. However, as part of these articles the foundation was also laid for Britain's oldest orchestra. Signed by Lieutenant Colonel Phillips, the first article spells out that 'The band to consist of eight men, who must also be capable to play upon the violoncello, bass, violin and flute, as other common instruments'. Ever since, the Royal Artillery and most other military bands have demanded dexterity of ability in their musicians. They were to 'be obliged to wait upon the commanding officer so often as he shall desire to have musick, without any hope of gratification'. Above all else they were to be soldiers first and not mere embellishments; this is still the case today. When George IV was Prince Regent he sometimes sang with the Royal Artillery's Band and Orchestra and he even joined them with his violoncello. Anton Dvorak was a friend of the director of the orchestra, Cavaliere Zavertal, and used to visit the regiment's home at Woolwich frequently. At this time the Band and Orchestra were often required to perform for Queen Victoria at Windsor, and they performed Dvorak's New World Symphony for the first time. Whilst the Royal Artillery Band and Orchestra was the first established orchestra but the Hallé Orchestra claims to be the first professional orchestra that still performs today.

OLDEST ORGAN

There were church organs in Britain during the 10th century: Bishop Alphege installed one at Winchester with 400 bronze pipes and St Dunstan, the architect of England's Coronation, granted one earlier to the abbey of Malmesbury. The oldest complete organ in the world was built in 1390, at Sion in Switzerland, but recently a strange piece of wood, stored for years in Suffolk's Wingfield Church, was identified as a 16th century organ soundboard. The date is difficult to establish but experts estimate somewhere between 1530 and 1550. Recently, a new organ has been built around the original soundboard. Every possible historical detail has been followed and therefore the instrument sounds very different musically from what we are used to today. Inspiration was taken from descriptions of organs in the Tower of London and at Coventry, now long gone but which were built in 1519 and 1526 respectively. The Reformation questioned the use of organs in worship, particularly in Scotland where the organ in Holyrood's Royal Chapel was derided as a 'kist [chest] full o' whistles'. Few survived Cromwell's purge of display and the new protestant liturgy. Those that did were later replaced with the introduction of two manual keyboard instruments and the ability to enclose pipes in a swell box.

OLDEST BRASS BAND

Metal instruments have summoned humans to respond since the earliest times. The horns of Egypt and the trumpets of Israel had a call upon the souls of men, as did the first brass band that played among the people of Stalybridge, just east of Manchester, in 1809. It was a dismal time for a town touched by the early effects of the Industrial Revolution and the continuing demand for troops to fight Napoleon's armies. But when Thomas Avison raised his baton for the first time in the improvised practice room at the shoe shop, he started a tradition of music that would sweep into its embrace most of the industrial and mining communities of Britain. The first performance of the Stalybridge Brass Band took place in 1815, just six days after Wellington's victory at Waterloo. The band saw action of its own four years later, when it was booked to play at a political rally of 80,000 people in Manchester's St Peter's Fields, which turned into the 'Peterloo Massacre', when the Yeomanry charged the crowd killing eleven and wounding 400. The meeting had been about the rights of working people, hunger and the need for reform. The band remains the rallying cry for the challenges Stalybridge faces in modern times; just as all the other bands that have followed have done so for their communities.

OLDEST ENGLISH POEM

The English language has developed like every organic thing and it is almost impossible to read the words of our early Anglo Saxon ancestors without training. Exactly which work is the oldest poem, amongst the sparse literature that has survived, may be difficult to gauge without definition. The three candidate works are the biblical poems of Saint Caedmon and the two epic poems *Beowulf* and *Widsith*.

Caedmon's poems are scriptural songs that were typically sung as part of early worship and therefore may not qualify. *Widsith* has been preserved in the Exeter Book but is dated to around the year 975AD. *Beowulf* is dated slightly later, in the year 1000, but precise dating for works like *Beowulf* and *Widsith* is fraught because both probably began their existence in memory not script, being passed from generation to generation in oral form. It was common practice for poetry to be recited and learnt rather than written down.

Looking first at Caedmon's famous poem, we learn about its inspiration in the account of the saint's life left by the Venerable Bede. Caedmon was a Briton rather than an Anglo Saxon, who probably started life as a herdsman before entering the monastic life in Whitby. It was common practice for hymns to be sung after meals but Caedmon was shy and hid in order to avoid this task. On one occasion he was hiding when a vision inspired him with words that he felt compelled and enthused to sing. The text of this poem survives and its first lines emphasise the difference between English now and then:

> *Nu sylun hergan hefaenricaes uard*
> *metudaes maecti end his modgidanc*

This is translated to mean, 'Now let me praise the keeper of Heaven's kingdom, the might of the creator and his thought'.

Widsith starts its 143 lines with an inspiring invitation,

> *Thus Widsith spoke, revealing a treasury of words,*
> *he to the greatest degree of the tribes over the Earth,*

> *and its peoples have travelled through; often he is in the*
> *hall received,*
> *valuable treasures …*

The poem rambles a bit with descriptions of unlikely trips by this egotist to Saracens, Medes, Persians and most of the Germanic tribes, where his arrival inspires a showering of gifts and honour.

Beowulf is regarded as the oldest English epic even though it was not written as a manuscript until around the year 1000. The assumption is that an Anglian bard living in the kingdom of Northumbria composed the tale in the 8th century. The poem is divided into two parts. The first describes Beowulf's fight with a water monster, called Grendel, and the monster's mother, while the second part vividly recounts the elderly Beowulf setting out again to slay a dragon. It describes his subsequent death and the funeral rites that were observed for such a brave hero. It is gripping stuff and set a literary trend for poets and writers ever since who seek to inspire all humanity with the bravery of heroes.

OLDEST ROCK ART

Sometimes the sheer antiquity of things can be almost haunting. This is the case when confronted with the oldest rock art in Britain, which is to be found on the border between Nottinghamshire and Derbyshire. The place is called Creswell Crags and it is probably the most northerly point in the world that was regularly visited by our Neanderthal ancestors. This narrow gorge is about 500 meters long and was hewn out of the surrounding limestone by a river. The action of the water left caves that were used for shelter by the hunters that walked north from the continent between 10,000 and 50,000 years ago.

At that time, the English Channel did not exist and so hunters would have followed the bison and deer herds as they moved north in the summer months. It is unlikely that the hunters stayed here long because the environment would have been very harsh, but on the wall of what has been named the Church Hole, they left paintings on the walls and ceiling. These depict what appear to be European bison or early types of deer, which are now no longer found in Britain. Scientists from the universities of Bristol and Sheffield teamed up with the Open University to investigate the date for these paintings. By analysing traces of radioactive uranium that they discovered in the limestone crust over the engravings, they deduce the work to be 12,800 years old. Tools and other artefacts dating from 13,000 to 15,000 years ago have also been gathered, documented and analysed. Sadly, the initial exploration of the caves, which started in 1870, was less cautious and more driven by excitement, and a great deal was overlooked and disturbed that would have proved useful today. It is no longer possible to enter the caves, as there are protective grills covering the entrance. However, there is a visitor centre that seeks to guide and educate anyone fascinated by the incredible thought of being so close to the paintings created by our ancestors so long ago.

OLDEST CLUB

Fraternity is not as popular as it was and the exclusive gathering of men is no longer fashionable; indeed it is almost illegal. The squares and streets around St James's Palace in London still have a number of gentlemen's clubs, which were once where the most powerful men in the kingdom met and discussed politics, finance and gossip. Many of these clubs evolved in the 18th century from taverns, coffee and chocolate shops, where groups of friends gathered for weekly meetings. The oldest of these is called Whites. In 1698, a chocolate shop opened in St James's Street called White's Chocolate House but it burned down 35 years later. When the new shop was built close by, it attracted a number of aristocratic friends, among which was the Duke of Devonshire. In 1736, they became the founding members of the club that adopted the old shop's name. It moved to its present location, a fine house towards the top of St James's Street, in 1755. There was a rush of applicants to join the new club and its competitor, known as Brookes's. Whites handled the increase in membership by running a two-tier arrange-ment for a few years. The famous bay window was added to the frontage during the Napoleonic War, in 1811. Perhaps the most famous member to sit here and observe those passing by outside was the urbane critic of fashion, the dandy George 'Beau' Brummell.

OLDEST SOCIETY

The oldest society in Britain, and probably the world, first met in secret. Philosophers, academics and influential noblemen gathered in both London and at Oxford, generally on Wednesday afternoons. In letters of the early 17th century, reference is made to the 'Invisible Society',

which underlines the dangerous political times before the Civil War. A German called Theodore Haak first gathered this society together at the Bulls-Head tavern in London's Cheapside; meanwhile, in Oxford, the Philosophical Society met in the Warden's rooms of Wadham College. At the Restoration in 1660, the first journal of the society was started. The meeting was held on 28th November and Mr Wren gave a lecture on 'Physico-Mathematicall Experimentall Learning'. The following week a member brought news that Charles II had heard about the meet-ings and approved of the society. Gresham College became the official meeting place and in October 1661, the king joined its membership. It therefore became The Royal Society of London for Improving Natural Knowledge. No longer a secret, the society became a leading influence upon philosophy and learning.

OLDEST CHORAL SOCIETY

In the West Riding of Yorkshire, Halifax sits beneath the Pennines and between Huddersfield and Bradford. It was one of the main centres for the woollen and worsted industries and had been an important part of the cloth trade since the 15th century, before which it was just part of the ancient Royal Manor of Wakefield. This is where, in 1817, just two years after Napoleon's threat to Britain was defeated, the people of Halifax came togeth-er to form what is now Britain's oldest Choral Society. A local musician, called William Priestly, had the idea and the necessary character to draw in willing recruits. His musical abilities, coupled with the literary skills he had developed, ensured that the first members of the body were inspired by the best traditions of music. The Halifax Choral Society grew during the remainder of the 19th century and played a significant role in the town's life. In 1863, members took part in celebrations to mark the opening of the new Palladian style Guildhall, designed by Sir Charles Barr, and there was always room for the society to take part in religious and imperial celebrations in the town. In 1901, a new hall was constructed and named after Queen Victoria, who had died that January. Inside there was a home for the society and this became the setting for its regular concert season. Today the Halifax Choral Society has joined up with the North of England Chamber Orchestra in order to deliver half of its annual series, a fitting crescendo to the plans hatched nearly two centuries ago by William Priestly.

CHARITIES

OLDEST HUMAN RIGHTS ORGANISATION

The British Empire was once celebrated for stretching so far around the world that the sun could never set upon its shores. In recent times this boast has been subsumed by a reaction against imperialism and its colonial consequences. However, one matter is worthy of universal note and this was achieved in part by Britain's oldest charity. This was Britain's abolition of slavery in 1833, and its consequent implementation throughout the empire: a policy that spread beyond the colonies to reach the conscience of the whole world.

The first abolitionist society met in 1787, two years before the French Revolution, and their lobbying pressure led to an end to slavery in mainland Britain in 1807. After the Napoleonic war, radicalism took root and in 1832 the Great Reform Act spread change throughout society. Abolitionism grew and the following year the Abolition of Slavery Act was passed. But this legislation was flawed because it turned slaves into apprentices, which were exploited almost as much. Abolitionists succeeded in persuading Parliament to abolish apprenticeships three years earlier than planned, in 1838. Following this successful influence, the British and Foreign Anti-Slavery Society was formed the next year. Britain's Navy followed up abolition with patrols set on intercepting slave boats and the diplomatic efforts of the country concentrated on abolition. Despite this, the society is still working hard today at rooting out slavery around the world.

OLDEST CHARITY

An old sea captain and an artist founded the oldest children's charity in Britain during the 18th century. Their work was soon supported by one of the most successful composers of the day, and many other artists took their example and supported its work. Sensitivity to the well-being of children is particularly high in western society at the moment; however, this implicit responsibility was not always taken so seriously. In the late 18th century Captain Thomas Coram was horrified by the number of unwanted children forced to survive on the streets of London. He gathered a number together and provided a home, care and support, with the help of the famous artist, William Hogarth, who sold some of his work to raise funds for this project. They petitioned King George for a Charter in 1739, because nothing was strictly legal in those days without one. It was forthcoming and the Foundling Hospital was established. The Master of the King's Musik, George Frederick Handel donated an organ for the Hospital chapel, played at its opening and left a copy of his Messiah to the archives. By 1920, the building and its philanthropic concept was outdated. A new location was found for the charity, which also changed its name to the Thomas Coram Foundation for Children. Today, it goes by the more embracing name of the Coram Family, which is just what the sea captain wanted it to be.

CHURCH AND MISSIONARY SOCIETY

The current strength of religious adherence across the United States of America might have something to do with what Thomas Bray regarded as timely intervention in the moral welfare of the British Colonies in the 17th century. His actions resulted in the formation of Britain's oldest Church and Missionary Society.

Thomas Bray was born in Shropshire in 1656, and became what was called a Divine, one who is devoted to serving God. As a priest he was spotted by the Bishop of London and tasked with evangelising the American colony of Maryland, as the Anglican Church's commissar. He first established the Society for the Propagation of the Gospel, which targeted the souls of American Indians. The year before Thomas sailed to America, his friends met in London's Lincoln's Inn on 8th March 1698. They formed a society to support his work which was determined to 'counteract the growth of vice and immorality' in the colonies. This work required books and scriptures and so libraries were developed. Thus the Society for Promoting Christian Knowledge was formed, still known as the SPCK.

The publishing arm of this society is today the third oldest in Britain, after the presses at Cambridge and Oxford. In many towns and cities across the United Kingdom there are shops that sell Christian literature, in a manner that supports other philanthropic promotional and supportive work.

OLDEST CONVENT

Religious intolerance was rife in Britain after the Popish plot to blow up Parliament in 1605 was foiled at the last minute. As a result, Protestants detested and distrusted Roman Catholics; something that grew in its intensity with the development of Puritanism. Against this background, Mary Ward bravely started a Catholic society for women just four years later called the Institute of the Blessed Virgin Mary and modelled on the Society of Jesus. This monastic order established schools for Catholic girls but its work infuriated Pope Urban VIII in Rome, because its members taught without wearing conventional nun's habits. One of the early adherents of Mary's institute was Frances Bedingfield, who went on to establish the Bar Convent in York in 1686, which is now the oldest convent in Britain. With a Catholic king, James II, on the throne this was a good time for new Catholic foundations but the Glorious Revolution, two years later, swept him and his Catholic sympathies from power. As a result, the Bar Convent went through trials and hardship, including mass imprisonment in York's foul gaols, as it struggled to meet the original call that inspired its foundation. That call had come from Sir Thomas Gascoigne, who had said, 'We must have a school for our daughters'. Today the convent thrives in a beautiful Georgian building, but no longer has direct links with the city's children.

Sister Gregory in the chapel of the Bar Convent in York. The chapel has a false roof and windows on one side to disguise it. Now only five nuns remain but the convent flourishes by offering, in addition to spiritual retreats, a busy café and a thriving bed and breakfast business.

EDUCATION

Students at King's School Canterbury in front of the Norman staircase and war memorial. The gown worn by a scholar dates from the 16th century when purple was deemed to be a studious colour.

OLDEST SCHOOL

The King's School that nestles in the buildings that surround Canterbury Cathedral, is Britain's oldest. The first act of almost every missionary in early history, who managed to survive the challenge of converting pagan warriors, was to found a school, in order to confirm the Faith and proselytise future generations.

It is no surprise therefore that St Augustine established a school at Canterbury when he arrived from his monastery of St Andrew in Rome in the year 597AD. He was acting on Pope Gregory's instructions to convert King Ethelbert of Kent. Or so we are encouraged to believe by the Venerable Bede, who wrote a century later that St Augustine 'did not defer giving his teachere a settled residence in his metropolis of Canterbury, with such possessions as were necessary for their subsistence'. Bede went on to confirm the school's existence by describing how Siebert of Essex, in 631, founded a grammar school on the template of Canterbury.

Some believe that it was the Greek archbishop, Theodore, who started the school on 27th May 669, before his journey around England with the Latin-African monk called Hadrian. This journey supposedly marked the start of a united and obedient church in the country and so its ability to teach may have inspired the foundation. It was in the period when this unity was most tested, during the Dissolution, that the ancient school became King Henry VIII's concern. In 1541, he established that there were to be 50 King's Scholars and thus, in time, the name of King's School Canterbury identified this Anglo Saxon as the forefather of all English schools.

OLDEST GRAMMAR SCHOOL

It is possible that the Royal Grammar School of Worcester has evolved from a school that existed at the time of the first Cathedral Church in the 7th century. If so, then it is definitely the oldest grammar school in Britain. In 679AD, a diocese was established to provide a focus of worship for the people of the *Hwiccas* tribe. This caused great discord because the diocese was within the already established bishopric of Litchfield. It is believed that when the Cathedral

church was built, either Bishop Bosel or Bishop Oftfow then established a school that stood just outside the Cathedral's boundary wall.

Nearly 600 years later, Bishop Walter de Cantelupe established posts for teaching chaplains in order to serve at a school in Worcester. This could have been a further stage in the school's development. The date that is accepted as the unquestioned start for the Royal Grammar School was 1291. The evidence results from an argument between the parish of St Nicholas and the school. So intense was the dispute that Bishop Giffard was required to intervene. In his judgement, the school's headmaster is named as Stephen of London and he was the first in an almost continuous line of incumbents up to and including the present day. In 1561, a Royal Charter named the school as The Free School of the City of Worcester. It was free because it was no longer tied to the monastic orders that Henry VIII had dissolved.

Since the 7th century Council of Constantinople, the Church had ordered that all priests should take in children and teach them. This was reiterated by King Ethelred in the year 994AD, when he instructed that 'mass priests ought always to have in their houses a school of disciples, and if any good man desires to commit his little ones to them for instruction they ought gladly to receive and kindly teach them'. Royal association with the education of British children is maintained today through the responsibilities of The Queen's ministers and inspector. The school in Worcester carried the name of the first Queen Elizabeth until 1991 when it simplified the name to the Royal Grammar School, Worcester.

OLDEST CAMBRIDGE COLLEGE

The story of the oldest college in Cambridge may spring from an argument in 1256 between Hugh de Balsam and Henry III. Who should enjoy the temporal (secular) benefits of the diocese of Ely? Hugh had been canonically elected to be Bishop of Ely by the monks but awaited confirmation from Pope Alexander IV, while Henry wanted to grant the lands to John de Waleran.

The Pope confirmed Hugh's election in 1257 but several years were spent sorting out the damage John had done in the interim. Part of Hugh's responsibility was for Cambridge and the growing community of monks and clerics that had assembled in the town. Hugh at first sought to separate the scholars from the monks because Henry III's charter stipulated rule that was too narrow. When this was not successful, Hugh copied the example set in Oxford by Walter de Merton who faced the same problem when he had established Merton College. Hugh issued a charter in 1284 and bought two buildings that could accommodate a Master and fourteen 'worthy but impoverished Fellowes'. This act established Peterhouse College, which was the first college of the University of Cambridge. It was named after St Peter, who had been the rock on which Christ built his Church. The name came from St Peter's church but may have gained Hugh's approval because he hoped that his college would be similarly rocklike in the academic sense. More than seven centuries later it remains at the geographic centre of the university but still forms a relatively small and intimate part of the community. When Hugh died two years later in 1286, his bequest was immediately invested in more land and a new Hall, which still survives today.

Peterhouse is not only the oldest college in Cambridge but also the smallest. Seen through this archway is the chapel, which plays an important role in the life of the college.

OLDEST UNIVERSITY BUILDING

Merton College, Oxford could be the oldest university college, at the oldest university in Britain. It is almost definitely the location of the oldest university building. The library claims to be the oldest to be continuously used by students and is one of the original buildings put up around the famous Mob Quadrangle, which include the College Chapel, the Hall and the Master's Lodge. The founder, Walter de Merton, was Chancellor of England between 1261 and 1263. He served Henry III and must have been partly responsible for the king's decision to revoke the Provisions of Oxford that led to Simon de Montfort's military uprising. On stepping down, Walter established the 'House of the Scholars of Merton' in Surrey, in 1264, which moved to Oxford ten years later and became Merton College. Walter himself returned to power

as Chancellor in 1272 in order to help the new King Edward find his feet. It was soon after the college had been established at Oxford that Walter, then Bishop of Rochester, fell from his horse while crossing the river Medway and died. The buildings that form the nucleus of his college were put up in the 14th century and the library, which is the oldest of these, was erected in 1373: this therefore claims to be the oldest university building. Since the 1970s, the college has been the setting for an odd custom. Each year, when the clocks change from British Summer Time back to Greenwich Mean Time, the undergraduates spend an hour walking backwards, while drinking port. It is called the Time Ceremony. A satire on other academic ceremonies, it takes place where time has marched a steady and otherwise fairly uninterrupted path since the library was built.

The timeless view of Merton College and Chapel seen from across Christchurch fields. Behind these buildings is the oldest quadrangle and Mob Quad. Merton also has the oldest statues in Oxford.

OLDEST SCHOLARSHIP

It is perhaps refreshing to note that the man responsible for establishing Britain's oldest scholarship in the 14th century was not considered an academic by all his contemporaries – only by the Popes of the day under whom he suffered. Born of very humble stock south of Winchester, he was sent by a benefaction of the Lord of the Manor to the new priory school opposite the Cathedral, and thus academic generosity was an example set in his upbringing. However, William of Wykeham was outstandingly capable. 'At this time there ruled in England a priest Sir William of Wykeham that by him everything was done and without him they did nothing', wrote the distinguished historian, Froissart.

William rebuilt Edward III's castle at Windsor and there is an inscription attributed to Wykeham in St George's Chapel – *hoc fecit Wykeham* – 'Wykeham made this' or indeed, 'This made Wykeham'. He transformed it into a magnificent fortress and 'college' for the newly founded Order of the Garter, and then went on to earn the appointments of Royal Secretary, Keeper of the Privy Seal and to become Chancellor of England. In 1366, when petitioning Pope Urban V for the post of Bishop of Winchester, King Edward dismissed William's lack of scholarship and lauded his sheer capability. The diocese was granted and brought with it great wealth; 'Canterbury is the higher rack but Winchester is the deeper manger' said Bishop Edington, the outgoing Bishop of Winchester. The new bishop had plans. After overcoming the hiatus of Richard II's accession, William became a patron of education, establishing New College at Oxford in 1379 and then three years later a College in Winchester. The college was established for 70 scholars, three chaplains, two schoolmasters, ten Fellows and all were ruled by a Warden. The buildings were finished by 1394, and it is said that at 9am on 28th March, the first scholars were admitted. In order to win a place in the college each candidate had to sit a competitive examination, called The Scholarship Election, which takes place in the first week in May. The Election is therefore the oldest scholarship.

While Winchester College has grown considerably from its small foundation, the College remains the heart of the school. The scholars still occupy roughly the same buildings and form of lodging. They share their main rooms (Chambers) in order that the younger years can learn and be supervised by their older peers from whom they capture much intellectual and cultural aspiration. The Master in College is their guide and holds an appointment that sits between the scholars and the Warden, who, with the Headmaster, must supervise the greater school, with its 600 'Commoners' or non scholars. Scholars still benefit from assistance with fees, just as William of Wykeham intended. One final lesson is imparted to scholars from their founder's motto, 'Manners Makyth Man', which is probably the oldest motto in English.

OLDEST GIRLS' SCHOOL

John Whitson was a Bristol merchant who had three daughters at a time when little was done to educate girls; unfortunately two of them died fairly soon after birth. It is not clear whether this was the inspiration that led John to leave money for the establishment of a school for poor girls but, after a lifetime in business and service both as a member of Parliament and Mayor for Bristol, he left a large sum for the project. It is called the Red Maids' School and claims to be the oldest surviving school for girls in Britain.

John wrote his will in 1627, within months of being stabbed through the head by a miscreant in court. The knife passed through his nose, cheek and mouth, so he left money for a sermon to be given in respect of his survival from this attack. Two years later, at the age of 72, he died when his horse stumbled; he fell off and an exposed nail entered his skull. The school might have opened sooner had not John's third wife understandably contested a will that left her with almost nothing. Bristol's Common Council of Bristol was able to start plans in September 1634 for the new Hospital of Mr Alderman Whitson – the word hospital then being used for many charitable houses. One of the first items purchased, for a shilling, was a 'lookeinge glasse for the Children in the Mayden hospitall'. There were to be 40 'poore women children' who would be taught English, sewing and any other laudable work. The Mayor was to see that the mistress had money to dress the girls in red. Each year the girls dress in their red cloaks to process through Bristol, from the church where John was buried to the cathedral. The head girl lays flowers on the tomb as a gesture of gratitude from another generation helped with the best possible education. The school has now moved to a new location in Westbury-on-Trym, just outside Bristol.

SPORT

OLDEST SPORTING CLUB

When a horse race is run, or its result brought into question, it is to the oldest sporting club in Britain that the matter is referred. The Jockey Club is as aristocratic as the sport it administers, with quintessential English characteristics running through its own bloodline. Today it sets and enforces the rules of racing, licences and registers its participants, sets and enforces standards at all British racecourses, including the veterinary and medical cover provided and it protects the sport's integrity.

It all began in 1752, when a lease was taken out by a number of owners and breeders on a coffee room at Newmarket in Suffolk. This heath was the home of racing and these friends, who met to enjoy the sport, also gathered at the Star and Garter Coffee House in London's Pall Mall. King Charles II had inspired a great enthusiasm for racing in Britain and slowly their club gathered influence. At first they gained authority over the turf at Newmarket, where a series of judicial decisions supported the Jockey Club's power of 'Warning Off'. This was first upheld in 1827, when a Mr Hawkins was told to leave Newmarket Heath for swearing at Lord Wharncliffe. This tenuous precedent, which emphasised the aristocratic weight and influence of the club's members, was recognised in a deferential age and admired. Other racecourses submitted disputes to the Jockey Club for adjudication and it was necessary for the club to establish rules by which all courses they supervised should operate. Sixty-six rules were laid out in 1858 but were overhauled in 1871. By this time its authority was established and the Jockey Club continued to guide racing through difficult times such as the doping scandals of the 20th century.

OLDEST SPORTING TROPHY

Each year since 1677, the oldest sporting trophy in Britain has been contested, at Musselburgh, near Edinburgh. Called the Musselburgh Silver Arrow, it must be shot for by Scottish toxophilites, or archers. These are no ordinary bowmen – they are called the Royal Company of Archers, and they also act as the Queen's Body Guard at ceremonial events in Scotland. Attending these parades they wear the distinctive knee-length, forest green uniform, and feathered bonnet designed for them by the historian and romantic, Sir Walter Scott. He was re-inventing Scottish history for the visit of George IV to Scotland, in 1822; the first by a monarch since the Jacobite rebellion.

Throughout the Middle Ages archers were vital in warfare. Robert the Bruce depended upon his archers holding fast in the face of Edward of England's notorious bowmen during the frantic Battle of Bannochburn, in 1314. James IV was not so fortunate when he faced the English army in 1513, at Flodden Field. His body was found surrounded by his dead archers, and so he was buried with them.

With the advent of gunpowder, archery became more of a recreation and practising the skill was encouraged and became a social sport. This was particularly so in Edinburgh where archers had been admired for centuries and the dominant hill, now called Arthur's Seat, was once known as Archer's Seat. Each year the shooting members of the Royal Company meet at Musselburgh and march to the competition as a military body. Here the clouts, or targets, are in place and the match begins. They use longbows, which were the weapons that won France for Henry V in 1415. There is more than just the prize for the best shot. The winner receives the Silver Arrow from the Queen at Holyrood, while his fellow archers are on duty outside for the garden party. The winner also wins the esoteric and seldom claimed right to graze a goose for the year on Musselburgh Common.

OLDEST BOWLING GREEN

Moles are never popular, and it would be fair to say that their destructive work would be particularly tragic at Southampton's Old Bowling Green, which has been nurtured, rolled and cut for over 700 years. This turf is arguably the most venerable of its kind because it is Britain's oldest bowling green. It was in 1299, during Edward Plantagenet's reign that the first Master of the Green was appointed, and records exist that confirm the game was played on this ground during that year.

The land was part of the Warden's garden, in the God's House, or St Julian, Hospital, which was laid out in 1187. The hospital was a charitable infirmary providing lodging for the needy that was established with money from Gervaise le Riche, a wealthy merchant who must have benefited from the fact that his king, Henry II, ruled over

a vast territory of which the kingdom of England was just a part. Trade would have been profitable, especially from a port town such as Southampton, which offered convenient access to the king's extensive dukedoms in France. At this time the Royal Court was often at Clarendon, near Salisbury, or at Winchester and therefore not far away.

In 1220, the Hospital's staff supposedly played a game in the Warden's garden that involved wooden balls, but it is impossible to claim that this was what became known as bowling. The garden was stipulated as a bowling green when the first Master of the Close (or Green) was appointed in 1299, but no record of the incumbent's name survives. Edward III transferred God's House to the newly founded Queen's College at Oxford, in 1343, which was named in honour of his wife Queen Philippa. It remains the possession of Queen's College to this day, although Edward's successor and grandson, Richard II, moved to restrict the game by statute in 1388, in order to promote more military activities that were falling into disuse.

In 1511 the word 'bowls' appears for the first time in a Statute of Henry VIII. His dread power was bent on enforcing the restrictions of previous monarchs. It was his further legislation, in 1541, that seems the most vindictive and prescriptive. He forbade any working people from the game and this law, which included professions such as artificers, labourers, apprentices and servants, was not repealed until 1845. Licensing was used to enforce this spite, and it provided a useful resource to the Treasury. No doubt the Master of the Green was required to cough up. Bowls games fell under further suspicion during the Reformation and Queen Mary withdrew licences from some clubs that seemed to be using the sport as an excuse for illegitimate assembly.

It is odd that such a gentle game should have attracted so much powerful attention but it did not seem to discourage the bowlers of Southampton's Old Bowling Green. On the contrary, in 1776, Mr Miller started a competition for a silver medal, which began a unique

'Sir' Bert Baker dubs Don Weaver a 'Knight of the Green', the winner of a bowls ceremony that was founded in 1776 and has been played annually ever since. Winners of the competition can be addressed as 'Sir' within the club. The Mayor, Sheriff and Mace-Bearer of Southampton look on.

At Mitcham Cricket Club, it is not possible to reach the pavilion without crossing the busy A23. Nor is it possible to visit 'The Cricketers' and 'The Burn Bulloch' pubs without the same, dangerous journey. The latter is named after a Surrey player who ran the pub for many years.

tradition of the Knighthood – the winner of the game is made a Knight of the Green. In the confines of the club he is also addressed as a knight and in the 700th anniversary year, 'Sir' Mike Rich was appointed Master of the Green.

The turf is what makes the game special, and those treading it today are aware of its history. The worst calamity to hit the green was the Blitz. Goering's Luftwaffe concentrated its firepower on the strategically important port of Southampton. Known to all as the 'Gateway to the Empire' it was a symbol of British international power that Hitler wanted to crush. Two bombs landed on the Old Bowling Green on 13th August 1940. One landed on the turf itself, creating a crater six feet across and another razed a wall and destroyed part of the pavilion. Despite this, the club met to hold its annual Knighthood competition. With the return of peace, the only danger to this hallowed and historic ground in Southampton might be the shocking evidence of a mole to spoil the summer's sport.

OLDEST CRICKET CLUB

Few games are more English in nature than cricket. The oldest club claims to be Mitcham Cricket Club, in Surrey, where the oldest continually used cricket ground has provided the club with a home since 1685. Another claim comes from Hambledon Cricket Club, which framed rules for the modern game in 1750.

The source of this sport may be extremely old. A 13th century manuscript, that is part of the collection in the British Museum, contains a drawing that shows two men playing with a bat and ball. Whether or not this, or the reference in Edward I's wardrobe account in 1300, to a game called creag, are the precursors of the game may never be proven but, by the height of the 19th century, it was the favoured English summer pastime. It was also an intrinsic colonial export, which now involves a world-wide varsity of nations.

Mitcham Cricket Green was the possession of the Dean and Chapter of Canterbury until 1923. An extraordinary consequence of the pre-Reformation habit of landowners granting land to the Church in return for an eternity of prayers from the living clergy. The oldest reference to the word 'cricket' links the game to Surrey as well. In Russell's *History of Guildford*, the city's parish of Holy Trinity enclosed land for the game in 1550, only for Queen Elizabeth to order this land to be laid waste in 1593.

OLDEST RUGBY CLUB

Another sport that claims ancient origins and possible Roman participation is rugby. The game also shares a link with Blackheath in south-east London. Here the Guy's Hospital Rugby Club used to meet and play. The Guys team supposedly first played together in 1843 and claim to be the oldest Rugby Club because in 1883 they published the forthcoming fixtures for what was described as their 'fortieth season'. Interestingly, the title of oldest rugby club is also claimed by the Blackheath Football Club, which was formed by old boys from the Blackheath Proprietary School in 1858. Four years later both claimants, the Guys and Blackheath teams, shared the same dressing room at the Princess of Wales Hotel. The Blackheath claim has more documentary evidence but is not so old. It qualifies because the club was immediately opened to unrestricted membership.

The story of modern rugby football began when William Webb-Ellis was playing a game of Association Football at Rugby school in 1823. Suddenly he reached down and grabbed the ball 'with a fine disregard for the rules' and ran for the line. The tradition is venerated among players and affirms the sport's name.

Blackheath had considerable influence in the Victorian organisation of the sport and its rules. In 1862, the club had a famed rule 10 included, which limited the behaviour of players in a scrum, or scrimmage. This is when the forward players of both teams pack together by locking their heads and pushing to gain possession of the ball. The Blackheath Club rulebook states that 'though it is lawful to hold any player in a scrimmage, this does not include attempts to throttle or strangle'.

OLDEST RUGBY GROUND

In 1895 the relatively new game of Rugby Football was split in two, and 12 years later, in 1907, the Rugby Football Union bought Twickenham, which now claims to be the oldest rugby ground in Britain, although the field at Rugby School where the game began in 1823, is probably by logical deduction the oldest of all.

By the late 19th century, the game of rugby had quickly caught on in the northern counties of Yorkshire and Lancashire, where it was the sport of working men. In the south, by contrast, Rugby Football was taken up by the

Guy's Hospital is the oldest rugby club but membership was restricted to the Hospital. Membership of Blackheath, founded in 1858, was open to all. Blackheath was a founding member of the RFU and it still thrives in today's professional game. At one time, there were no referees – the game was played by gentlemen who knew the rules! Here, dressed in black, they win a line-out against Manchester at their Rectory Field ground.

middle classes. The split came when the working class northern players could no longer survive financially as amateurs. The Rugby Football Union in London stood its ground and so in 1895 the northern clubs formed what was to become the Rugby Football League, a professional body that promoted wages and compensation for injuries. The Rugby Football Union continued to field the national team in a growing imperial and gladiatorial contest.

In 1907, committee member William Williams purchased the 10.25 acres of market garden that were to become known as the 'Billy Williams Cabbage Patch'. Twickenham was previously a royal farm owned by Henrietta Maria, the distrusted Roman Catholic queen of Charles I. In 1908, two stands were erected to the east and west of the field, each with a capacity of 3,000 spectators. The field was used to graze horses in the First World War and a civil defence depot during the Second. Now the vast east and west stands dominate the landscape and the Twickenham name has world renown.

OLDEST FOOTBALL CLUB

The Nottinghamshire 'Magpies', of Notts County have the honour of being Britain's oldest football club. They were formed in November 1862, and played their first game at Cremorne Gardens. Football is virtually a religion in the United Kingdom, as in the rest of Europe, providing both social cohesion and a tribal identity for most towns and cities across the land. The game has provided a rallying point for communities in times of hardship. It has also provided flash points for stress and a focus for local pride. Fans follow their teams with the same courage and loyalty that Henry V inspired at Agincourt.

Football had been played in Britain since Roman times. In 1175, mention is made of a tradition of football games being played every Shrove Tuesday, though the reason for this is lost in time. Tudor, Stuart and Hanoverian monarchs all passed laws aimed at restricting the sport because of its brutality, but in

1862, the Notts Foot Ball Club was started in order to create a regulated and regular focus for the community's sport. Soon afterwards, in 1888, Notts County became one of the founder members of the English Football League. The foundation of the League and the regulation of association football established a standard that was supported with the evolution of similar leagues around the world.

The club's distinctive livery of black and white earned them the nickname 'The Magpies'. In 1903, John Savage was playing for the Italian team, Juventas, and when they were looking to replace their pink shirt, he asked his friend in Nottingham for advice. Almost immediately a black and white Notts County shirt arrived in Turin and Juventas liked its 'aggressive and powerful' appearance. This shared identity continues today and creates a bond between the teams. Football that first united communities towards a common goal now tries to bond nations in a single net.

OLDEST FOOTBALL GROUND

The devoted fans of Northwich Football Club fought a long battle to protect their pitch from invasion, but in the last few years this struggle has been lost and the property developer's bulldozers have moved in on Britain's oldest football ground. Originally the pitch was the home of the 3rd Battalion of the Cheshire Rifle Volunteers, who regularly met for drill and training for marching and parades. As a result it was called the Drill Field. Some of those hardy volunteers may have been members of the new football club that was formed in 1874. It was named after the area and the reigning monarch as Northwich Victoria. The next year the team started to use the Drill Field for its matches and practice. The field was in continuous use from this date until the final match, which was the Mid-Cheshire Senior Cup Final between Northwich Victoria and Congleton Town football clubs on 3rd March 2003. It was then that the financial battle for survival was lost and the reign of

Meadow Lane Stadium, now the home of Notts County, founded in 1862: the oldest professional football club in the world. In 2003, the club was saved from extinction by local business men and its passionate supporters.

The grandstand at the finishing post of Chester Races –- the oldest course in Britain. If you don't want to be in the stands, a good view can be had from the old Roman walls. Chester is a compact course that has become fashionable – race-goers, not only from Chester, like to dress up for a day at the races.

Northwich Victoria's Drill Field as the oldest football ground, not just in Britain but also in the world, came to an end. The Football Association confirmed the team's belief that they had the oldest ground in 1989, but even this claim to fame could not rally the sort of funds needed to meet the mounting debts and implement the increasing safety standards that were demanded by the Nationwide Conference. The team's ambitions may be partly to blame because Northwich Victoria wanted to enhance its status as a Nationwide Conference club. This was only possible with a new ground, which had to be paid for by sacrificing the club's historic and cultural home to the developers' plans.

OLDEST RACECOURSE

Horse racing still takes place in an old harbour at Chester, which is Britain's oldest racecourse. Roman legions moved north in Britain during the last century before Christ. They built a fortress where the city of Chester now stands, called Deva.

In those days, the meandering River Dee flowed close to the walls we see today and the Romans established a harbour where the river was broadest, which became the second largest port on England's west coast. In the Middle Ages the harbour was called the Roodee after an island, or 'eye', marked by a cross, or 'rood', which was left visible at high tide. Sea levels dropped and the harbour dried out leaving flat land that gently sloped towards the river's new path. This was used by the inhabitants as a leisure space and, although horses may have raced here long before, the first formal race took place in 1539. In that year a silver bell was offered to 'that horse, which shall, runne [stet] before all others'. Horse racing replaced football, which had been banned six years before. The Chester racecourse is still one of the most important in England. Its regular race meetings are watched by crowds from the city walls that sit upon the ancient Roman foundations, which are now more than 2,000 years old.

OLDEST HORSE RACE

In the 12th century, Crusader knights who had witnessed the speed of Arabian mounts brought back captured horses to test them against domestic breeds. This is probably the first way in which racing took place. Today the Kiplingcotes Derby claims to be the oldest horse race in Britain. It is run on the flat in Yorkshire across the same

four miles of lanes, between Etton, near Market Weighton, and Londesborough Wold Farm. When it was first run, in 1519, Henry VIII had reigned for 10 years and England's horses were expected to be either strong for work or manoeuvrable in battle. Speed became increasingly important with the discovery of gunpowder and the development of carriages; as a result horses were carefully bred and the best way to assess them was racing. Charles II sent his Master of the Horse to buy foreign horses in order to win the races he established at Newmarket. Royal patronage encouraged the sport and Queen Anne founded Ascot in 1702 as a fashionable social race meeting that included the advent of betting, something that would become a national obsession. The race at Kiplingcotes takes place on the third Thursday in March every year. It probably assumed the suffix of 'Derby' after the Earl of Derby established the most famous flat race in England by that name in 1780.

OLDEST CLASSIC RACE

Perhaps the worst year for those seeking to build the British Empire was 1776, the year in which the Declaration of Independence was signed in the American Colonies. For racing, though, it was the year in which the oldest classic

race was run for the first time. Except for 1939, the St Leger, as the race is known, has been run in every year since. Anthony St Leger was educated at Eton College before going up to Peterhouse at Cambridge University. He joined the army as an officer, serving in the 124th Regiment of Foot, and he became a Lieutenant Colonel, at a time when such promotions sprang from the purse. His regiment was disbanded and so he took on an estate at Firbeck, near Rotherham, where he bred horses for racing. To keep himself interested, he served as Member of Parliament for Grimsby from 1768 until 1774 and in the following two years he hatched a plan with the Marquess of Rockingham for a two mile race for three year-old horses to be run on Cantley Common at Doncaster. On 24th September 1776, the race was run as a sweepstake, with a stake per horse entered of 25 guineas. The winner was Allabaculia. Three years later the race was moved to the new course at Town Moor and it takes place there still, although it is now run over just one mile, six furlongs and 132 yards. People came from all over Yorkshire to attend the race. Miners, factory workers and farm labourers took time off to make the journey and mix with aristocrats, trainers and breeders. In 1903, Edward VII began to attend, completing the social spectrum. In 1977, the horse Nijinsky won what is called the 'Triple Crown', which are the Derby, the 2000 Guineas and the St Leger.

OLDEST HOCKEY CLUB

South of Greenwich is Blackheath, an open table of land stretching south and surrounded by London's south-eastern suburbs. Here Henry V and his victorious army were welcomed back from Agincourt in 1415, and today it is where Britain's oldest Hockey Club still meets.

The Blackheath Hockey Club claims to have been formed from boys at the Blackheath Proprietary School in 1840. This was 35 years before the Men's Hockey Association was formed to lay down the rules that revived a national interest in this ancient game. Hockey was certainly played in some form by the Romans, using hooked sticks on frozen ground or on the ice. It was popular in most of northern Europe; in Scotland it was called 'shinty' and in Ireland it was called 'hurley'. In both of these countries it was generally played upon the hard, sandy sea shore. The Blackheath Hockey Club's minute book opens in 1861. Like everything the Victorians did, there were rules and formal records. It is for this reason that the evolution of the game can be followed with certainty from this date but there are no records of ancient gatherings of sportsmen with crooked sticks. As with many sports, the inclusion of women players in hockey was terribly delayed. At Blackheath they only started the Ladies Hockey Club in 1982.

left
The Kiplingcotes Derby is a four-mile hack to the start and then a four-mile gallop back over the gentle rolling hills of East Yorkshire. This is the course of the oldest horse race. Held on the third Thursday in March, and coinciding with Cheltenham National Hunt Festival which draws a crowd of 250,000, Kiplingcoates attracts 100 spectators – some contrast!

above
The Kiplingcotes Derby was won in 2005 by Harriet Bethal on Wolfé.

Ashraf Barkat and Jonathan Shipman of The Monmouthshire Polo Club practice on the lawns in front of the ruins of Ruperra Castle near Cardiff. There is only a hint of the glamour associated with the Guards Polo Club of Smith's Lawn but both clubs are united in their passion for the sport.

OLDEST POLO CLUB

Ashraf Barakat runs the Monmouthshire Polo Club, which is the oldest in Britain. His ancestors were Moslem warriors that rode out of Arabia in order to proselytise India. Centuries later, a genetic love for horses survives in his veins and he is working to revive the club that Captain Francis Herbert founded in 1872. The Captain brought the sport back from a tour of duty with the 7th Lancers in the British Raj and established it on his brother's estate, near Abergavenny. The foundations of polo began during the 4th century in Persia, where King Sapoor II first played at the age of seven. 'It's hard going in Monmouthshire', Ashraf admits, 'there are only a few

members at the moment but now that hunting has been banned, I am sure that interest will grow. And you don't have to be rich, you just need a properly trained polo pony and once you sit in the saddle and hit the ball, it's a bug and it's difficult to get it out of you.' Other polo clubs were founded soon after Herbert's Monmouthshire Polo Club. Among them, one at the Hurlingham Club in London, where the first polo match was played in 1874. A year later the Hurlingham Polo Committee drafted the English Rule book that permeated its influence back across the Empire, through Malta and out to India. Lord Mountbatten, the last Viceroy of India, wrote his own treatise on the sport, under the pseudonym 'Marco' and it was a favoured game of princes and officers throughout the colonies. The Cirencester Park Polo Club was founded in 1894, and claims to be the oldest club to operate without a break. It is also highly regarded as an affiliated High Goal club in the Hurlingham Polo Association's Blue Book, whereas Monmouthshire is rather decried for its size and lack of members, but not for its enthusiasm.

OLDEST HUNT

Hunting in Britain was a way of life long before the organised hunts we know today came into existence. The Holcombe Harriers from Lancashire claim that Edward I hunted with their pack in 1304, and James I granted them the right to wear scarlet coats after riding with them in 1617. The Sinnington Hunt has been pursuing foxes over Yorkshire's North Riding since the 17th century and claims to be the oldest hunt of its style in Britain. Sinnington territory is bounded by Thirsk, the river Derwent and Pickering but it better describes its bounds by the names of its neighbouring hunts: among which are the Bedale, the Bilsdale and Farndale. The pack was probably formed by George Villiers, the second Duke of Buckingham in the 1660s. His real pleasures away from politics were hunting and racing at his Hemsley estate in Yorkshire. His passion for the chase was celebrated long after his death in the county's hunting songs. Today hunting in England and Wales may end, as it has in Scotland. During the evolution of the human race, survival depended on the ability to hunt. Perhaps for this reason, some people still thrill at the chase because it is part of their instinct. This is more often the case among country people, who live amongst nature and are exposed to its seasons, its needs and its balance. An activity that occupied the Saxons and their Norman conquerors became the distraction of Plantagenets — the obsession of Henry VIII later evolved to become the principal means of vermin destruction to landowners.

The hounds of Sinnington Hunt near Gillamoor. The Sinnington hunts over interesting country. On Saturdays, they are on the southern hills and valleys of the North York moors and on Wednesdays, they hunt the flat farmland south of the A170. As with many hunts, the members have hunted together for many generations, contrary to misheld belief, it is a completely classless social gathering.

The Royal Burgess Golf Club in Edinburgh was founded in 1735 and is the oldest golfing society. Red, as seen in the painted glass window of the clubhouse pictured right, is still the club colour as it was when the club was first opened. Scotland is the spiritual home of golf, so if you love the game you often have to play in miserable weather.

OLDEST GOLF CLUB

Many of the world's golfers journey to Scotland to play in the home of their sport. Quite naturally, it is the location of the oldest golf club in Britain. The provenance of the game is to be found here and so too is the regulating authority. But the two are not co-located.

Roman emperors played a game using a club and ball, called *paganica*, and it is accepted that almost every civilisation has derived fun from whacking a ball with stick. Golf in its modern form is supposed to have first emerged in Scotland in the 15th century – it led the king to worry that it would interfere with the practice of archery. The game was called 'goff' and James IV, who was killed at the battle of Flodden in 1513, played it, as did his son and granddaughter, Mary Queen of Scots. The oldest club is called the Royal Burgess Golf Society, which claims to have been founded among tradesmen players in 1735. For the first century of their existence they played beneath the ramparts of Edinburgh Castle, on Bruntisfield Links, no doubt missing a fixture or two when Prince Charles Edward and his Jacobite army of Highlanders entered the city in 1745. The year before that, a rival club, the Honourable Company of Edinburgh Golfers was established and then, in 1754, the nation's most famous golf club, the Royal and Ancient Golf Club of St Andrews was founded. From the clubhouse beside the sandy links on Scotland's eastern shore, a reputation has developed. The 'R and A' is now recognised by organisations from over 110 countries as the arbiter of the sport's rules and it organises the Open Championship.

OLDEST ATHLETICS CLUB

Birmingham has the oldest athletics club in Britain and it came about because of a badly organised competition in the 1870s. Competition is a human instinct and it derives from the need to hunt in order to survive and fight. The ancient Greeks are closely associated, through the history of the Olympics, with the development of athletics. The word athlete derives from one who seeks to compete for a prize and the ancient culture of Greece praised winners as heroes. There is little difference today. English medieval athletics was made up of rugged ball games, wrestling and the play of warlike skills. So popular were they that kings passed edicts against sport in order to promote archery, which was the ultimate skill of warfare in the Middle Ages.

At Aston Hall, near Birmingham, in the 19th century land was set aside for sport. Aston Villa Football Club started meeting here in the meadow before relocating, and the county cricket club met here before moving to Edgbaston in 1886. The running track was laid in the late 1870s and a race meeting was held but it was badly organised, and discontent marred both the competition and the prize-giving. The participants convened and established their own club in 1877, calling themselves the Birchfield Harriers. By organising themselves into a club they established the first of its kind. Athletics clubs are now located in most towns, cities and some villages. The Birchfield Harriers count among their achievers names like Geoff Capes, Bob Weir, Kelly Sotherton and Blondell Thompson.

OLDEST CYCLE TRACK

It was possibly the development of a 'free wheel' device, which enabled the drive wheel to rotate independently from the pedal chain that led to the boom in cycling at the end of the 19th century. This design saw off the precarious 'penny farthing', with its enormous front wheel and tiny stabilising rear wheel and produced a practical bicycle that both men and women could safely use. The new design was brought out in 1885; it had pneumatic tyres and looked roughly similar to bicycles today.

With the surge in popularity that came from this new vehicle, competition for speed followed. In 1892, the first velodrome, or dedicated cycle racing track, was built in London's Dulwich, called the Herne Hill Velodrome, or Stadium. It claims to be the oldest in Britain. Cycling clubs developed all over the country and were unified under the National Cyclists Union which, following the French lead, had been established in 1878 in order to lobby for improvements in roads. Hitherto these had only been roughly maintained for horse and carriage.

The Tour de France remains the world's most famous cycle road race, the first winning yellow jersey being given to Maurice Garin in 1903. That year, Herne Hill pioneered the Good Friday Meeting. A gathering for enthusiasts, it still continues despite war and other interruptions. Interest in track racing declined in the late 20th century but Jason Queally's gold medal at the 2000 Sydney Olympics revived interest and he took part in the Herne Hill Good Friday meeting to confirm the trend.

OLDEST TENNIS COURT

Lying on his death bed in 1542, close to the oldest tennis court in Britain, which he had built between 1539 and 1541 at Falkland Palace, Scotland's King James V moaned 'It cam wi' a lass and it will gang wi' a lass'. He had been defeated in almost every way possible. His uncle, Henry VIII, had crushed the Scottish army at Solway Moss, his body was collapsing under nervous exhaustion and news arrived that his second wife had given birth to a daughter. The Royal House of Stewart had sprung from Marjorie, the daughter of King Robert the Bruce and now he was leaving a weak kingdom in the hands of a seven-day old princess. The kingdom would surely not survive.

However, like the open air tennis court and its nearby chapel, the daughter was to live long in the national conscience. Mary Queen of Scots rarely used her father's tennis court, known in Scotland as a *caichpule*. Her son, James VI, was a keen player of tennis, or *caich*, until his call to the English throne in 1603. Arriving in England he found the older tennis court of Henry VIII at Hampton Court. It had been built in 1528, but was radically altered in the 17th century, unlike Falkland. Henry VIII was supposedly playing tennis at Hampton when Anne Boleyn was executed.

OLDEST SWIMMING POOL

Swimming should be an ancient sport for an island race. However, the sea was not harnessed for recreation or exercise values in any real way until the 19th century. The oldest seawater pool was called the 'Historic Roman Seawater Baths' at Lymington, in Hampshire. William Bartlett was the builder in 1833, so it was anything but historic or Roman. The original shell was superseded by a renovation in 1929, but the original structure had signalled the trend that would motivate a generation to seek the sea for medicinal and recreational health. It was not far from here, on the Isle of Wight, that Queen Victoria built Osborne House and had a bathing machine of her own.

The oldest freshwater pool, which still survives, is called Pells Pool and is at Lewes in East Sussex. It was built in 1860, and is fed by a natural spring just beside the banks of the River Ouse. Cirencester open-air pool also uses water from a natural spring, although this is now heated, and was built in 1869. There were six artificial pools in London before this time when, in 1837, the National Swimming Society held the first swimming competitions. England was the first modern society to develop swimming as a sport and it grew in popularity. All over the country pools were built, though it was the advent of chlorine in the water that made conventional baths both practical and healthy. By the time that the Amateur Swimming Association was established in 1880, there were 300 clubs in the country.

OLDEST SWIMMING CLUB

Glasgow is a vibrant city, and in the Charing Cross area of the city, which was once residential, there is the oldest swimming club in Britain. The city's businessmen founded the Arlington Baths Company in 1870, the same year that the first sanitary inspector was appointed for the city. It was built by John Burnett and consisted of a 21 metre pool and two separate bath and changing areas. Known by locals affectionately as 'the auld steamie', it grew to include a Turkish Bath for its more esoteric members in 1875. At this time, its membership grew to exceed 600 and the increased income enabled a further development in 1893. Andrew Myles was commissioned to add a reading room and billiard room, thus making it a perfect gentleman's recreation for the late 19th century. It has remained unaltered since a further development in 1902, though in 1903 the company changed its name to the Arlington Bath Club. The club's clientele and the city it serves, on the other hand, have altered beyond recognition.

OLDEST YACHT CLUB

Just south of Hyde Park in London is a modern building that looks a bit out of place. No. 60 Knightsbridge is the home of Britain's oldest yacht club. An earlier yacht club was founded in 1720, in southern Ireland, when the Cork Harbour Water Club was established to race small yachts.

In 1775, George III's brother Prince Henry, who was Duke of Cumberland, became interested in yachting and offered a cup as prize for a sailing competition on the River Thames. The duke was Admiral of the White, which was one of the Royal Navy's squadrons, and he could see the advantage of promoting nautical skills. Races between the bridges of Putney and Blackfriars races for both sail and row boats were common from the early 18th century but Cumberland's patronage put the sport onto a proper footing. The first group of yachts to compete for his cup were called Cumberland's Fleet and later, in 1823, they were renamed His Majesty's Coronation Fleet. When William IV came to the throne in 1830, the sport had grown through the development of the resort of Cowes, on the Isle of Wight. This club became the Royal Thames Yacht Club, and its members have enjoyed several locations but in 1961 the present building emerged.

Cirencester open-air pool was built on land given to the town by Lord Bathurst. Both Pells Pool in Lewes and Cirencester have had chequered lives – they were privately built, taken over by the local council and are now run by enthusiastic community associations.

OLDEST HIGHLAND GAMES

The historic defeat of England's King Edward II at Bannochburn, on 24th June 1314, altered irrevocably the status of Scotland and the expectation of its people. Under the command of King Robert the Bruce, the Scots mustered an army, inferior to the English in size and weapons, which conclusively won the day. It is no wonder, then, that the victory is marked each year by a games meeting that is the oldest of its kind. It takes place in the village of Ceres, in the county called the Kingdom of Fife.

Knowing that Edward II's army was coming to relieve Stirling Castle, Sir Robert Keith, who was Great Marischal of Scotland supposedly mustered Scottish archers on what is still called the Bow Butts in Ceres. Here they practised for the coming fight. The expectation of defeat must have been high as the men left to march the 40 miles to Bannochburn. Thus, the return of

victorious warriors to Ceres was cause for rejoicing. Ever since, excepting some interruptions, the Ceres Highland Games have been held on or near the date of Bruce's victory. The meeting originally lasted two days, with a market held on the first and then one day for competition, which was called Plack and Penny Day. The games still test strength and agility, as they originally sought to when their purpose was to prepare soldiers for battle under the feudal system. However, the tradition has evolved from tests of combat, to riding agility, dancing, the sack race and, until 1866, the scary challenge of climbing the Greasy Pole. This was a fir tree stripped of bark and coated in thick soap with a prize ham at the top for the winner. Bannochburn is rooted in the conscience of a re-invigorated Scotland, a country that has embraced the ideals of independence, ideals the men of Ceres marched away to defend nearly 700 years ago.

PUBS AND INNS

OLDEST PUBS

There are few in the list of oldest things that champion as many claimants as the oldest pub. For a number of reasons, it is not possible to determine which of the many who advertise this unique status, actually is the oldest. How the judgement is made or defined is just one of the difficulties in selecting the oldest. It could be the pub that occupies the oldest building, the one that is a built over the site of an ancient place where beer was once served in Saxon times or the place that can claim continued use of the same building for the same purpose until today. The term Pub, or Public House, adds to the confusion because it is a relatively modern one. In the Middle Ages there were alehouses, taverns and inns. Each provided something different. The first two provided fairly simple fare and therefore their buildings were not substantial. However, inns were where food and drink preceded an overnight stay, while horses were stabled close at hand. This required the hostelry to be well-constructed and therefore many buildings have survived. While some of the oldest pubs appear here it is the oldest inn, which has been in use as such since it was first constructed, that will be dealt with first.

The George Inn, Norton St Philip

The George Inn, just south of Bath, in the Somerset town of Norton St Philip, has been an inn for over 600 years. It was named after the patron saint of England, who had been a strong influence upon the crusaders that left these green valleys for the Levant. It was originally built in the 14th century to accommodate travellers attending a trade fair, which had been moved from near Bath to Norton in 1345. The monks at Bath Abbey had complained about the noise from the inn and, taking heed of this, the monks of the small priory in Norton built it sufficiently far away to avoid interruption to their devotions. The ubiquitous noise complaints of the 21st century are therefore nothing new and nor is the British habit for heavy drinking.

Even in the 14th century, constables of the manor courts were vexed with the centuries old problem of over-drinking and disorder in England. The problem made worse because ale was a safer drink than water, which was generally foul and diseased, so everyone seeking their daily quota of water was in fact consuming alcohol. After the Black Death had swept the country, the population was even more fearful of water-borne disease. Ale was not expensive, it was easily brewed and it was safe to drink. With drink at the heart of British culture it is no surprise that, in 1551, Edward VI's

Whilst none of the original buildings exist for the majority of the oldest pubs discussed here, The George was built as a pub and the original building is still in use as a pub.

parliament legislated the first licensing system to regulate what became public houses.

Perhaps it was in the George Inn that the king's collector of wool taxes stayed, in 1401. He had come to inspect the markets at Norton, which were booming from trade along the Salisbury to Bath road. However, the market was fuelled by liquor and a disagreement developed; the hapless tax collector was stabbed a hundred times. Centuries later it provided lodging for the diarist Samuel Pepys, and the Duke of Monmouth, who was passing through with his army set on defeating the Catholic James II. The room where Monmouth planned his attack the next day is still named after the ambitious illegitimate son of Charles II. Today this inn, which was designed to bring further income for the monks of Norton, is still able to attract supplementary funds as a film location. Films that have used the authentic setting include *the Canterbury Tales* and *Moll Flanders*.

Ye Olde Fighting Cocks, St Albans

Two years after King Offa of Mercia established the first Benedictine monastery at St Albans, in 795AD, Ye Olde Fighting Cocks pub claims that its history of providing ale began in a local dovecote. The pub is beside the River Ver and close to the Abbey, which contained the bones of Saint Alban, England's oldest saint. It served the monks, who may well have brewed its ale, and it also would have been an ideal place for pilgrims to the tomb to take refreshment before the journey home. The name suggests the activities that alcohol and boredom provoked – cock fighting took place in a pit around which the punters would watch and place their bets. Today this pit is used as a bar because in 1849 the sport was stopped by legislation. At this time, the pub changed its name to The Fisherman but old habits are difficult to quell and once again it holds its old English name. The river flooded in 1599 and the old building had to be rebuilt. The claim here is that it has been the location of a pub for 1300 years, which is why it is listed as the oldest pub in the *Guinness World Records*. However, it is no longer housed in the original building.

below
The proven date of the existence of a pub on the site of Ye Olde Fighting Cocks is 795AD.

Eagle and Child, Stow-on-the-Wold

But for the disqualifying fact that for 16 years the pub was closed to business, the Eagle and Child, at Stow-on-the-Wold, could be the oldest. It claims to have opened for business in the year 947AD. However, a pub that has not maintained permanent business is judged by some as no longer in the running. There was an Iron Age fort on the rounded hill top where Stow-on-the-Wold now stands. Set at the apex of the Salt Way and the Cotswolds Ridgeway, a Saxon community followed and developed here. The original pub is now incorporated in the Royalist Hotel, which claims to have been founded originally as a hospice in the year 949, by Duke Aethelmar. This also makes it a contender for the oldest hotel. To help prove its claim, many Saxon discoveries have been made in and around the building, including an old shoe and some crucifixes.

right
The proven date of the existence of a pub on the site of the Eagle and Child is 947AD.

Ye Olde Trip to Jerusalem, Nottingham

Castle Rock was the site of Nottingham's royal stronghold. Around its base there were caves that, since Saxon times, were used for habitation and storage. From these caves, passages reach up through the rock towards the original medieval castle built here by William Peverill in 1068. The pub that now abuts the rock is called Ye Olde Trip to Jerusalem and claims to be the oldest pub in England, on account of the fact that within its walls are some of these castle caves, where ale was brewed for the garrison and where it must have been made available to the people of the town. Much of this claim is difficult to support with evidence but there are strong links between Nottingham and King Richard the Lionheart. The crusader king came to the throne in the year the pub claims to have started business, in 1189. It was soon afterwards that he set off on the Third Crusade to the Holy Land taking soldiers from all over England. Many might have passed by Nottingham and taken a 'trip', which meant a rest, in middle English. Evidence does give grounds to the claim. The nearby Brewhouse Yard was administered by the Prior of the Order of St John, part of the old Crusader Order of Knights Hospitaller. And there may have been a pub called The Pilgrim. When the castle was built the river was directed to the foot of the rock. This would have provided the water supply and the caves had the steady temperature needed for brewing. The facts may never confirm the claim but there is definitely a hint of evidence.

left
The proven date of the existence of a pub on the site of the Old Ferry Boat Inn is 1100AD

above
The proven date of the existence of a pub on the site of Ye Olde Trip to Jerusalem is 1189AD.

The Old Ferry Boat Inn, Holywell

On March 17th every year there is an added attraction at the Old Ferryboat Inn, in Holywell. The ghost of a girl called Juliet Tewsley, who was buried in the building in 1050, is supposed to haunt the place in search of the woodcutter, Thomas Roul, who apparently broke her heart. The pub claims that its foundations were set here a century before beer was first served on the premises in the year 560AD. Today it is an idyllic thatched, white-washed building located beside the Great Ouse, where it winds north from Huntingdon towards the Wash. Its route is the more gentle and majestic because this is fenland and there is little elevation from the sea to this point. The ferry that crossed the water here has long gone and the provenance of the village name of Holywell explains why this place was so important to the faithful for rest as they journeyed to Ely and Cambridge.

Bingley Arms, Bardsey

Heraldry and the display of Arms are a recent invention compared to the history claimed by the Bingley Arms, in Bardsey, north of Leeds. Pubs often adopted the armorial bearings of their feudal lord, though in later times the arms or name of a local or national hero was more often used. This pub is mentioned in the Domesday Book, compiled by William the Conqueror's agents in order to better understand the kingdom he had seized. The pub is described as The Priests Inn and when its details were entered into the tome it had already been in existence for some time. The claim is that Samson Ellis, the first known member of the family, was brewing ale there in the year 953AD. As with many of the older pubs there was a religious foundation close by. In this case, it was the Abbey at Kirkstall, which is now part of greater Leeds. For the monks, the pub provided a stop on their route to St Mary's of York. Perhaps it was for this reason that a Priest's Hole exists in the chimney. The Reformation made outlaws of many religious men and here was a safe hiding place. In 1738, the Saxon building was sandwiched by more building and in 1780 the name changed to the Bingley Arms.

OLDEST PUB IN WALES

On the edge of the Black Mountains, north of Abergavenny, is Wales's oldest pub. There are no other claimants to the status in the country. Records refer to the alehouse beneath Skirrid Mountain in 1110. It was probably established earlier, but from this date some court hearings, which often took place in alehouses, are recorded. The unfortunate criminals on this occasion were James and John Crowther; two brothers accused of robbery and stealing sheep. John was sentenced to death and immediately hung from the beam while James was imprisoned for nine months.

Vindictive treatment of the Welsh by Edward I and his successors bred contempt and in 1400, Owain Glyn Dwr broke ranks with the English to lead the cause of his countrymen. Before he attacked, Glyn Dwr is said to have marshalled his rebels on the cobbles outside the pub. The mounting stone he and his men used is still there and, ironically, was used by many successors to Edward, including some who held the title Prince of Wales, which Owain had claimed back temporarily from heirs to the English crown. The courts work continued in the pub up to the 17th century and the beams are still scarred by the ropes that ended many a hearing. This building has been altered but its foundations and structure remains the original.

OLDEST IRISH PUB

Where else in the world could Sean's Bar be located? It is a true Irish name for the Athlone pub that claims to be the oldest in Ireland. However, it was renamed only recently. Since its presumed foundation in 1630, when the merchant William Moorehead owned the building, the pub was called the Three Blackamoor Heads, in reference to the Moslem Arabs that conquered southern Europe. Much of the existing building dates from the known existence of the pub in a deed of 1725, just before the stage coaching service was established to Dublin. It is much altered inside but the atmosphere is still electric.

OLDEST SCOTTISH PUB

The heroic Scottish rebel, Rob Roy, may have spent time drinking in the Clachan Inn because it was close to the centre of his operations against the Duke of Montrose. The pub is located in the village of Drymen on the south-eastern side of Loch Lomond. It lays its claim to the date of its licence in 1734. At this time Scotland was not a settled country because it was the period between the two Jacobite Risings. Rob Roy, who was of the MacGregor clan, grasped the opportunity provided by the Jacobites to try and recover his Balquidder estates. He had been evicted because of proscription and had been forced to steal cattle for survival. He created a battle-ground between the two rival dukes of Montrose and Argyll. Eventually he was captured and taken to Newgate prison in London. He was sentenced to transportation in 1727 but this was dropped and he did finally return. Perhaps in his quiet times, he came to the Clachan before the licensing of premises began. Today the Clachan attracts visitors from around the world keen to see the incredible landscapes afforded by Loch Lomond, which Queen Victoria enjoyed in 1869, and to enjoy the best of Scotland's beer in its oldest pub.

The oldest pub in Scotland proudly displays its licensing date on the front wall of the building.

OLDEST INN IN SCOTLAND

Colin Campbell of Glenorchy acquired the land at the
head of the River Tay in the early 16th century. He
constructed a fortress to guard the area, which he called
the castle of Balloch; this was replaced by his successors
by the much more magnificent Taymouth Castle. Nearby
he founded a new village by establishing an inn, which is
now Scotland's oldest. The Kenmore Hotel, as it is
known today, was built to provide lodging for travellers
encouraged to bring trade to the area and pass along the
side of Loch Tay to Killin and Crianlarich. It opened its
doors on 3rd November 1572, 10 years before Sir Colin
Campbell died. The Campbell line was elevated to the
peerage, as Earls of Breadalbane in 1681. The third earl
developed a model village around the established inn,
which is now a conservation area. It thrilled the romantic
imagination of the young Queen Victoria, who travelled
to stay with the Breadalbanes on one of her first visits to
Scotland in 1842. In her *Leaves of a Highland Journal*, she
wrote, 'At a quarter to six we reached Taymouth … There
were a number of Lord Breadalbane's Highlanders, all in
the Campbell tartan, drawn up in front of the house, with
Lord Breadalbane himself in a Highland dress at their
head. The firing of the guns, the cheering of the great
crowd … the beauty of the surrounding country, with
its rich background of wooded hills, altogether formed
one of the finest scenes imaginable. It seemed as if a
great chieftain in olden feudal times was receiving his
sovereign. It was princely and romantic.' No doubt many
of the retinue stayed in the Kenmore Hotel, as the poet
Robert Burns had done in 1783, when he inscribed the
poem he had just written on the chimney breast in pencil.

OLDEST PUB SIGN SYMBOL

When the Romans invaded Britain they changed its
culture completely. Perhaps the most influential change
was the introduction of a national administration, which
linked the disparate parts of the island to a centre and

then on to Rome. Through this network came the Roman way of living and, in particular, of trading.

It was customary for professional Romans to advertise their trade above the premises with a sign. These were generally made of terracotta. However, a wine shop was marked by a bunch of evergreens. This was copied in Britain and branches were tied together and hung above the door using an ale stake, when the brew was ready to be drunk. Pubs were named gradually and symbols were simple, like the pagan sun, moon and stars, or the Christian cross. Richard II ruled in 1393 that all pubs must have a sign so that the ale tasters could identify them for checks. This inspired many to adopt the king's heraldic badge, the white hart. The symbolic white animal represented the king's piety and so it is an ironic invitation for the masses to drink heavily. The system evolved from the local feudal baron's coat of arms, to reflect whatever symbol was currently in vogue. The list of 'oldest pubs' included in this book is an example of this and today some pubs celebrate contemporary style or humour, like the 'Slug and Lettuce'. The Bush Inn has, however, the longest surviving symbol for a pub sign which links to the worship of Bacchus in the Roman Empire.

OLDEST HOTEL

Before assessing the two claimants for oldest hotel, it is worth understanding what a hotel is and how the name came about. It was an evolutionary process. Both hotel and hospital evolve from the Latin word, *hospitalis*, from which we also have hospitality, something we all understand. Long before medicine developed, hospitals were places where the poor and suffering were housed; hotels were private homes available to visitors. The latter would often be found in a monastery, where guests of the abbot or prior would stay. Originally, the place where travellers paid for their lodging was called an inn. Inns were found at crossroads, or at suitable stages on the main roads: they also appeared close to the Royal Court in London as a dormitory for students of law. By the 16th century when monasteries were dissolved and their buildings put to new uses, the term hotel was adopted by the better inns and became a way of identifying quality to the traveller. Therefore, there were buildings called hotels long before the hotel we understand came into being. Hence, it is difficult to identify the oldest hotel. The Old Bell Hotel at Malmesbury, in Wiltshire, claims to have been in

business since Abbot Walter built it in 1220, which is a little short of 800 years. However, the early life of this hotel was as the private guesthouse of the abbot. The Old Hall at Buxton dates much later but came into use as hired lodging. It was built by Bess of Hardwick over the foundations of an earlier hostelry, known as the Auld Hall. The new building was designed for a very different guest in 1573: the royal prisoner, Mary Queen of Scots.

The Old Bell Hotel in Malmesbury is said to be the oldest purpose-built hotel in Britain, and sits on the edge of the Cotswolds in the oldest borough (see page 104).

FAIRS

The original purpose of fairs was to trade at the end of the harvest. There was always merry-making as well, but now having fun is the only purpose. Nottingham Goose Fair is the last big fair of the year before the operators retire for the winter. It would be a miracle to see a goose here – even in a burger!

OLDEST FAIR

Markets have been held in almost every town and city since law and order established the free movement of people and goods. Markets that were held on special occasions were called fairs because other attractions were put on to draw in customers. Since Saxon times, some towns held fairs to coincide with religious Saints' days, so that traders could observe the liturgy and celebrate the feast. It is not possible to establish which of the fairs still held now have roots in Anglo Saxon practice. However, two fairs make claims to be the oldest in Britain: the Goose Fair in Nottingham and the Summercourt Fair in Cornwall.

Edward I referred to a fair on St Matthew's Day in his Royal Charter to the city of Nottingham in 1284, but the assumption is that the tradition would have existed for some time before this document – possibly as far back as the Danish occupation. The belief was that farmers from as far away as Lincolnshire, Norfolk and Cambridgeshire brought fatted geese for sale. In order to do this they would coat the birds' feet in tar and sand in order to protect them on the long journey to Nottingham. In 1541 the Goose Fair was listed in the Borough records as taking place on St Matthew's Day, the 21st September each year. However, in 1752 when the Gregorian calendar was introduced into the United Kingdom and the months were realigned, a number of days were lost from the year and the fair was moved from 21st September into October. The Goose Fair is still a wildly busy affair, but it must have been even more chaotic, with the noise and bustle caused by so many geese. The birds are acclaimed as effective 'guard dogs' and with thousands of them in Nottingham's square, the sound must have been shocking and the smell probably worse. There would also have been musicians, jugglers and pickpockets to entertain the crowds, and people could congregate around the stocks and pelt miscreants with whatever came to hand. This was the 'shop window' for the Vale of Belvoir and the valley of the River Trent and the inns would have been overrun with demand.

Meanwhile, near Cornwall's Newquay, the Summercourt Fair claims to be the oldest because it can be traced back to 1201. Like the Goose Fair, it is also traditionally held in

September at the end of the harvest – a time of preparation for the cold winter months and a time when, since pagan times, there was a tradition for merrymaking. Cornwall has held a unique identity in England since before Roman times, because its tin was the source of wealth and envy. Consequently few parts of the country have known commerce for as long as this county, part of which is also a

Royal Dukedom. The fresh farm produce and livestock still draw the crowds today, and will be of interest to the present duke, the Prince of Wales.

The Crown issued more than 1500 Royal Charters for the establishment of fairs around the country between 1199 and 1350, in order to control the revenue these trade marts generated. To a large extent this process merely legitimised activities that had been in practice for generations reaching back to before the Norman Conquest. Fairs were vital and utilitarian in medieval life, but they have become almost irrelevant to the way business is done today. The supermarket and the television now provide all the produce and entertainment that was once only available when the fair came to town.

BUILDINGS

REMAINS OF THE WEST
WALL OF THE NAVE
XIII CENTURY

TOWNS AND BUILDINGS

OLDEST COUNTY

If Hengist and Horsa were to visit Kent today, its boundaries would not be so very different from the early kingdom that the former was to rule from the year 455AD. While many parts of England have been divided and renamed over the vicissitudes of time since the Romans left, Kent has kept its identity and, to a large extent, its original name. It is therefore England's oldest county name. The Celtic word for this county, which was used in the year 51BC, was *Cantium*, which probably meant either 'coastal district' or 'land of the armies'. It was through these lands that Julius Caesar and the Roman Empire advanced and from them that their power waned when the legendary King Vortigern grasped power in the 400s. Vortigern needed help to suppress the northern Picts and Scots, who were encroaching south to take advantage of the power vacuum. This help came at some point in the middle of the 5th century from the Angles and Saxons, among whom were Hengist and his brother Horsa. The former supposedly became the first king of Kent, though it is when Ethelbert was king that history of the county becomes more documented. This is when St Augustine arrived in the year 597 and baptised Ethelbert as the first Christian English monarch in Canterbury. The word Canterbury itself translated as 'the town of the people of Kent'. From this time, England gradually evolved from a heptarchy of many kingdoms into a single monarchy, but the boundaries of the ancient kingdom of Kent managed to survive. The only significant incursion of territory was in the top left-hand corner of its triangular shape, when the growth of London's metropolis required a transfer of land.

OLDEST BOROUGH

The word Malmesbury has a meaning, which is 'Stronghold of a man called Maeldub'. Maeldub was a monk from either Scotland or Ireland who established a hermitage for his disciples here in about the year 635AD. Among his pupils was Aldhelm who went on to become the first abbot of the abbey that was built.

previous pages
Glastonbury Abbey is the oldest abbey and, under Norman rule, was the most powerful. The Abbot's kitchen is seen beyond the ruins.

right
The market square in Malmesbury. The town was given its charter by Alfred the Great in 880 but it was his grandson, Athelstan, who made it the centre of his kingdom and is buried in the Abbey.

'Bury' means a place or stronghold, which implies that an area was fortified in some way, and the word 'borough' therefore suggests an evolution of the same word. The Anglo Saxons used the word to define a place where the leader lived, which had special significance because its administration enjoyed special powers and privileges. 'Borough' was also one of the administrative divisions used by Anglo Saxon monarchs when distributing authority in their land in order to establish order and justice and gather revenue.

Malmesbury claims to be the oldest borough because of a charter given by King Alfred the Great in the year 880. He gave this status in reward for the town's efforts in defeating the Danes. From this charter came the privileges and authority through which the abbot and the secular overlord were able to wield power. In the Domesday Book, Malmesbury is one of just two boroughs in Wiltshire. In fact it was not until 1645 that the town became a free borough, ruling itself with its own alderman and burgesses.

OLDEST TOWN

Emperor Claudius built the oldest town in Britain in Essex, where Colchester stands today. Julius Caesar had already invaded the country in 54BC but in the year 41AD the new Emperor Claudius was looking for a great victory to secure his popularity in Rome. His chance came from a request for help from Verica, a British chieftain. He was being harassed by another tribal leader, Caratacus, king of the Catuvellauni, who lived roughly where Colchester stands today. The emperor answered the call and came with a vast army, including elephants, to seek out and destroy Caratacus. After eventually capturing him, Claudius sent Cataracus to Rome in chains, Claudius then demanded that a fortress be built over the enemy's camp, which was then called *Camulodunum*, and this in time was developed into a city for retired Roman centurions.

The logistical project was overwhelming and required stone, gravel, wood and other building materials, which were gathered from throughout the area. Never before

The town hall and high street of Colchester in Essex, the oldest town in Britain, founded by the Romans and still surrounded by an impressive wall. Lincoln and Marazion in Cornwall, both claim to be the oldest Saxon towns.

The spa complex on Scarborough's South Bay, seen to the left of the picture, was designed by Sir Joseph Paxton in 1850 and built around the natural spring that flows to the sea.

had bricks and mortar been used in Britain. It became what the Romans called a *colonia*, a town for veterans and their families. Claudius named it *Colonia Victricensis* (Colony of Victory) and a vast temple was built there in which the emperor's effigy in bronze was raised for worship. Little remains of this place, but its impact on the surrounding indigenous natives resulted in the Iceni risings, led in traditional matriarchal fashion by Queen Boudicca. In Colchester today, the remains of the Norman castle stand on the foundations of Claudius's temple.

OLDEST SEASIDE RESORT

Health has always been an important aspiration in life and the present craze is therefore nothing new. Similar desires to follow a more pure, wholesome and invigorating lifestyle helped to establish what is probably Britain's oldest seaside resort. Scarborough had been an important site for the Romans as its large, impressive peninsular was an ideal place for a feudal

bastion to protect the shoreline between Whitby, in the north, and Filey, to the south. Nowadays, as then two sandy beaches stretch either side of the promontory. The postcard setting sounds as attractive today as it must have been in 1620, when a local woman called Mrs Farren began to market the water from two springs that bubbled to the surface close to the southern beach. The tonic properties of these waters were advertised for their healthy qualities, and the public came in large numbers to drink in the goodness that was promised and to enjoy the location, its fresh air and general feeling of wellbeing. One of these springs produced a mineral water rich in natural salts, which might have had some beneficial effect on the drinker. However, it is less easy to see what pleasure can have been gained from the other – it was a laxative. This makes one wonder, with the benefit of both hindsight and the culture of health and hygiene in which we now live, quite what its source actually was. The impressive Spa House built with the income that flowed into Mrs Farren's coffers was not

too far away from the other houses in Scarborough, which could lead to one possible conclusion.

So it was that the town began a trend of 'taking the waters', which was the initial attraction of seaside resorts across Britain before it was considered wise to swim. It was later on that bathing became popular, especially in Victorian times: Scarborough was ready for the boom when it came.

OLDEST COLONY

Strange as this may sound, the British Empire was formed largely by accident. Vast parts of the globe were accumulated on the back of trading companies, vesting long term responsibilities upon Britain for the administration of her territories, as European powers vied for lands in the expanding world.

The oldest British colony is Bermuda, which is made up of nearly 100 small islands that were taken into British possession in 1609 by Sir George Somers, who named them the Somers Islands when he was shipwrecked there.

They are better known by their original name, Bermuda, which was given to them by Juan Bermudez, a Spanish seaman who was the first man to be shipwrecked there in 1515. The islands are formed where the summit of a vast mid-ocean volcano breaks the surface of the Atlantic, so the sea all around the islands dips to a great depth.

Sir George Somers took Bermuda into the administration of the Virginia Company, which had been given a charter to develop part of America by King James I in 1606. The Company administered Virginia until 1622, when the Indian Massacre forced the king to make Virginia, and thereby Bermuda, a Crown Colony in 1624.

Over the years, the status of Bermuda has evolved along with its successful tax-shelter economy. It became a self-governing overseas territory of the United Kingdom in 1968, but total independence was rejected in a referendum in 1995. Despite its remoteness and small size, Bermuda thrives and proudly maintains its links as a colony.

PEOPLE AND BUILDINGS

A 'beehive' house, on the Dingle peninsula, is made of stones but no mortar. This type of dry-stone building was common between the 7th and 12th centuries.

OLDEST BUILDINGS

The Orkney Islands are a set of islands about eight miles north of the British mainland, and preserved there is one of the a remarkable collection of Neolithic settlements. During the last century, a number of these remains have been unearthed or exposed by the same wind and storms that covered them up many millennia before. These are the oldest buildings in Britain (some are almost the same age as the Great Pyramid of Giza) and they have been given World Heritage status.

Perhaps the most inspiring of these is the chambered cairn of Maeshowe, which dates from about 2700BC. It is close to a concentration of sites located around the isthmus between Loch Stenness and Loch Harray. The Maeshowe had already been found before the Victorians discovered it in 1861, because inside the chamber was some Viking graffiti. This confirmed a Norse saga that the tombs existed, and that they were referred to then as the Orkahaugr.

The most remarkable of these locations is to the south on Sandwicks Bay O'Skaill. This is where the storms cleared the earth from the long lost settlement that is now called Skara Brae. It is possible to see almost exactly how the Neolithic people lived because the preservation has been so complete. Each house has the same layout and the stones have been gathered and set with care.

The Dingle Peninsula, on the west coast of Ireland, also has many archeological sites, such as bronze age Wedge tombs, Iron Age forts and over sixty ecclesiastical sites including 'beehive' shaped houses. There is also evidence that hunter-gatherers settled in Ferriter's Cave near Ballyferriter in 3600BC. Nearby Gallarus Oratory is a marvel of a dry-stone building.

OLDEST PARLIAMENT

It is said that a place left alone will change slowly, if at all. This is certainly true of the Isle of Man, nestled between Britain and Ireland and broadly ignored by both. As a result of this, the Manx people have been able to keep the oldest parliament in the world — it has met, without a break, since it was established more than 1,000 years ago. Called the Tynwald, its constitutional structure is of less interest than the place it has always met. On a plateau close to the town of Peel there is a small village, called St Johns. Here there is an open field with a church and, some distance to the west, a man-made mound. The provenance of the mound is not known. It could have been a burial site or a memorial to the Norse god Thor. It is made up of four seat-sized steps with a flat top that is about six feet across. Of course, the business of this busy parliament is normally done indoors in the city of Douglas but every mid-summer, on 5th July, the Tynwald meets back at the mound. This preserves the right of the people to gather,

hear the laws passed in the previous session and redress any grievances that they might have.

The Vikings seized the island in the 9th century and probably established the Tynwald soon after. In the Norse language *thing* means an assembly and *wald* means field. It is also the source of the word hustings, used during elections, which is a house assembly. In Iceland too, where a similar parliament was established, it is called the Althing, or national assembly. The town of Dingwall in Scotland is so named because this was where the Vikings located another *thing-wald*. The Vikings ruled Man until it was ceded to King Alexander III of Scotland in 1266. From 1405 until 1736, the Stanley family were Lords of Man; for 29 years the Dukes of Atholl took over before the title was vested in the British Crown in 1765. None of these overlords chose to interfere with the Viking parliament. The Queen is now 'Lord of Man' but the island is independent of the British Parliament. The Manx people keep their Tynwald, its traditions and continue to meet each year at its ancient unexplained mound of earth.

OLDEST INHABITED BUILDING

Two castles, one in England and another in Scotland, claim to be the oldest inhabited buildings in their respective kingdoms. In England the owners of Berkeley Castle claim that it has been in the same family since the start of the 12th century, and at Traquair House in Scotland a similar age is claimed but with the incumbent family living continuously at the site since 1491. Inevitably both had historic royal links that predate the 12th century and were constantly part of the nation's royal story because of the locations they dominated.

Berkeley Castle was first recorded as a possession of Godwin Earl of Wessex, who died in 1053; presumably his hapless son King Harold inherited the castle, but he was defeated and killed at Hastings in 1066. Here the Norman story begins and it was not long until, around the start of the 12th century, Roger de Berkeley took responsibility; his descendants live in Berkeley today. It is remarkable that a single family should never fall out with the vicissitudes of royal whim – something that unseated

The Hon. Tony Brown, Speaker of the House of Keys, stands on the earthen tiers of the Viking Parliament at St. John's in the Isle of Man. The parliament, which is called Tynwald, still meets here for one day – Tynwald Day – in July each year.

most families from their abodes during history – even more remarkable considering that one king was brought to Berkeley and murdered. Edward II was deposed by his wife and her lover in favour of his son, Edward III, and it was not long before the prisoner was murdered. The act was performed with a red-hot poker and was notoriously awful and distasteful. However, the new king forgave Thomas the 8th Baron of Berkeley for any involvement in his father's murder. The castle has been a celebrated part of England's defences against Wales and it sits beside the Bristol Channel between Gloucester and Bristol. It retains all the features that romantics seek to discover in a castle that has been first a fortress and second a home for nearly a thousand years.

Traquair is no less romantic, indeed, its setting in the Scottish Borders acts as a remarkable embellishment to claims that the castle stands where a heather hut once stood in the 10th century. It is located close to the convergence of several important routes through Ettrick Forest, which may explain why Alexander I stopped here and stayed long enough to issue a charter – a fact which suggests the heather hut had been replaced by something a bit more substantial. Unfortunately the battles with England inevitably drew in Traquair and the castellated house was used by Edward I of England, known as the Hammer of the Scots and by his less successful son Edward II, who would end his days at Berkeley. The family that live in Traquair today bought it for a couple of pounds. The Earl of Buchan, who was the king's uncle, then gave it to his son James Stuart in 1491 but he fell at the battle of Flodden. Catherine Maxwell Stuart is the chatelaine today and, like all those who are privileged and yet burdened with the responsibility of maintaining a great house, she works hard to attract visitors to enjoy this remarkable inheritance. Like Berkeley, Traquair has the unique added magic of unbroken habitation and single-family ownership.

OLDEST CONTINUOUSLY INHABITED HOUSE

In August 2003, one of Britain's leading magazines, *Country Life* set out to find the oldest house in Britain that has been lived in continuously since its construction, and not turned over to either institutional use or some other purpose. It invited its readers – the kind of people who might live in an ancient abode – to submit houses for consideration. After establishing certain caveats, like the removal of ancient Royal castles and palaces, monasteries and places built on the ruins of much older buildings, the list was narrowed to a handful of continuously lived-in buildings that date from around the 12th century. Unfortunately, this set of criteria removed any candidate buildings from Scotland, Northern Ireland and Wales.

It is difficult to prove many things dating from these distant times because maps and documentary evidence are scarce. However, the ability to date the timbers used in construction is one of the few empiric measures science has developed in this field. For instance, it was possible to accurately date the pre-historic Sweet Track (page 176) in this way. The *Country Life* article named two buildings. It established that the oldest timber-framed house in Britain is Fyfield Hall in Essex. Its timbers were assessed to date from a felling in 1178; a time when builders did not treat or weather the wood but used it immediately as green timber in the building. The oldest stone domestic structure to be continuously inhabited from its construction was assessed to be Saltford Manor House, which is near Bristol in Somerset. The evidence for the building's age comes from its architectural links to the stonework in Hereford and Bristol Cathedrals – it includes an outstanding Norman window in the main bedroom. Hereford was completed before 1150 and we know that Bristol was built between 1118 and 1148. Saltford Manor was originally part of the lands associated with the earldom of Gloucester and because it has never fallen into disuse this house is considered to be the oldest inhabited home in Britain.

OLDEST CATHEDRAL CHURCH

The word cathedral is an adjective and not a noun, and 'cathedral church' correctly describes a church with a cathedra, or bishop's throne. Probably the first use of this description occurred in the year 516AD, in the papers covering the council of Tarragona. Pope Gregory the Great despatched Augustine with a mission to Kent. He landed at the Isle of Thanet in the year 597AD and was looked after by Bertha, the Christian wife of King Ethelbert. Augustine went on to christen Ethelbert and many others, so the Pope sent Augustine a pallium, a simple woollen scarf worn over vestments to symbolise the metropolitan powers of a bishop. Therefore, wherever St Augustine placed his seat would be a 'cathedral church.'

Services are held in the summer months and there is a pilgrimage in July to St Peter-on-the-Wall, Bradwell-on-Sea, Essex. This is a really tranquil and spiritual place and some of the most fertile land in Britain. The coastal marshes are used by thousands of migrating birds. There were plans to build a wind farm nearby, which would have shattered the peace of the place but St Paul's Cathedral, which has owned the land since 604AD, managed to defeat them.

The first cathedral church St Augustine selected was on the site of a Roman temple, where worship to pagan deities had been practised for centuries. This is exactly where the cathedral church stands today. It is correctly called the Metropolitical and Cathedral Church of Christ Canterbury. Inside there is a stone throne, which is still used by the current Archbishop of Canterbury. No pallium has been worn since Henry VIII severed links with Rome, although one still dominates the archiepiscopal Coat of Arms. Today's Archbishop is known as Bishop of Canterbury, Archbishop of the Province of Canterbury and Primate of All England, while also recognised as head of the worldwide Anglican communion.

The cathedral church of Canterbury grew as its importance and wealth increased. As the first established bishopric raised by the Pope, the building is the oldest cathedral church. However the dispute between Archbishop Thomas Becket and Henry II altered the fortunes and shape of the place. Henry II asked forlornly if anyone would rid him of his tiresome old friend and adversary and four knights, picked up on his exasperated words and arrived at the time of vespers to literally execute the king's wish. Thomas became a saint and the king was thrashed at the tomb in penance. Subsequent visits from British and European pilgrims to see the tomb and ask for intercessions brought wealth and the building grew. Today its splendour overpowers all who visit Canterbury. The Cathedral Church towers over everything, just as the influence of this place still

reaches to all the far flung countries of the world that have an Anglican communion. Every day since its foundation, the holy ministry has taken place, just as deities were worshipped here for centuries before St Augustine. This is not only the oldest cathedral church, it is one of the oldest continuously used Christian sites in Britain.

OLDEST SAXON CHURCH

The story starts at the Abbey of Lindisfarne, which can be found on the exposed southern shore of Holy Island, just off the eastern coast of Northumberland. Here St Aidan established his monastery in the Irish tradition in the 7th century AD. Aidan built his community with the permission of King Oswald of Northumbria in around the year 634AD. Two brothers served him, called Cedd and Chad. Both went on to become missionary saints and Cedd went to the southern kingdom of the East Saxons. He landed in the year 653AD close to the Roman fort of Othona, which had been built by Carausius in the year 285AD, and which is now found on a promontory between Southend-on-Sea and Clacton-on-Sea. On the site of the ruined fort, Cedd built his monastery and the church of St Peter-on-the-Wall is all that remains of the 7th century abbey. It is therefore considered to be the oldest Saxon church in Britain. Unfortunately it was not always used as a church. The Vikings ransacked the coast on their frequent visits and the villagers built a new church in Bradwell-on-Sea, a little further inland. Masses and the liturgy were celebrated in

the ancient building until the 17th century, when it fell into disuse and was turned into a barn. In 1920, the church of St Peter was restored and re-consecrated. It is now respected for the symbolic witness it bears to the early aspirations of the Saxon Church.

OLDEST ROMAN CHURCH

Bertha was a French princess who crossed the channel to Kent in order to marry its king, Ethelbert. She was a Christian but he still worshipped pagan gods. Concerned for his wife, the king gave her the use of a church close to Canterbury, where she could celebrate her religion with the Bishop she brought from Paris, Bishop Liudhard. This church is now believed to be the oldest church in Britain to remain in continuous use – it is certainly the first church to have been established by direction of a Roman pope. Missionaries had reached England, Scotland, Wales and especially Ireland long before Bertha married Ethelbert, but they were of the Celtic Christian faith that was superseded by the events that followed this marriage.

It is not clear whether Bertha's church was in fact a former Roman building that was converted for use, because the structure today gives few clues as to the provenance of its stonework. However, Liudhard consecrated the church to St Martin of Tours, one of the most exalted of French saints. When St Augustine arrived in Kent in the year 597AD, he was welcomed by Bertha. St Martins was made available to him and he prayed here while he prepared to convert the king to Christianity. Where the king's baptism took place is not certain, but some say it was in St Martins, at the tub shaped font that still welcomes those entering Christianity today. This may have been the most significant baptism in English history as it was to influence the whole land with the message of Christian acceptance it delivered. In due course, Augustine established himself in Canterbury and founded his cathedral church. In the shadow of that magnificent edifice and its growing power, St Martins has quietly served its parish on the hill just a short distance away. The general appearance of this church is unremarkable and there are no clues to mark this place as the Mother Church of England and of the whole Anglican Communion.

OLDEST DIOCESE

Prince Deiniol the Blessed established himself in north Wales's Gwynedd some 20 years before he was granted the land he craved to build a monastic idyll. It was the year 546AD and so the style of religious community was

The Venerable Bede refers to there being a church on the eastern side of Canterbury, in use at the end of the Roman occupation. Many Roman bricks remain in the structure.

very different from the orders monasticism that were developed later in France. This land formed the basis for the modern diocese of Bangor and therefore it is probably the oldest in Britain; it may also be the oldest cathedral church in competition with Canterbury. King Maelgwn gave the land to Deiniol, or Daniel, built the church and enclosed the central area with a wattle fence, which was called a bangor – giving the city its name. About 5000 monks worked here in what was called a *clas*, or Celtic monastery. They followed the Celtic faith in Christ which was somewhat different from the one that would soon arrive from Rome. From here, monks went out as missionaries to spread the word. They set up satellite cells in places like Holyhead, Penmon, Cadfan and Tywyn, but their work was not always popular, and the king of Northumbria once put a large number of them to death in Chester: a martyrdom that did nothing to quell the remaining monks' determination to spread the word of God. The Christian message was not embraced widely, though most people in Wales tolerated the believers. The assumption is that the king asked Deiniol to be his bishop and thus he would have been consecrated before Maelgwn died. The date of this consecration marked the start of the oldest territorial diocese in Britain and most evidence suggests the year 546AD or shortly before because, one year later, a dreadful disease spread across the country and killed the king.

The Lady Chapel, often called St Joseph's Chapel, is part of the ruins of Glastonbury Abbey. There has been a church of some kind here since, some say, the 3rd century. It is still a spiritual place, and it is easy to imagine how it was before Henry VIII ordered the destruction 1000 years of human endeavour during the Reformation.

OLDEST ABBEY

Each year, at Christmas, a very special present arrives for the Queen. It is a sprig cut from the flowering Glastonbury Thorn – a tree that still grows in Glastonbury's churchyard and was supposedly propagated from the original thorn bush. According to legend goes that Joseph of Arimathea, who had buried Christ's body after the crucifixion, was sent to evangelise Britain by the disciple Philip. He came to Glastonbury in the year 63AD and stuck his stick into the ground. It immediately took root and burst into flower at midwinter. It is also said that he established the first church here with his band of eleven followers and consecrated the ground with Christ's blood. The danger in believing this magical story is that abbeys competed for business, provenance and sanctity in the Middle Ages and this was a splendid selling point. St Patrick supposedly established monastic life here in the year 443AD but the first British monastery was built in 601 with King Ine establishing the first Saxon abbey in 708. A fire swept through these buildings in 1184, but Henry II ordered his Chamberlain to build the vast abbey church, which is now in ruins. It was the largest abbey in Britain and its considerable riches attracted Henry VIII during the Reformation, when everything was destroyed. Among the tombs lost were those said to contain King Arthur and his queen Guinevere. But this may be as fictitious as all the other legends that the Abbots promoted to attract pilgrims and their money to Glastonbury.

OLDEST MOSQUE

It was not legal to be a Muslim in Britain until 1812. The prejudice was an ancient one, born of inter-religious misunderstanding and fuelled by the fiery hatred of the Crusader Wars. Despite the ban, many Muslims did visit and live in the country before this date. They were often seamen serving on the boats that toured the colonies and sailed into Britain's ports. Although many of these believers established zawiyahs, or prayer rooms, the oldest mosque in Britain, which is in Woking, was not opened until 1889. It was named after the principal benefactor Begum Shah Jehan, who was ruler of the Bhopal, one of the princely states in British India. It is still the centre of the Muslim community in the town. Islamic influences in the country may have been imperceptible until the 20th century but there are coins from the reign of King Offa, in the 8th century, that are inscribed with the Arabic 'There is no God but Allah'. No one can explain this aberration in minting but it suggests a marked respect for the Islamic faith.

Doctor Leitner commissioned the Shah Jehan Mosque to stand beside the Oriental Institute he established. It was built with stone from Bath and Bargate according to designs influenced by the art and records kept in the British Library. This brought some imposing Indo-Saracen architecture to Surrey's verdant suburbs, including an impressive dome and minarets. The institute died along with Dr Leitner in 1899. However, in the 20th century, new life was to fill Woking's magnificent building, when the first Islamic preacher arrived in Europe. Khwaja Kamal-ud-Din reopened the Mosque in 1913 and established the Woking Muslim Mission. Four years later the first English Qu'ran was published.

In the aftermath of two World Wars the Empire drew in its boundaries, leaving unresolved strife. This was particularly so in India, where the race for independence divided the sub-continent geographically, and tore at the religious soul of the nation. A large immigration began of displaced Muslims caught up in the violent insurrections that followed. Both sides of the Indian religious divide were affected. Later, when Asians were displaced from African Colonies, they too found a refuge in Britain and the number of faithful grew.

The Islamic focus shifted from Woking after the intervention of the British peer, Lord Headley, who was President of the British Muslim Society. This aristocrat converted to Islam and made his pilgrimage to Mecca in July 1923. He prefixed his name with the honours of Islam, calling himself Al-Haj Lord Headley al-Farooq. In 1910, he and Syed Ameer Ali established the London Mosque Fund. Thirty-one years later the money was sufficient to build the first London Mosque on Commercial Road in Stepney. In 1944, the Government gave land at Regents Park for a mosque in return for a grant of land in Cairo, from the Egyptian Government, where Anglican Christians could live and worship.

In the 1960s Muslim immigrants came to Britain in increasing numbers and the need for more places of worship meant that mosques appeared in the main cities of settlement. A large number of the new families arriving in Woking were from Pakistan. As a result, in 1968 Sunni Muslims undertook the management of the Shah Jehan Mosque and they appointed the President of Pakistan as Chairman of the Trust. The country now has a strong foundation of Islam, and the roots of this tradition will always look to Woking for its source.

The leafy skyline of Woking is interrupted by the dome of the oldest mosque. Professor Lestner who could speak 50 oriental languages, built the mosque and it was paid for by His Highness Begum Shah, ruler of Bhopal. New buildings have been added since, to serve the ever-increasing community.

OLDEST SYNAGOGUE

It is recorded that Jews first came to England soon after the Norman Conquest of 1066, when William the Conqueror brought them over from Rouen. With such longstanding provenance in the country, it seems odd that the oldest synagogue in Britain, which is called the Bevis Marks Synagogue, was not opened until 1701. The reason for this is perhaps not well known in Britain but it is the same one that besmirches the history of most European countries during the last millennium: it was anti Semitism. For more than 350 years, from 1290 until 1655, Jews were forbidden to live in England.

The relationship between Christians and Jews in the British Isles started well. Perhaps one reason why Rome decided to send missionaries to Britain was because Pope Gregory saw the slaves brought to Rome from there by Gallo-Jewish slave traders in the 6th century. St Augustine was sent to the Pagan monarchs of Saxon England and the foundations of a Christian culture were effectively laid. In early Norman times Jews and Christians lived in harmony. Henry I reaffirmed what were called the Laws of Edward the Confessor and granted a charter to the Chief Rabbi in London, Rabbi Joseph, explicitly granting Jews special freedoms of movement, trade and immunity from certain tolls. The first recorded issue to arise that could be interpreted as stemming from religious difference, came during the great anarchy, during King Stephen's reign. The house of a Jew was burned down in Oxford because the owner, who was apparently burned alive inside, had not paid expenses to the monarch. Blood libels began all across Europe soon after Pope Urban II called for the First Crusade – part of the rhetoric deployed by prelates keen to encourage the faithful to Jerusalem was the outrageous allegation that Jews had killed Christ.

In the boldest move led by a Norman baron keen to make his fortune, Strongbow conquered Ireland in 1170. Arguably it began the most painful feud in the history of these islands but it is interesting to note that Strongbow's adventure, which his king was compelled to sanction, was bankrolled by Josce, a wealthy Jew from Gloucester. The unfortunate Josce was heavily fined by Henry II for his involvement in the mission.

When Richard the Lionheart was crowned at Westminster Abbey, in 1189, Jews joined in the loyal throng that came to pay homage. The leaders of the Jewish community attempted to enter the abbey but were ejected because superstitions prevented non-Christians from attending. In the frenzy of misunderstanding that followed, it was rumoured that Richard wanted Jews put to death and a hideous pogrom followed. Although Richard was said to be furious, he took no action because of the large numbers involved. Once he had left for the Crusades, the situation grew worse, particularly in York, where many Jews killed themselves rather than submit to conversion to Christianity or murder. Ironically, the Jews of England were expected to find a large proportion of Richard's ransom. However, Jews were granted certain privileges in financial matters and the Ordinances of the Jewry, settled in 1194, brought their business in line with support from the kings' judges. In towns and cities, Jews exercised their rights and many streets still bear the name, 'Jewry' to mark where Jewish business and activity took place.

During the 13th century, the Jewish people in England became possessions of the king. This status was beneficial to the Crown because it raised revenue and to some extent it protected the Jews from danger. However, as the decades passed, they were overwhelmed with taxation and kings looked elsewhere for resources. In 1275 Edward I forbade Jews from lending. This deprived the community of its source of income and many left the country. Three years later the king imprisoned all Jews and many were executed. Finally, in 1290, Edward commanded that all Jews were to be exiled. They had to flee with what they could carry and only a few were permitted to sell their homes.

It was not until Cromwell ruled the Commonwealth that a Dutch Rabbi petitioned for the ban to be lifted. Despite gaining no support from his Council, Cromwell enabled the first Jews to re-enter the country in 1655. Slowly, they returned from ghettos they had occupied elsewhere. With care, the community was re-established among a population that was fevered with the effects of

The oldest synagogue, Bevis Marks, was built in London's Aldgate in 1701. On the eastern wall is the Ark, the 12 columns represent the 12 tribes of Israel, the 10 candlesticks represent the 10 commandments and the 7 chandeliers, the days of the week.

Puritanism and Civil War. The first London community met to worship in a private house. Nothing remains from this synagogue but the pews.

In 1701, the first purpose-built synagogue in England was opened in the City of London. Called the Bevis Marks Synagogue, it was built over the former home of the Abbot of Bury St Edmunds. It reflects the style of churches that Sir Christopher Wren built following the Great Fire of London. The decoration inside is stark, simple and symbolic. The 12 pillars represent the tribes of Israel from whom these pioneers of revived Jewry descended. They have become a thriving community across the land. Ironically, the synagogue survived the dreadful bombing of the Second World War, while European Jews faced incomparable peril. However, it suffered badly in two IRA bombing attacks during the 1990s. Surrounded by the skyscrapers of the financial district, this venerable building still contains the pews used by the Cromwellian Jews. They remind the community of the determination of their forefathers and of the vicissitudes of their history in Britain.

OLDEST ALMSHOUSE

Duke William of Normandy was outraged when Lanfranc, the Italian Benedictine from Pavia opposed his marriage to his cousin. In time, Lanfranc was won over and went to Rome in 1059 to beg leave for the duke's marriage. William remembered this after the conquest of England in 1066 and four years later William called Lanfranc to become Archbishop of Canterbury. He served until his death in 1089 and it is believed that in around 1085 he founded what could be the oldest almshouse in Britain, at the north gate to his cathedral church in Canterbury. Lanfranc was consecrated as archbishop on the day the church commemorates the execution of St John the Baptist, which may be the reason that the new foundation was named after the saint. The original building, which was divided for men and women needing alms and support, was sustained by grants of land which provided a steady stream of income: however, it was destroyed by a terrible fire, probably during the reign of Edward III. The oldest building remaining inside the gates is the kitchen, which dates from Tudor times. Its heptagonal staircase from the old ground floor kitchen up to the first floor dining room is a remarkable feature. Most of the current lodging was built during the 19th century and has individual kitchens and bathrooms which provide independence for those lodging in the almshouse. There are other almshouses all over the country and some might argue that their claim is older. It is not possible to confirm or refute these, but the evidence for St John's Hospital in Canterbury is strong. The oldest buildings still extant in an almshouse are probably those at Winchester's St Cross Hospital. Henry de Blois founded it around the year 1136 and the church was started in 1135.

OLDEST ROYAL PALACE

Very little remains of the palace built by Edward the Confessor on the Isle of Thorns beside the River Thames. However, its foundations have been absorbed into the fabulous soaring Palace of Westminster which was built when the medieval buildings burnt down in 1834. Known better as the Houses of Parliament, the building is possibly one of the most recognised in the world, with its famous clock tower that is named after its hourly bell, Big Ben.

It is thought that the Romans built a temple here in a clearing where the Britons had already been worshipping Pagan gods for centuries. It was originally marshy ground that was bounded by islets, formed from gravel banks deposited as Ice Age glaciers thawed. Edward the Confessor sought Papal leave not to make his obligatory pilgrimage to Rome in the 11th century and, in dispensation, was instructed to found a monastery. He selected the Isle of Thorns because it was some distance upstream and west of London's city walls. Here he built what was called the Minster in the West – now known as Westminster Abbey. Between his church and the river Edward built his residence, which has evolved from an inhabited royal home to become the seat of Parliament. While the eyes of most visitors are drawn to the exciting Gothic profile that the Victoria Tower and Clock Tower provide, it is the more squat and plain Westminster Hall between them that has survived a truly remarkable age. This must be the oldest ceremonial building in Britain. Its walls date from those built by William II in 1099. At that time, the scale of this building was extraordinarily bold. It is no less awe-inspiring today.

Some of the greatest events in the nation's history have been played out between its walls, such as the trial of Charles I and the enthroning of Oliver Cromwell as Lord Protector. Until 1830, the coronation of all monarchs involved a procession that started here and a banquet afterwards. More recently, sovereigns and their consorts have lain here in State before their ceremonial funeral. The hammer beam roof was added by Richard II and is one of the oldest in Britain.

OLDEST COUNCIL HOUSE

As a royal prince, Edward, Earl of March, was anguished by the sight of his inadequate cousin Henry VI on the throne. Henry was a guileless man and incapable of kingship. As a result of his weakness, the French crown and possessions that had been won on the battlefield of Agincourt by his heroic father Henry V were gradually lost. Henry eventually had a breakdown and advisors squabbled over who should take power. Something had to happen and Edward decided to rise up and take the throne. The showdown between Edward and Henry took place at the Battle of Ludlow in 1459. Perhaps there is no obvious link between this battle and the oldest 'council house' in Britain but two years later, when Edward became king, he gifted a small inhabited chapel to Ludlow.

The building was built as a chapel in 1190 and dedicated to St Thomas Becket, who had been murdered only 20 years before. The de Lacy family owned the manor, which included the small chapel in its bounds. In the following century the manor was passed to Roger de Mortimer, the man who cuckolded Edward II, and through him it passed to Edward. In 1459, at the battle of Ludford Bridge in Ludlow, Henry sought out and defeated his rebellious cousin and routed him from the town. However, in 1461 Edward returned to England and this time overcame Henry to become Edward IV. The manor's possessions were no longer of interest to the new king and he donated this small royal property immediately to public ownership, to Ludlow's Borough.

The chapel was part of this gift and was administered by the town as part of the housing assets. With the development of councils in Britain, Ludlow Council administered the property and the policy by which it was rented. The value of the oldest council house could no longer be overlooked at the turn of the century and in 2001 this ancient building, the chattel of a king, was put on the market.

OLDEST PUBLIC LIBRARY

For Europe, 1848 was the year of revolutions. In almost every country unrest shook the establishment and it looked for a time as if the status quo would topple. Two significant events also occurred in Britain during that year. The first threatened to bring revolution to the country, and was caused by the Chartist movement. This was made up of discontented working class activists, who sought to force Parliament to accept its demands or face the consequences. As it turned out the consequences did not come to much. The second, was the establishment of the first publicly-

The Borough Council took over privately-owned Warrington Library when it established a town museum in 1848. In 1857, the library was moved to this purpose-built building. The public have been free to use it as a reference library ever since.

funded reference library in Warrington, which is now housed in the oldest purpose-built general library building in Britain. It is debatable which of these two happenings was more radical for the evolution of British culture. However, the library has probably had a more lasting effect than the Chartists, because it opened at a time when building libraries for public use was an aspiration of many literary figures. It is often said that reading is knowledge and

The Roman Baths in Bath, with the abbey beyond. The picture was taken just before the baths complex underwent major restoration. Today's building professionals still marvel at the skill of the Roman builders.

knowledge is the key to all things. If this is true, then the public had a rich source to read from. The collection of books that was made available in the new library, had been started in 1760 for the tutors at the Warrington Academy. Among them was the chemist and Methodist minister Joseph Priestley, who became a teacher at the academy in 1761 and was one of the scientists to discover oxygen.

Two years after the Warrington free reference library opened in 1850, a librarian called Edward Edwards was busy in London helping to draft legislation that would make libraries available to all. He became known as the 'father' of the public library movement. In 1852, he achieved another major step in the quest to make knowledge available to all. This was the year that the first member of the public was allowed to freely enter a library in Manchester. This library, which is in Campfield in the centre of Manchester, claims to be the oldest library to be supported by public rates, a step which assured the provision of knowledge to all. The significance of this leap in public responsibility was marked

by the presence of some great luminaries at the Campfield opening, including the great Victorian authors Charles Dickens and William Thackeray.

OLDEST BATHS

In a country of chill winds and inclement weather the sight of fresh warm mineral water, bubbling to the surface at a quarter of a million gallons a day, must have caused the earliest inhabitants of Britain to marvel. It was the work of the gods. Thus it was no surprise that the Romans established a settlement here and venerated their own gods through this phenomenon of nature. Quite logically, Bath is the oldest bath in Britain. The Romans combined their deities with those worshipped by the Celts, dedicating the baths that they built over the spring to Sullis Minerva. The engineering of these builders demonstrates a deep understanding of heat management and water flow, which is still considered to be impressive by heating experts today. The Romans called the town Aquae Sullis and merchants came from all over the Roman Empire to join the local inhabitants in taking the waters. The story goes that in pre-Roman times an ancient leper prince, called Bladud, came to the springs and was miraculously cured of the disease. The curative powers of the water may have had something to do with the faith of those who drank but also to the purity of its source. The water surfacing today landed as rain on the nearby Mendip Hills more than 20,000 years ago. It rises up from a depth of 10,000 feet and flows out at exactly 46.5 degrees centigrade. The buildings decayed after the Romans withdrew from Britain and apart from the fabled Arthurian Battle of Mount Badon, there was relative obscurity for the waters during the medieval period. The spa town came to life again when the Georgian Royal Family visited – immediately, a trend was set and the town's fortunes surged. The old monastic buildings that had guarded over the Roman heritage were altered by the architecture of the day and the wealthy poured into the Pump Room to take their tonic. Lepers too were wheeled into the bath in bath chairs. The bath is now a World Heritage Site and tourists flock to view the history that trickles through the steamy stones. Arrangements for a new generation to take the waters are in hand.

OLDEST HOSPITAL

Henry I was used to his courtier Rahere making jokes because he was said to be a favourite of the king's and a jester. However, when Rahere returned from a penitential pilgrimage to Rome and asked if he could build a priory and a hospital for the sick, because of a vision he had seen, Henry took the request seriously. The hospital he founded, which is affectionately known as 'Barts' is located near the meat market in London, and is the oldest in Britain. Rahere caught malaria on his pilgrimage and prayed for the energy to return to England before he died. While he did so, St Bartholemew supposedly appeared in a vision and told him to return and build the priory and hospital. What was more, the apparition told him that he would live to see the project finished.

In 1123, building started with Henry's support at a place outside the city walls, known as Smoothfield, which is now called Smithfield. Ten years later Henry gave the hospital its first Royal Charter, which made Rahere prior and stipulated that the monks should live by Benedictine rules. It went on to put the sick undergoing treatment under the king's protection, a promise not always upheld by his successors. The hospital was often involved in national

events, perhaps never more critically than when the young Richard II faced the Peasant's Revolt outside the gates in order to parlay with its leader Watt Tyler. Henry VIII dissolved the priory and left the hospital to decay until he was persuaded to grant a fresh Letter Patent in 1546, so that care for the sick could resume. The hospital appointed its first regular physician during Elizabeth I's reign, but unfortunately Dr Lopez was falsely implicated in a plot to poison the queen and was hung, drawn and quartered. The hospital became part of the National Health Service in 1948. The 1992 Tomlinson Report signalled closure, but in 1998 the new Labour Government saved the oldest hospital in Britain to continue its work.

The Henry VIII gate in Smithfield is the entrance to Bart's Hospital which has treated the sick for 900 years. The Great Hall is one of the more notable rooms and there are two murals by Hogarth on the stairs, which he painted for free. The medical school has now been merged with St Mary's and Barts is to specialise in the care of cardiac and cancer patients.

OLDEST OPERATING THEATRE

Before 1847, surgical operations were carried out with no anaesthetic at all. Surgeons were judged by the speed with which they hacked off a limb or removed an offending growth. The sounds and smells of surgery were as ugly as one can imagine. For comfort in this terrifying struggle for life, the patients resorted to alcohol, crude opiates and a piece of leather to bite on. At the oldest operating theatre in Britain, which is maintained as a museum in London's St Thomas's Hospital, the macabre nature of early operations can be seen for the spectacle it was.

In 1815 the Apothecary's Act stipulated that apprentice surgeons should attend surgical operations in order to learn their craft. Perhaps it would have been better for them to visit the butcher. This theatre is in the roof of St Thomas's Church, a church dedicated to St Thomas Becket, the Archbishop of Canterbury killed in 1170 by four knights, on Henry II's implied instructions. This strange location was chosen because the space was level with and adjacent to the women's ward, which it served. Into this roof space came a congregation of students that were ranged on elevated benches around the ominous wooden table. They stared down, from every vantage point, at the surgeon and followed each incision of the scalpel, every bite of the saw and all the needle's stitches. This audience is why the operating room became known as an operating theatre. It was a show, but it was an improvement. Before the new theatre was opened in 1822, operations had been performed in the open wards, which may not have done much for patients' morale.

OLDEST ANIMAL HOSPITAL

The British obsession with animals has engendered a society driven by their welfare in every sense. At the start of the 20th century, as the world of medicine was developing at a tremendous rate, the first animal hospital was opened in London's Victoria. It is probably the oldest animal hospital in Britain, and in 2001 it completed a massive refurbishment to enable it to provide any degree of animal care and surgery that may be required. The original hospital was opened in 1906, but there was no idea of the increase in demand that would develop. Nowadays, the hospital receives something close to 25,000 consultations a year. Run by the Blue Cross, which is an animal charity, the hospital follows the guidelines set by the trustees. In a similar fashion to the National Health Service, the Blue Cross will provide treatment to animals when the owner can't afford to pay the vetinary bills; it also finds shelter for the animal if it is unwanted or abandoned. The hospital plays its part in educating the public about the needs of animals – a constant battle as the responsibilities of owning a pet are often overlooked and continues to build a bond between animals and their owners in accordance with the British cultural love for pets of every kind.

OLDEST PRISON

Lancaster was virtually an independent part of England and, until relatively recently had its own laws and courts. This is because the area around the city of Lancaster was made a royal dukedom that had 'palatinate' power – which meant the Duke of Lancaster could act under his own authority with no need to consult the monarch. At the centre of this authority stood Lancaster Castle, where since 1196 there has been a prison of some sort. The cells today are less foreboding than the dungeons of the past, but unbroken continuity makes this the oldest jail in Britain. There are now 232 prisoners under Category C training status in the newly refurbished site, which was opened in 1955, but this place still shows sinister signs of the days when capital punishment was meted out. Death was once the sentence for petty crimes, like horse stealing, and it was only in 1868, that hangings stopped being a public spectacle. Lancaster's last hanging was in 1910 but its reputation as Britain's 'Hanging Town' had been won long before. The dukedom of Lancaster still exists but since 1399, when its displaced duke returned to claim the throne, it has been held by the monarch: today the Queen is Duke.

OLDEST TELEPHONE KIOSK

There was a competition in 1924 to find a dignified design for telephone boxes that the General Post Office would then place in almost every town, village and on most major crossroads in Britain. In 1920, a very standard design had been introduced, which was made by Somerville and Company and called 'K1', or Kiosk Number One. The competition four years later produced many designs and was judged by the Fine Arts Commission. The winning entry came from the architect Sir Giles Gilbert Scott and it was not the first major competition he had won. In 1903, his design was selected for the massive Anglican cathedral church in Liverpool. Inside this building today, tucked away at the back as a humorous reference to its architect, is one of Giles Gilbert's first telephone kiosks. It was called 'K2' and, after some constructive discussions between the architect and the customer, the design went into mass production. There was an outcry in some areas when the red kiosks were put up, but the colour was selected for ease of recognition which was intended to help in times of emergency, but in some cases the kiosks were painted green to meld with the landscape. However unpopular they may have been in the 1920s, there was another public outcry after the privatisation of the telecommunications industry meant that many phone boxes were replaced by modern designs. As a result, some of those that survive are protected. The oldest of the K2 kiosks is at the National Gallery in London.

OLDEST POST BOX

A few months before the Battle of Waterloo, in April 1815, a novelist was born. His name was Anthony and his parents were Thomas and Frances Trollope. The young Anthony endured a succession of English schools before entering the civil service as a postal surveyor. Although he is now more famous for writing some of the most highly respected literary works in the English language, Anthony Trollope was also deeply engaged in the plans to improve the postal system of the United Kingdom.

In 1844, the letters of a political refugee called Mazzini were intercepted and read, resulting in outrage and thus plans to make the post secure were hatched. Part of this process was to arrange a safe way for people to leave letters that could only be collected by a postman. The post box was the answer for every area that did not have its own post office. Anthony, as a postal surveyor, was involved in testing out certain designs, the first of which was trialled in the early 1850s. Some were not considered suitable but the one that has survived was a favourite of the novelist's. Hence it was that on 8th February 1853, the oldest post box in Britain was placed in Union Street in St Peter Port on the island of Guernsey. It still has its original livery colour of maroon, though the Post Office in Guernsey has adopted blue for all the others. Ever since this first post box was put in place, others have been cast in iron and marked with the reigning monarch's cipher. This caused problems in Scotland after Elizabeth II came to the throne. In the first years of her reign, which almost exactly marked the centenary of the post box, Scottish nationalists took to burning or blowing apart post boxes that held the cipher of a second Elizabeth: to them she was the first.

OLDEST CLOCK

Time rules monastic life as the offices of prayer divide every day. Candles and the sun's slow move across the heavens measured the hours at Salisbury Cathedral, in Wiltshire, until 1386 when the bishop installed a mechanical clock that is not only the oldest in Britain but probably also in the world. Ralph Erghum became bishop of Salisbury in 1375, and two years before he left there, he engaged a clockmaker to construct the clock. There is no face to the mechanism but it strikes the hours. It originally had a foliot balance with a verge escapement but these were replaced in the 17th century by a more robust recoil escapement and pendulum. A century later, it was moved to the central tower of the cathedral when the clock tower was removed. It was totally decommissioned in 1884, when a replacement was installed. Left to decay, the ancient timepiece was brought back to life in 1956. After leaving Salisbury and taking his appointment as Bishop of Wells, Ralph Erghum built another clock in his new cathedral. They were probably both built by the same craftsmen but the clock at Wells, which was probably built in 1392, has a readable face.

Neil Fitchet collects the mail from the oldest post box in Britain. The Union Street post box has remained in its original colour – most post boxes in Guernsey are now blue. Guernsey postmen wear shorts all year round!

OLDEST WEATHER VANE

Swivelling on its spike, high above a 14th century church in East Sussex, is the weathervane that claims to be the oldest in Britain. The church is dedicated to the Assumption of Blessed Mary and St Nicholas in Etchingham, and the successive generations that have worshipped there have reiterated this claim of antiquity. The claim is based upon the heraldic representation of the founder's Coat of Arms that can be seen in the design which is typical of the style and history of the age in which the church was built. Sir William de Etchingham started building the church in 1366, as a statement of his faith. In the 4th century the fear of an eternity spent in Hell drove the wealthy to build their own churches in order to secure God's forgiveness and ensure a place in heaven. Perhaps to make doubly sure of eternal salvation, the church at Etchingham was built on an extremely grand scale, especially when compared with the size of the rest of the village. It was constructed within the moat of Sir William's manor and, when he died, on 18th January 1389, his body was laid to rest in the newly completed church. The family had a long association with the nearby abbey at Robertsbridge and there would have been an arrangement made for the monks from there to come to the new church and say prayers for the Etchingham souls buried inside. It is assumed that the weathervane had already been put into position on top of the pointed sloping roof, which crowns the tower, when Sir William was interred. The Reverend Leslie Hook, who was Rector of Etchinham in the 1950s, wrote that 'The weather vane, dating from the latter part of the fourteenth century, is a great rarity. It is probably the oldest in the country. It is of copper, shaped like an inverted banner, with its ornamental fringe at the top. It is pierced so as to display as escutcheon … the arms of the de Etchynghams.' Today's incumbent is the Reverend Robert Dixon, who makes the pertinant observation that, 'It seems that the existence of the weather vane and its style is simply down to the vanity [of Sir William] and in keeping with the building as a whole. Believe me the de Etchingham Coat of Arms is everywhere!'

The weather vane at the top of the tower of the church at Etchingham in West Sussex.

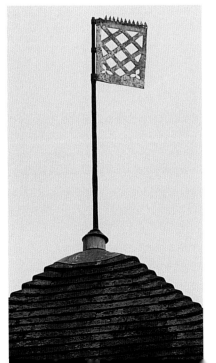

OLDEST SEWER

Experts in public health warn that the sewage system in most British cities will soon require extensive renovation. While many of the Victorian sewers are reaching the end of their life, in York the city still relies on one that the Romans built. This is probably the oldest sewer in Britain.

The need to remove human waste and excreta from living accommodation is instinctive. As the nature of living evolved from rural dwellings, where everything could be safely buried, to urban locations, this require-ment became a more pressing health problem. In Britain, as in most of Europe, the Romans pioneered the solution. They built efficient sewers that flushed everything into the nearest river – in Rome itself sewers still exist that flushed the imperial court's waste into the River Tiber.

The dangers of not treating sewage became clear from the many epidemics and plagues that hit cities in Europe during the Middle Ages, but it was not really until the Victorians faced the massive problems of post-industrial urbanisation that the sewer system in most cities was established. The Roman sewer in York was probably begun soon after Quintus Petillius Cerealis became the Governor of Eboracum, which was the name for York in the year 71AD. In the three and a half centuries that the Romans garrisoned the city, a considerable building programme took place. Some of this survives but the sewers may be the only part of their grand plan for the city which still fulfil their function. As the York city plan-ners consider how to tackle the coming need to replace the sewage system, it is ironic that they will probably not need to touch the oldest part that the Romans built. It has lasted for 2,000 years and may yet stand the constant flushing of another two millennia.

OLDEST LAVATORY

Close to the House of Lords, in London's Palace of Westminster is a tiny room with a valve closet, or 'thunderbox'. Some say it is the oldest flushing valve closet lavatory in Britain that is still in full working order. It was installed close to the Royal Robing Room when the Palace of Westminster was rebuilt after the fire of 1834, in order to provide Queen Victoria and her successors with a convenience when attending the State Opening of Parliament. There may well be older valve closets in the United Kingdom that are not widely known about because they are privately owned and quietly serving a new generation.

An early attempt at a water closet was made for Queen Elizabeth in 1596 by her godson, Sir John Harington, who made her what he referred to as a 'necessary'. The very first valve closet arrangement was probably brought into use in the mid-18th century. But it was in 1778 that Joseph Bramah's design became the template for all that followed. Joseph was a famous locksmith in Piccadilly who perfected a similar complex system of levers in order to produce his perfect lock.

Britain has a fine history of lavatories. The oldest in the world is probably the system discovered at Skara Brae when wind and storms off Orkney threw off the covering of a late Neolithic village. Its houses had been left in extraordinary condition after over 5,000 years. At one place there is what seems to be a sluiced latrine. If the assessment is correct this must surely be the oldest in Britain.

OLDEST PUBLIC LAVATORY

When Sir Christopher Wren was buried in London's St Paul's Cathedral, which he had designed and built, no grand sarcophagus marked the place. Instead, on his simple tomb was the inscription, 'Reader, if you seek his monument, look around you'. This powerful invitation might just as easily inspire the search for Britain's oldest public lavatory. It can be found by looking around you because it is the great outdoors. The instincts in all of us require somewhere to go, several times a day, and our ancient forebears had no shame in playing their part by giving back to nature what it had provided, wherever the urge occurred. However, as human beings began to reside together in buildings, the need for hygiene and respectful consideration for health increased. Old castles provide a thrill of amusement for most children when they see the privy. It is generally a simple seat overlooking a void in some overhanging room, which juts out from the high wall of a tower, directly above the moat. This solution to the need of public convenience may have been simple, logical and effective but over time it was not very healthy. The people of York in the 14th century used an arch in the old Ouse Bridge. One satisfied customer left money in his will for 'a light in the common jakes at the end of Use Bridge'. In the 16th century, councillors stood on the riverbank beside the Guildhall, and due to society's devel-

oping sense of propriety, they voted money 'to erect a wainscot around the pissing place'.

Cities demanded sewers as the Industrial Revolution drew large populations from rural areas into the urban slums. Despite attempts to improve drainage the increase in water closet usage led to London's Great Stink in 1858. As a result, planners began to address the critical need for treating sewerage and providing the public with conveniences. London's first is now probably the oldest functioning public convenience in the British Isles. This is at Oxford Circus. It was built in 1885, has been renovated twice — it was most recently given an 'anti-crime facelift' in 2005 at a cost of £300,000. Ironically, Sir Christopher Wren built St Paul's for a little over twice this amount.

Beside the Royal Robing Room in the Palace of Westminster is the oldest lavatory. Pugin designed the door furniture, the cornice and the air vent, but not, sadly, the lavatory roll holder!

STRUCTURES

Greensted Church is probably the oldest wooden building in Europe. Work was begun on a church here by St Cedd who was also responsible for the church at Bradwell-on-Sea (see page 112).

OLDEST WOODEN BUILDING

If you ever require reassurance that well-prepared and seasoned wood can stand the test of time, visit the oldest wooden building in Britain at Greensted by Ongar. Run your fingers along these walls and ponder on the claim of this tiny church that it is in fact the oldest wooden building in Europe. The oldest timbers were probably put in place here in the year 645AD and the nave extensions, which still stand today, were built in 1060, six years before the Battle of Hastings. The name of this village is a clue to its history – it is a Saxon word that means the clearing of green. In the pre-Christian days the East Saxons worshipped their pagan gods in small huts set up in wood clearings. St Cedd, who had been trained in the Celtic monastery at Lindisfarne, came here on his missionary travels. Perhaps his message was more attractive to the locals than the Roman words of St Augustine, which had been resisted as alien dogma by many. Early Christians in this part of England during the 9th century faced endless assaults from the Danes. Believers were often murdered, like the Saxon martyr King Edmund. The Normans were a fierce breed and came to this part of England with considerable skills in stonemasonry, and the church has some examples of what the Normans did in the flint footings along the chancel wall. Fortunately, they left the original building alone and apart from essential maintenance, the building is hauntingly unchanged. It is possible to imagine the thatched roof back upon the walls and the door through which the early faithful passed.

OLDEST WOOD AND PLASTER CHURCH

During the Dissolution of the Monasteries in the 16th century the Vicar General, Thomas Cromwell, took most of the chantry chapels in hand. It could have been the end for the oldest wood and plaster church in Britain, and possibly in the world, but good fortune preserved this jewel for future generations. Chantry chapels were generally built in cathedral churches so that special prayers for a specific person could be said. Individuals who wanted to protect their souls after death established these chapels and funded priests to pray for them in perpetuity. The church defined the number of prayers needed, to ensure that the saints would intercede with God for eternity. This was attractive to medieval knights who had not lived entirely within the rules of the Church.

For Sir John de Davenport of Henbury, in Cheshire, the prospect of an eternity in purgatory was sufficient for him to endow a church with 60 acres of land and to fund enough priests to pray for his soul and that of his son Vivian, in 1343. The land was farmed and the profits and tithes were paid to the chantry priests. The church that father and son built was at Merton, now called Marton, which was a short distance south of their home at Henbury. It was built on what is believed to be a prehistoric mound, which may well be a burial place. The fact that this was already a respected holy site may have influenced the

choice. Interestingly, at a time when stone was used for most building work, the builders chose wooden frames with lath and plaster to complete the structure – it is remarkable that a building exposed to the elements for so long should still look pristine. In the belfry were four bells; only three remain and the oldest of these is inscribed 'God save the Queene and Realme 1598'. Under the belfry lie two stone effigies of knights, replete with their crumbling heralds. These are supposed to be the two founders, John and Vivian. It was the intervention of the Davenport family that saved the building from Cromwell, buying back what their ancestor had already built and paid for. This must have

been galling, but worse to see the loyal Chantry priests dispersed and the endownemt seized by Henry VIII.

OLDEST IRON-FRAMED BUILDING

There is no tall building on the breathtaking New York sky-line that does not owe something of its bold construction to the ingenuity of Charles Bage. In 1796 he pioneered the first iron-framed building in the world because he was keen to build a factory for his friend, the industrialist John Marshall, that was not susceptible to fire.

The Flax Mill at Ditherington on the outskirts of Shrewsbury is the oldest iron-framed building in Britain

Many oak trees grow around Marton in eastern Cheshire (see page 40) so timber was readily to hand when the church of St. James and St. Paul was built in 1343. It is worth taking a closer look at the work of those very skilled craftsmen who were only using rudimentary tools when they built this timber structure.

The interior of the oldest iron framed building in the world. Ditherington Flax Mill had to be fire-proof so it was built using cast iron columns and beams with stone screed floors. English Heritage have bought the derelict building, so it is saved for the future. What it will be turned into has yet to be decided.

Louis XVI and offered all guests en suite bathrooms, double-glazing and other comforts, and Arthur Davis and Charles Mewes put this 'into effect. Edward VII regularly dined in the restaurant and it is still used by the Royal Family for certain events.

King Edward also visited the oldest steel-framed building in Britain, which is Skibo Castle. Andrew Carnegie bought Skibo as a summer home where he and his wife could raise their only daughter and hold large house parties. His story is extraordinary. Andrew was born

and in the world. Flax was grown locally and in Northern Ireland and it was processed to form a yarn that was badly needed for the uniforms of soldiers fighting in the Napoleonic Wars. The production process was very dust-intensive and this was dangerous because it created the perfect conditions for fire — often the fate of flax mills in traditional wood-framed factories. Ditherington is located beside a canal that was once part of the most important national communications infrastructure which helped to drive the Industrial Revolution. Iron was readily available because the first smelting site that used coke was at nearby Coalbrookdale. Charles wanted to produce a vast open-plan space for the milling equipment, which could be well-ventilated with high ceilings. His structure began with a frame constructed using cast iron girders. Wrought iron would have been better, but at the time this was far too expensive and Charles did not know the shortcomings of cast iron under great tension and compression. The market for flax fell away and so its production here ended in 1886, when the building was converted into a malting that brewed beer. It was finally left vacant in 1987, but English Heritage has now taken on responsibility for Charles Bage's building. Meanwhile, the steeplejacks who work high above the avenues and streets of New York can know where their skills were first pioneered.

OLDEST STEEL-FRAMED BUILDING

At opposite ends of the country and in totally different settings are the first two buildings constructed with a steel frame. The oldest English building is in London but the oldest of all is in Scotland's northern county of Sutherland.

London's Ritz Hotel was built in record time. The foundations went into the ground early in 1905 and on 24th May 1906 the hotel opened its doors to the most lavish interior yet seen in the capital. The hotelier Cesar Ritz had the inspiration for a hotel that echoed the style of

into relative poverty in 1835. His father was a weaver in Dunfermline who sought a better life for his family by emigrating from Scotland to Pittsburgh, when Andrew was just 13 years old. In 1901, Andrew retired to the land of his birth as one of the wealthiest men in the world, having made a fortune in oil, iron and steel – he was known as the 'Steel King'. Andrew searched for a suitable grand home. Skibo was suggested and after much persuasion, Andrew finally visited the crumbling former castle of the bishops of Caithness. He loved the southerly facing land looking out over the Kyle of Sutherland, the purchase was immediately made, and he set about building his perfect mansion. Impatiently he opted for a steel construction, which was popular in America. He had his own steel milled in Pittsburgh, sailed across and constructed according to plans drawn up in Inverness in 1899. The poured concrete and steel structure enabled Andrew to move in during 1901 and the building was completed by 1902. Faced with Dornoch stone, it is now a private international residential club and provided the location for Madonna's wedding.

The restricted site available to build the Ritz Hotel forced the use of a steel frame. The hotel was designed to look like a Parisian building and was the first in Britain to have en-suite bathrooms. It has been one of the most luxorious hotels in London since it was built a hundred years ago.

The Normans built a chain of stone fortifications along the English and Welsh border, of which the keep of Chepstow Castle was the first. The castle was extended in 1190, and the wooden doors built then are still standing today.

OLDEST STONE-BUILT CASTLE

Records are sketchy in the immediate aftermath of the Norman Conquest, and therefore it is not easy to be sure when the first stone foundations were laid for the many fortresses that were built after 1066. That said, it is worth considering what posed the greatest danger to William the Conqueror on securing his English crown. It is probable that the Great Tower of Chepstow Castle in Wales is, by a whisker, the oldest stone-built castle in Britain. The origination of the word castle is another clue. It came into England's vernacular when Edward the Confessor imported Norman knights as mercenaries, so that he could establish castles in Herefordshire and keep the Welsh at bay. Possibly these knights discovered the rugged cliff by the River Wye and began building before 1066. Soon afterwards, William fitz Osbern arrived. He was one of the Conqueror's most trusted knights. It was no surprise that he was rewarded with plenty of land for his bravery. The territory he got was akin to modern Herefordshire. With it came the military responsibility for holding ground against the Welsh. Thus some historians date the start of Chepstow Castle's Great Tower to 1067, because the new baron would have wanted to establish his stronghold immediately. Fitz Osbern died in combat in 1071, and the Domesday Book states that 'Earl William built the castle at Estriguil', or Chepstow. As the foundations for the Tower of London were not laid until 1078 and Windsor's two years later still, until more evidence can be found, Chepstow's ruined keep is probably the oldest.

OLDEST FORTIFICATION

The Picts inhabited the north of what later became Scotland, and in many parts of the Highlands and on Orkney there are brochs, which were fortified dwellings built to sustain the simplest existence and withstand tribal attacks. Any one of these might be the oldest castle in Scotland. Just west of Glasgow a giant rock narrows the Clyde beside the tributary of the River Leven. The ancient Britons used this volcanic plug as a fortress; at that time it was called Dun Breatann, which means Fortress of the Britons. Today it is called Dumbarton Rock and it is the oldest fortification in Britain.

Many historians assume that even before the Britons came to Dumbarton the ancient tribes chose this feature because of its safety from attack while using the land around the base for their settlements. The first documentary evidence for the use of the rock is a letter, which St Patrick wrote to the King of Strathclyde in the year 450AD in protest against a raid by the Britons of Dumbarton on his converts' settlements. The Britons ruled most what is now south-western Scotland, other kingdoms surrounded Strathclyde. In the north were the Picts; to the northwest, roughly where Argyll is today, was the kingdom of Dalriada ruled by the Scots, who were settlers from Ireland. To the south in Northumbria and Cumbria were the two kingdoms of Rheged and Elmet. The greatest danger came from the sea and in the 9th century the Vikings arrived and defeated Strathclyde. They lay siege to the rock for several months before starvation and thirst defeated the Britons. It is said that Olaf the White and Ivar the Cripple needed 200 longships to carry the spoils of war back to Dublin. The fortress was adapted over the years to meet the changing needs of warfare and it became a vital link in the Hanoverian chain of strongholds from which to suppress the Jacobites. It was only vacated by the British armed forces in the 20th century.

OLDEST MUNICIPAL BUILDING

It is thought that Exeter has the oldest site for a municipal building in Britain. Its Guildhall stands where it is believed that the first city building stood around the year 1160. Reference to the site is made in a deed of the time, but it is possible that it had already been here for many decades. The nature of municipal government has changed completely since the early Norman feudal structure took hold in this region. Around it the city's dwellers gathered to celebrate and trade in the Llamas

Fair, which was established by Royal Charter and is still opened each year with the same text that was first read out here in 1330, during the reign of Edward III. The majority of the Guildhall that is visible today was built in the 15th century, though there are extant references to construction on the site in 1330, when the Llamas Fair words were first used. Sadly it is believed that none of the original building remains visible above or below the ground. Like all Guildhalls, Exeter's was where the Mayor and his council were able to regulate the activities of the guilds that worked and traded in the city. The hall would have been a market and, like the Great Hall at the Palace of Westminster, which is much older but served a very different function, it was also where the court met and justice was done.

Exeter Guildhall has been at the centre of civic life for the last 800 years. The Mayor's parlour is on the first floor and every Easter, the Senior Mace Sergeant hoists the Lammas Fair Glove from the balcony. The Guildhall is used for city council meetings, Mayoral banquets and general civic functions.

The architect of the Palm House in Belfast, pictured here, later used the same technology to build the Great Glass House at Kew Gardens.

century. However, the chapel was destroyed in 1737, in a ritual act of barbarism by Bishop Henry Egerton, who spent £50 on the deed when, it was said, he could have restored it for just £10. It is no longer possible to see the soaring timber beams of the great hall without clambering into the roof space but they are still part of the building and represent what is considered to be the grandest of the remaining 12th-century timber buildings in the country. Nowadays the Church of England is continually reviewing its assets following poor investments made by Church Commissioners, and huge losses incurred towards the end of the 20th century. There are no remnant temporal trappings for the Bishop of Hereford in the bishop's palace. He no longer fills the stately rooms as a potentate, but instead has a modest flat and shares the rest with other members of the clergy. Today the Bishop's Palace gives no clue to the riches it contains. From the outside it is, as the last bishop put it, 'singularly unimpressive'.

OLDEST CURVILINEAR GLASSHOUSE

The sight of the Palm House in Belfast's botanic gardens is remarkable. It is the epitome of design and practicality that marks many Victorian buildings, and was the signature of its architect, Sir Charles Lanyon. His vision required not just a curvilinear iron frame but also specially prepared curvilinear glass from Dublin. It is now the oldest surviving house of its kind in Britain, though it was superseded in design and daring by the Palm House in Kew Gardens that was built shortly afterwards. The Belfast Botanical and Horticultural Society decided that a Palm House was required in the mid-1830s and it was built to Sir Charles's design by Richard Turner, a builder from Dublin who had a great deal of experience with glass. Work on the building began in 1839 and was completed the next year. 'It's a lovely building which still provides a home for the plants that befits the enjoyment of our visitors' explains Reg Maxwell the manager of the botanic gardens, 'It isn't big but it's very intimate and you feel you are in amongst these plants and you're touching, passing and brushing them as you walk through the three sections'.

The three sections start with the first of two wings extending from the central dome. In this wing, which is called the Cool House, there are many vibrant and colourful plants set in pots that are continually changed in order to provoke a sense of awe. This opens into the dome, where the taller tropical and sub-tropical plants thrive. The sense of space is not great but the effect is just as Sir Charles

OLDEST SECULAR BUILDING

A secular building is one that is not strictly religious and therefore it may seem odd that a bishop's palace should qualify. However, even though most bishops' palaces have chapels within them, the buildings themselves are not consecrated for worship.

Hereford's bishops palace stands beside the River Wye in the lee of the magnificent cathedral church. The great hall was built in 1186 – a testament to the wealth and power of the bishops at that time. This was the year that William de Vere was consecrated as Bishop of Hereford and although we are not sure of its state, it is likely that the palace was in some disrepair when he took it over after all the fighting that had occurred during the Anarchy. The plan was to set the great hall in a scheme of three adjoining buildings – a chamber block, the hall and the chapel that Bishop Robert Losinger built at the start of the 12th intended. It has what Reg Maxwell calls the 'wow factor' and was designed to give the best aspect for visitors. Finally, the door opens into the Stove House which is the last wing, where plants that need constant heat are nurtured. The collection was replaced after extensive refurbishment work between 1977 and 1980 and many of the plants came from places like Kew and Sheffield Botanical Gardens. There may be older glasshouses, which include simple lean-to designs but no cathedral to horticulture quite like this one in Ulster.

OLDEST LIGHTHOUSE

The invasion of Britain by the Romans required strategic support and logistical supply. The narrowest part of the Channel is the Strait of Dover and therefore Dover was adopted as the best place for a convenient harbour and defences. In order to help ships and boats find their way over from Gaul (the name the Romans gave to France), two large lighthouses were built on either side of the port – only one remains above ground. It stands to a height of 13 metres, which makes it the highest standing Roman building left in Britain. It is also the oldest lighthouse in the country, although it has not been lit for centuries. The Eastern Pharos, as Roman lighthouses were called, is preserved in the grounds of Dover Castle, which has been one of the most important fortresses in England's defence since the invasion by William the Conqueror. The octagonal tower and its pair, the Western Pharos, which can only be identified by its foundations, were probably built around the year 140AD. This was the time when the Roman's fleet of ships, called the Classis Britannica, used Dover as a port. It is unlikely they were here because of any danger to the shipping route, and the evidence suggests that the fleet was often away on military campaigns for the Emperor. Centuries later the remaining Eastern Pharos was converted into a bell tower for the church of St Mary-in-Castro, with bells brought from Canterbury sometime before 1252. These were removed to Portsmouth in the 1700s and the tower again fell into some disrepair. As part of a major national attraction, the Eastern Pharos tower is a protected building.

OLDEST LIGHTHOUSE AT SEA

Henry Winstanley was furious when one of his ships foundered on the rocks at Eddystone reef, 14 miles outside Plymouth Harbour. This flamboyant shipping merchant could not afford to lose vessels and it was heartbreaking to the families of his crew, notwithstanding the cargo that was lost. He is responsible for building the first lighthouse on a British rock out at sea. The lighthouse standing at Eddystone today occupies the oldest site of a sea-based lighthouse off the nation's coastline. It was 1696 when Henry started work. It was very dangerous as the rock is never far clear of the water and the weather in the English Channel could blow up at any time. Work went steadily until the following year, when a French ship stopped to take him prisoner. England was at war with France but when Louis XIV heard about the circumstances, he had Henry released saying, 'France [is] at war with England not with humanity'. In November 1698, the first light shone out and the project was completed the following year. Henry was so proud of the structure he resolved to stay in the building during a storm. His wish came true in 1703, but the storm was so great that the boat sent to bring him home found the lighthouse destroyed. First John Rudyerd and then John Smeaton built replacements, but in 1882 James Douglass built the tower that stands today.

The 80ft Roman lighthouse, in the grounds of Dover Castle from where, on a good day, France can clearly be seen.

Outwood Windmill on the Surrey Downs was built a year before the Great Fire of London. It is still milling flour that can be bought when the mill is open to the public on Sunday afternoons in the summer.

OLDEST WINDMILL

It is possible that Britain may be on the eve of a revival in the use of wind power. Using clean energy drawn from the elements is an aspiration once more, even if the prospect of unsightly wind farms is not popular. But perhaps this was also the reaction when Britain's oldest windmill was erected in 1665.

Whatever public perception was then, today the sight of Outwood Windmill is elegant and charming. There had been windmills in Britain long before Thomas Budgen from nearby Nutfield began work to build what is called a Post Mill at Outwood. This means one that is constructed around a central wooden post, so that it can be swivelled in order to meet the breeze.

The owner now is Sheila Thomas, who still mills flour as often as time and the wind allows. For her the mill is a venerable lady that is still alive in every way, 'There is a magical feeling when she is working and the wind is turn-ing her sails. She is alive through the creeks, rumbles and groans'. It is a vast and perfectly balanced machine. The sails, which are called sweeps, need to face the wind. To do this the entire windmill must be turned by lifting the anchoring steps and using a post to lever the structure round. Due to the perfect balance around its vast central post, it takes just one person to turn the great lady into the wind. The sweeps turn beautifully made wheels, constructed from wood, which drive the two stones that grind grain into flour. The grain is hoisted to the top, poured into bins, and gravity feeds it through a damsel, which evenly distributes the grain through a hole cut into the centre of the runner stone. The runner stone rotates above the stationary bedstone and this action mills the grain into flour, which then falls into sacks below.

Sheila described the windmill on the 45th anniversary of being its owner and guardian. During this time she and her late husband have invited school children and interested people in to marvel at the remarkable structure. 'She talks to you', explains Sheila, 'and if you listen she tells you what she wants. When the wind changes or the gusts are too great, she makes sounds to let you know'. The milling process is logical but the precision and craftsmanship involved is breathtaking. Feeling and smelling the fresh flour that has been warmed by the grinding stones you can sense the lady's conversion of the elements into natural power.

OLDEST FOUNTAIN

Wherever fountains play there is something fresh and alive about a place. In Scotland Britain's oldest fountain still plays in a deserted palace that was once magnificent. Built originally as a castle beside Loch Linlithgow by King David I in the mid-12th century, it was a convenient stronghold between Stirling and Edinburgh. Cromwell destroyed most of it, and what remained standing was consumed by fire when Bonnie Prince Charlie stopped here during the 1745 rebellion.

Linlithgow Palace was the favourite home for most of the Stuart kings of Scots. The original fortress was burned down in 1424 and James I immediately built his dream palace. James V was Henry VII's grandson and was determined to further beautify Linlithgow Palace. He installed the octagonal fountain in the first part of the 16th century. It is surmounted by a representation of Scotland's crown, the oldest in Britain and believed to contain the circlet used by the Countess of Mar to crown Robert the Bruce at Scone in 1306. On special occasions the fountain could be converted to flow with wine.

James V supported the French as part of the Auld Alliance between Scotland and its oldest allies. This infuriated Henry VIII and a meeting between the two in York failed to find resolution. The English army invaded and James was defeated. A few days before he died of a broken spirit in Falkland Palace, his wife, Mary of Guise, gave birth to a daughter at Linlithgow. She was to become Mary Queen of Scots. No doubt the fountain played with wine on her birthday in December 1542. During restoration a time capsule was placed in the fountain with objects to mark Linlithgow at the start of the 21st century.

OLDEST DOOR

If St Botolph's Church in Hadstock, Essex, was indeed the ministry built by the Danish king, Cnut, or Canute, which was consecrated in 1016, then its macabre door may indeed be the oldest in Britain. Legend developed in the locality

that the skin nailed across the timbers had been torn from the back of a pirate and fixed to the church door as a warning to other would-be marauders. It was a serious crime at that time to ransack, burgle or desecrate a church because of the sanctity of ecclesiastical buildings. Flaying may have seemed logical in a scale of punishments that lacked the sense of human rights accepted today. However, it was also a custom for the Saxons to line their doors with cow-hide, fragments of which have been found beneath the well-placed hinges of later Saxon and early Norman doors. There were other churches that boasted doors covered with skin, including Rochester and Worcester Cathedral and Westminster Abbey, and in each case there were similar claims of human provenance. What is true is the Anglo Saxon fear of Vikings and their longship raids along the coast – where it was possible, vengeance was taken. In 1002, for instance, King Ethelred ordered the slaughter of Danes as a warning after hearing of an assassination plot. In 1789, Sir Harry Englefield was passing through Hadstock and recorded the legend of the flayed pirate. Scientists assessed the evidence two years later, in 1791, when some of the skin that remained was taken to a nearby museum at Saffron Walden. Research concluded that it could be human. This only heightened interest in the story and increased the number of visitors. The myth of centuries was destroyed recently – the skin fastened to Hadstock's ancient door was in fact a Saxon cowhide.

It is remarkable that the oldest door survives, as it is still in daily use at the ancient church of St Botoloph in Essex, which has been re-modelled and repaired many times in its long life. St Botoloph is beside Icknield Way, Britain's oldest pre-historic pathway.

£3million has been spent restoring the oldest iron pier. Much of the work was done in Telford, the home of iron. Marlow, the hero of Jospeh Conrad's *Heart of Darkness*, left for Africa from Gravesend pier in the *Nellie*, a cruising yawl. Pleasure craft and the ferry to Tilbury now tie up alongside the pier.

OLDEST IRON PIER

The business of Parliament in 1832 was dominated by discussions of the Reform Bill. When it passed as the Great Reform Act it set in progress the modernisation of Britain's institutions and made unstoppable the move towards a democratic state with universal suffrage.

Parliament also dealt with another important matter that affected a town on the south bank of the Thames; it introduced the life of Britain's oldest iron pier. The Gravesend Pier Bill was introduced to a packed House of Lords on the 11th April 1832. In those days almost every major enterprise needed public money or approval from Parliament. There was little opposition to the plan and within two years the new iron pier was providing pleasure to the townsfolk in Gravesend. The name pier refers to the legs that provide support in buildings or bridges, and perhaps because the new promenade platforms that stretched into the sea needed reliable support, the name pier became generic. At Gravesend the sea was tempered by the narrowing estuary and the river's bend around Cliffe Marshes. The experience gained from the increasing number of iron ships that sailed the oceans in the

early 19th century held that, properly maintained, iron was better than wood and far more hard-wearing. The trouble with wooden pier supports was the same as wooden ships: they suffered from teredo, a mollusc-like sea worm that burrows into wood and therefore compromises the structure. This was the experience with the first promenade piers that were built. In the 1830s, the cost of labour was minimal and it seemed that this would always be the case and thus the large number of man-hours needed to maintain the iron pier would always be affordable. Unfortunately for the owners of Gravesend pier, one of the long-term effects of the 1832 Reform Act was to also give life to fundamental social realignment and an increase in labour costs.

OLDEST PLEASURE PIER

There is a great revival in progress. The oldest pleasure pier in Britain has been renovated, evolved and enhanced. It will bring to Southport the same fillip that the original pier brought to the town when it was built in 1860. Southport has been the main centre for spectacular leisure in the Merseyside region and it has had to cater for enormous growth. In 1860 the sea was regarded as the source of health and fitness but immersion was not always favoured. Also, the shipping industry that sailed liners regularly from Liverpool to America was becoming increasingly glamorous and more people wanted to enjoy a seagoing experience, but were unable to afford a trip to America. The pleasure pier was the answer. There was no seasickness and once you were a few paces from the shore it was like being at sea. The engineer James Burnlees built the pier using the 'pile jetting' system he had developed, which enabled each pile to be driven deep into the sand and gravel of the beach by using high-pressure water to help open the path to solid ground. One use for the pier was a paddle steamer service to North Wales and for this the travellers demanded both a shelter and food to sustain their wait. The shelter was built and in time became more of a small pavilion.

However, in 1923 the steamer service was suspended – the impact this had upon the pier's finances and future was considerable. What never ended were the demands of maintenance. The next blow for this popular promenade was the development of cheaper travel, which gave people of modest means the opportunity to take their holidays abroad rather than wandering the delights of Southport's sea front on the occasional wet day. Fire also destroyed some of its buildings and the pier was eventually shut down in 1998. Seven years before, the Southport Pier Trust had been started and the money raised with public support gave the impetus to revive and renovate this Grade II listed structure. The intent of this trust is to provide a more exciting destination to draw visitors out to sea along this amazing testament to engineering, and now that renovations have been completed, it is hoped that there is a long future ahead for the pier.

The grand opening of the 600 ft pier in Southport was in 1860. The pier was saved from demolition by one council vote in 1990. It underwent extensive repairs and was re-opened in 2002. It remains the second-longest pier in the country after Southend, which is the longest in the world.

COMMERCE

SHOPS

previous pages
Durtnells, the oldest builders (see page 160), working at Bedales' School in Hampshire.

right
Acid drops, Berwick Cockles, Black Bullets, Gobstoppers, Marry-Me-Quick, Miners' Mates, Mighty Imps, Pontefract Cakes, Snowies, Tiger Nuts, White Mice and Zubes are amongst the hundreds of varieties of sweets that Gloria Tordoff sells in this Aladdin's Cave of a shop which also does a roaring trade on the internet.

OLDEST SHOPS

Chester is full of oldest things because of its location and favoured site. It has also been left alone to evolve without too much pressure from the passing armies of warring nations or the discontent of aggressive kings. Perhaps as a result, it is the only city left with its encircling city wall almost complete.

The oldest shop fronts along Chester's Rows date from around the year 1274, and are probably the oldest collection in Britain. The surviving medieval Rows date back to the 14th century but others have been copied since. Trading had always been important to the city ever since the Romans used the port, and the Plantagenets mounted their campaign against the Welsh from this logistical centre. Warfare often brings wealth to opportunistic traders, and perhaps this led to the construction of the fine medieval houses that provide the oldest shop windows in Britain for modern-day browsers to enjoy.

The Rows are part of the scheme that divides the walled city into four, as the principal streets lead in the form of a cross from the centre to the original gates. Three of these, called Eastgate Street, Bridge Street and Watergate Street have Rows along their path, most of which were built as copies of the originals in the 19th century. They provide shopping at two levels with some open galleries on the first floor. The style of the buildings was repeated, giving the city a characteristic black and white timbered appearance along these streets. Tourism has been welcomed by the city, which has much else to offer including its Cathedral Church and Victorian clock. The influence of the Grosvenor family is also evident throughout the city, but the original 13th century Chester Rows and their 19th century pastiche copies are testament to an ancient city.

OLDEST SWEET SHOP

What child can resist the temptation of sweets? What adult for that matter? The days of large jars ranged on shelves filled with lollipops, humbugs and gobstoppers seem to have passed. Instead, the choice is one similar arrangement of confection after another whether they are in newsagents, supermarkets or beside garage counters. However, at the oldest sweet shop in Britain these nostalgic memories are a reality. The gingerbread door to Ye Olde Sweet Shop first opened into this heady glucose-filled atmosphere in the early 19th century. The shop is also the oldest building in Pateley Bridge, having been built on the High Street in 1660. A visit to buy some mints, aniseed balls or boiled sweets takes you into one of the many time warps in the Yorkshire Dales. Originally it was a farmhouse and its low ceilings, famous open fireplace and natural woods nurture the aroma of its contents. Sugar rationing bit into the business during the war but liquorice sticks grown near

Pontefract gave the children something to chew on. 'We stock all the old favourites', says Keith Tordoff, the confectioner, who is something of an expert, 'Lion's wine and fruit gums are the best – not too chewy and the best flavour. Also the original pear drops from Stockleys of Oswaldtwistle, which are still boiled in the original moulds'. There is an old wireless playing with music from the 50s, Avery scales to measure out the sweets and children are invited to press the keys of the old-fashioned cash register but, in a rare acceptance of changing times, this has been recalibrated to metric measures.

OLDEST BUTCHERS

Richard John Balson gets up early to stock his butchers shop in Bridport, on the Dorset coast. Unlike the meat sold in supermarkets, the produce he sells has hung for a minimum of three weeks in order that it matures and flavours. This tradition has been sacrificed elsewhere in pursuit of speed and vacuum packed redness. But hung meat and traditional products, like black pudding and faggots, are the essential parts of the service provided by Britain's oldest butcher. The family started trading meat here in 1535, when Henry VIII was busy dissolving the

Twenty years ago, R. J. Balson & Son in Bridport made two types of sausage: pork and beef. Now, they make 15 – a popular variety is Ostrich and Cranberry as it contains little cholesterol!

l–r: Richard Balson, his brother-in-law Rodolphe Boulay and his step-daughter Stephanie Pinkett.

monasteries of England. The Balsons set up their stall in the Shambles, or market area, close to where the Town Hall now stands and just 300 yards from where the present shop was opened in 1880. Bridport has been a trading town since before the Conquest: its historic products were rope, cable and hawsers for the Royal Navy. The first grant for fairs and markets in Bridport came soon after Balsons started trading, in 1593. The business has survived in the same family for nearly five centuries: each one has had to face the challenges of economic change. Today, Richard says, 'The biggest threat to business is from Sunday trading and double yellow lines'. It is also interesting that for the first time the family's son, Billy, is not planning a butcher's life. For him the attraction of London beats the butcher's life and long hours.

OLDEST CHEESE SHOP

It is easy to buy cheese today. Almost any shop can stock varieties from all over the world. But the cheese business was at its most exceptional when the purveyors out-performed transport constraints in order to deliver the rarest and the best brands for their customers. The oldest cheese shop in Britain prospered for doing just that. Originally, cheese was consumed on the farm or in the locality where it was made. In due course, buyers for the markets in London developed reliable suppliers from the countryside for their urban-dwelling customers. City folk were prepared to pay well if the quality was good and this is something that Stephen Cullum discovered, when he arrived from Suffolk to set up his cheese stall in London's Clare Market in 1742. Later in the decade he bought a shop

Napoleon to No. 3 for one of his secret meetings, before returning to France and establishing the Second Empire, as Napoleon III. In the cellars of this premises, while quaffing two bottles of French wine, the Emperor who would one day threaten to invade Britain planned part of his coup.

The business later merged with Rudds, makers of Cutty Sark Whisky. This provided the company with reliable shipping links and these were used to develop warehousing for their whisky to the Bahamas, in the Caribbean. When Prohibition ended in the United States, the company was perfectly positioned to cash in, and the profits soared. Further notoriety came when Britain faced its darkest hours. Berry Brothers & Rudd supplied Winston Churchill and the Houses of Parliament with wines. Today, No. 3 St James's Street still attracts customers from all over the world.

OLDEST CHEMIST

Scientific discoveries of the past two hundred years have moved medicine on from the days when pharmacists would prepare compounds and ointments using a pestle and mortar and ingredients from antiquated jars. Nowadays, at Reavley's, the premises which claims to be Britain's oldest chemist, in the Cotswold town of Burford,

left
Paxon & Whitfield, sandwiched between the gentleman's outfitters of Jermyn Street, stocks every type of cheese. When the Romans reached England in 55BC, it is said they developed a taste for Cheshire cheese although it was medieval monks who refined the art of cheese making.

below
Cedric Reavley stands in front of the family run pharmacy in Burford. The building has been a pharmacy since 1734.

in Surrey Street, then one in Southampton Street; all the time moving towards the west of London, where the Court was based and therefore the wealth could be found. He engaged a partner, called Paxton, in the 1780s because it was impossible to grow a business without sharing risk and pooling capital. John Whitfield joined the partnership a few years later and soon Stephen Cullum retired to enjoy the fruits of his labour. It is possible that this shop introduced Stilton cheese to London. Paxton and Whitfield, as the shop became known, earned the first of many Royal Warrants from Queen Victoria in 1850. It has been supplying cheeses to the Palace ever since, and it still surprises customers with the variety and quality of its produce.

OLDEST WINE MERCHANT

In 1698, the Widow Bourne opened a grocery shop beside St James's Palace, in buildings where Henry VIII's Real Tennis court probably once stood. In 1731, this area was re-developed and Bourne's descendants took No. 3 St James's Street, where the original business has been trading ever since. Groceries gave way to wine after a marriage between John Clarke's daughter and Mr Berry, a wine merchant from Exeter. Their son, George, became an apprentice at No. 3, having been nominated his grand-father's heir. His children, the original Berry Brothers, developed the grocery business into a thriving wine merchant. With the Royal Court as neighbours, their location could not be better for profits. There was a social advantage too. Unlike most tradesmen, who were never included at Court, vintners were accepted in aristocratic circles. Perhaps it was this trust that brought Prince Louis

Ede and Ravenscroft's shop stands in Burlington Gardens at the bottom of London's Savile Row, the home of English tailoring. They supply the offical robes for state occasions and for members of the legal profession and the academic gowns worn by graduating students. The heraldic symbols either side of the door mark the warrants this business has from the Royal Family. Amongst the customers is the Queen, who was fitted out for her coronation by these robemakers.

the pharmacist dispenses according to doctors' prescriptions, just like all other chemists across the country. Reavley's special product is a hand cream that Robert Reavley first made in the 1920s for his son to give to the women working at his workplace, which was a cement factory. Today, Reavley's Cream, with its mix of lanolin and glycerine, brings some notoriety to a building where cures have been offered to the public since the first lease was taken out on 16th July 1734. Before this date, the site had offered a different kind of cure, as the Crown Inn and a focus for Burford life. Nicholas Willet established the first pharmacy and it was run by his family until the 1840s, when the O'Reilly family and then the Ballard family took over the business. It was at the end of the First World War that Robert Reavley came to Burford from his pharmaceutical practice at Jarrow. He was an experienced chemist, having worked in India as well as the Northumberland coastal town. The pharmacy is still run by the Reavley family, and cement workers the world over can still rub cream from the oldest chemist into their hands. As the original advertisement said, it 'preserves and beautifies the hands'.

OLDEST TAILORS

Even in the chaos of revolution, the coronation on 11th April 1689 of two monarchs who had been imported to share the vacated throne required dignified splendour, and tailors and robe makers were kept busy preparing the robes needed for the participants at William III and Mary II's crowning. One firm that can trace its origin back to this event is now the oldest tailors in Britain, Ede and Ravenscroft. At the time of the joint coronation, it was a small business in London's Holywell Street, run by the Shudall family but they must have been in the industry before this time, because it was not easy to get a foothold into the specialist work of courtly dress-making. The cost of working with velvets, ermines and miniver required capital, significant skill and reputation.

It was not until 1811, when the country was again at war with France. that Joseph Ede indentured himself at Holywell Street. After the intervention of an uncle, called Thomas Adams, Joseph found himself the joint owner of the company, but in a new location, on Chancery Lane, where it remains today.

In 1831, William IV was crowned and Joseph was appointed to make the robes for his coronation and so in 1834 the company, now called Adams and Ede, received the king's warrant. There was much else beside the trappings of the Royal Court to keep the needles busy. The Courts of Justice also required ceremonial robes, as did the Church and the academic world. The monarch's robes were always made from the best of everything, with special dyes from the Mediterranean used to produce the royal purple velvet and extra long ermine tails to fleck the king's miniver cape. Joseph died the year after Queen Victoria's husband, Prince Albert, and, perhaps feeling sympathy for the widow running her husband's company, Victoria gave her royal warrant to the shop. It was soon renamed Ede and Son after Joseph's son took the helm. The last major evolution of the name came after the marriage in 1871 of Joseph junior to Rosanna Ravenscroft.

At the coronation of 1953 the business frantically worked to prepare the robes of the five ranks of the Peerage. Perhaps these robes will come out again at another coronation. If they do, there will be ceaseless activity to alter them, just as there was every year in the late 17th century in the run-up the annual ceremonies of the Order of the Garter. This is something that the staff employed by Ede and Ravenscroft still help with today.

OLDEST BOOTMAKERS

After limping all the way from Cornwall to London in 1848, the least John Lobb hoped for was a hearing, when he applied for work at a shoemaker's shop. The door was slammed in his face because dirty country folk were not welcome in London's West End. The young man was angry and swore that one day he would return; which he did, to establish in 1849 what is now the oldest bootmakers shop in Britain. Life had not been easy for John. His father tilled the soil and therefore this was his destiny, but the plan was cut short when he suffered a severe leg injury. John apprenticed himself to a local bootmaker in the fishing village of Fowey and, armed with his new skill, he set out to cross the country with his stick. 'We still have the stick he used on that journey here in the shop,' explains John Hunter Lobb, the Chairman and great grandson of the founder, 'he decided to go to Australia with his brother to mine for gold'. John got there but decided to make miners' boots instead. Some had small cavities in the heel to hide stolen gold. After successfully running a boot business in Sydney and marrying a rich Harbourmaster's daughter, John returned to London. His first shop in Upper Regent Street opened in 1866. Speaking from the present premises in St James's Street, today's John Lobb said, 'He contrived to get the Prince of Wales's foot measurements, made the prince some boots and got the Royal Warrant, which was a good start. He also entered every competition going and won medals for the superb shoes he made from the carefully made wooden lasts, which are still fashioned to the precise shape of each customer's feet'. The family have continued the business ever since, inspired by their ancestor and by the qualities of craftsmanship he set.

OLDEST GUNMAKER

Just off the New Kent Road, in Bengal Place, Benjamin Cogswell opened the front door of his new premises in 1770. His company has survived and is probably Britain's oldest surviving gunmakers. The first record of a gunmaker in Britain was in Norwich between 1577 and 1589, when Henry Radoe made snaphaunces, which were very early forms of flint guns. For Benjamin, military work was going to be important – there was a only a short time to go before the American War of Independence. Guns were increasingly required by soldiers, landowners, their keepers and those determined to duel. What Benjamin wanted to bring to the business was quality of workmanship and finish. Each of the early handmade pistols was crafted with design as well as function in the shape. Duelling was legal and gentlemen defended their honour by fighting to the death. A pair of Cogswell pistols would grace any second called to officiate at such a contest. In 1863 Benjamin's successor and namesake took Edward Harrison into the partnership and the company has traded under their names ever since. Quite soon after the company celebrated its 200th year, in 1970, the effects of recession proved too great and in 1982 voluntary liquidation was sought. Farlows of Pall Mall, the sporting and fishing business, bought Cogswell and Harrison the next year and ten years after that, Mike Cooley and Alan Crewe bought the company and re-launched the product.

John Lobb holds his grandfather's walking stick, and his sons Jonathan and William hold the tools of their trade. Both sons have served the long apprenticeship needed to become boot- and shoemakers. Most of the work is still done on the shop's premises in London's St James'.

Lock & Co in London is one of the oldest run family business in Britain. Hats go in and out of fashion but when you need to wear one, Locks can supply you with a hat for every occasion. They will even custom-make a hat, as they did in 1803 for Lord Nelson, whose doctor told him to wear a cocked hat with an eye shade to protect the sight of his remaining eye.

OLDEST HAT SHOP

The fortunes of Britain's oldest hat shop have never been better than they are today. 'All headwear sales are buoyant', says John Stephenson, the Managing Director, 'this has been helped by sales due to the dangers of sunburn. In fact last year was the best year we have ever had'. This is not just because of the diminishing ozone layer but because men wearing hats is once again becoming fashionable, and millinery still holds its popularity. When Robert Davis started his business in 1676, which is now known as James Lock and Co., hats were a necessity because they symbolised social position – a significant role of clothing ever since the Middle Ages. This carried on right up to the middle of the 20th century, when it was normal for a City gentleman to wear a top hat and his senior clerk a bowler, while the dustbin man wore a cloth cap. It was visible symbolism of the class structure and perhaps this is why headdress fell from favour in the 1960s.

The Lock family became involved in the hat business in 1759 when James Lock married the Davis heiress. The Locks were merchants that had made money importing tobacco and coffee from Turkey, and they had moved the family premises from the City to the clean air and open streets of St James's. Here they established coffee outlets for the wealthy gentlemen who had made the same move. The Lock family have worked in the hat business ever since. A visit to the shop is a step back in time – it is almost possible to imagine Nelson arriving for the fitting of the hat he wore at Trafalgar, or Churchill choosing the hat he wore as Prime Minister. All hats have a story and the heads of their wearers do too. Head sizes are increasing at three-eighths of an inch each half century, according to the records that go back to when the shop began trading.

OLDEST BOOKSHOP

The impressive entrance to Hatchards bookshop, at 187 Piccadilly near London's St James's, denotes exactly what you get inside. The doors were first opened in 1797, which makes it by far the oldest bookshop in Britain. It has both the character of a fully stocked library and the feel of being in something more like a home. Many of the staff have an expertise that is colourfully enthusiastic in their department and, unlike libraries, the hope is that you will not dally, read and leave, but that you will purchase as many signed copies as possible. Few shops could boast as many signings and many of the casual shoppers have their own biographies on sale on the ground floor. Authors today are still inspired to write about some of the shop's more famous patrons in history. Among them George III's consort, Queen Charlotte, who surprised many by how well-read she was. Instructed by her marriage contract, which was written in Latin, to leave for England immediately, join the Anglican church and be married according to Anglican rites, and never ever involve herself in politics, she did as she was told. Instead, she was a prolific student of botany and probably looked to Hatchards for the books she could not find in her husband's infamous library. The military saviour of the nation, Arthur Wellesley, Duke of Wellington, shopped here, as did other great Victorian Prime Ministers, such as Benjamin Disraeli. Heroes of the humanities, like Oscar Wilde, Rudyard Kipling and Lord Byron browsed the shelves and talked with the assistants for inspiration just as anyone can today.

OLDEST RECORD SHOP

In the Italian city of Bologna, Guglielmo Marconi made a discovery. It was 1894, and he was just 20 years old but the spark transmitter and antenna he had invented, which he called his 'black box', would become British Patent No. 12039 and revolutionise the availability of music over the airwaves. In October of that same year, another event took place that would be equally evangelical for the musical appreciation of Cardiff. Henry Spiller opened his shop in Queen's Arcade, which now claims to be the oldest record shop not only in Britain, but also the world. Just four years before, in 1890, the first coin-operated Juke Box was installed in San Francisco and the Berliner Gramaphone Co. had begun selling 7-inch hard rubber discs in 1893. So it was timely for Henry to start his business. To start with he sold phonographs, shellac phonographic discs and wax cylinders. The latter was a technology used to record Queen Victoria's first message to the empire. The shop passed from Henry to his son Edward during the 1920s. At that time, those who had survived the privations of the First World War were ready for some distraction and so the

business branched into selling musical instruments as well. For this work, Edward hired the famous accordionist and band leader, Joe Gregory. The long reign of vinyl was probably the heyday for record sales. The compact disc has followed with some success but the developments of electronic sales and downloads will present the oldest record shop and all those companies that followed its lead with a marketing challenge.

OLDEST BARBERS

It is odd that the oldest barber in Britain started business when the smartest in society would not be seen in public without a powdered wig. However, it was a boost for William Truefitt that when he opened his shop in London's Long Acre in 1805, it caught the king's attention. Then as now, the most trusted barber would leave the shop and visit the Palace to groom a royal scalp. Although George III was one of the first customers, this was no easy time for the monarch. He had already slipped into two bouts of madness and by 1810 he slipped into his final dementia. One year later, William established himself in Bond Street and called himself the Court Hair Cutter and Court Hair Dresser: the latter being more about the preparation and restoration of wigs than anything else. The Prince Regent,

above
It was a surprise to find Spiller's Records, the oldest record shop in the world, in Cardiff, a city not famous for being a centre of the global music industry.

left
Hatchards is the only bookshop that sells just books; it doesn't sell magazines, records, postcards or calendars. Authors come in on a daily basis to chat with the staff and check their sales and there are book signing sessions almost weekly.

Gino, one of Truefit and Hill's hairdressers, shaves another customer in the St. James' Street shop in London. The oldest hairdressers now has identical shops in Chicago, Toronto, Las Vegas and New York.

Prince George, was a dandy who provided steady business from his Court but as Wigmaker to the mad king, with his brother Peter, he established a reliable commercial reputation. This was good timing as the wig business flourished and so did the fashionable premises of the Truefitts. Wigs slipped from use and in their place the gentleman's coiffure developed in Queen Victoria's reign. Another barber was established in Old Bond Street, called Edwin Hill and Co. An amalgamation between the two companies took place after the Depression in 1935, establishing Truefitt and Hill. In 1994, the company moved to its present location on St James's Street; a short distance from the Court, which is much diminished in power, influence and size from the one the company initially served. The company still offers a totally unique and timeless experience that offers its clients a traditional, deferential and polite trim but nothing radical. For that, you should try the West End.

OLDEST RESTAURANT

Marco Polo was deeply impressed by the way the people of Hangchow used fine food as the focus for their social events in 1280. They gathered in bustling rooms where the heat of the kitchens and the exotic spices created an atmosphere that added to the pleasure of diners.

By comparison, eating was more a matter of subsistence in Europe at that time, where cultural practice saw wine or ale as the focus for pleasure rather than gourmet food, just as some still do today. Only the king and his Court feasted on tables groaning with delicacies, but this too was sternly regulated by the Christian penitential calendar that encouraged fasting as the route to salvation. Food was therefore tainted with guilt in the west. It is not surprising then, that its enjoyment as a social pastime in Europe was delayed until the Church discovered what could be done with a bit of seasoning and spice. It was then just a matter of time before those with wealth would discover the joy of good food. This reached the middle classes of Britain, freed from the rigours of Puritan restraint, during the 18th century. At this time France was particularly loathed, so it is ironic that its food was loved and the culture of French cuisine and wine was imported with delight. While many hotels developed restaurants, the oldest freestanding restaurant is probably Rules in London, which was founded in 1798 by Thomas Rule. At this time Napoleon was embarking upon his military campaigns and Britain feared the consequences and success of the French Grand Army. After 200 years the world is different and Napoleon's European dream more of a reality than the union of Britain, which would have been toasted back then as the foundation for all sanity.

OLDEST INDIAN RESTAURANT

The first Governor General of India in 1773 was Warren Hastings. He was suited to the task because he respected the existing constitution of the Moguls, and stood against the bare commercial exploitation that had forced the British Government to assume rule. His appointment and the Regulating Act that brought India into the British sphere, were to influence Britain's history, society and culture forever. Today the influence of this hegemony can be seen in the fact that the most popular dish eaten in Britain is curry.

In 1927, when the British Raj was at its apogee, Edward Palmer established the oldest Indian restaurant in Britain, which is called the Veeraswamy. His great grandfather was Military and Private Secretary to Warren Hastings. Edward had been sent to Britain to study medicine in 1880 but soon followed his love for spiced foods, which few in England had tasted. All his life, he had admired the cooking of his Indian grandmother in Hyderabad, where his grandfather was banker to the immensely wealthy Nizam, or ruler. Edward introduced these foods to London society, which was hungry for the exotic romance of India. In the mid-1920s he provided food at the Great Exhibition, which was a giant display of imperial culture and industry that took place in Hyde Park. The restaurant opened to enormous social approval and the Prince of Wales was a regular customer. An immaculate turbaned guard stood sentry at the door of the Regent Street location just as one does today. Great luminaries have been drawn to the restaurant, none more significant than Mahatma Gandhi, who had come to tell George V that it was time to quit India. The strong links between Britain and India are indelible and the love for the food of the sub-continent, which is now a national obsession, must stem in part to the work of Edward Palmer's restaurant. It has now been refurbished to a high standard and serves traditional and contemporary Indian food.

OLDEST POST OFFICE

Sanquhar, in Scotland's Dumfries and Galloway, has kept its Post Office going since 1763, and it is Britain's oldest. Located just north of the tollbooth, and at the centre of town life, it was convenient for the travellers passing north to Kilmarnock. This survival is particularly notable considering the popularity of internet communication and the sharp decline in the traditional use of letters.

This small Scottish Post Office is but a stepping stone in the British history of postal services. Inevitably, it was the king's business that developed the need for trusted messengers in the 13th century, to convey letters and money around the realm. The first Postmaster was Sir Brian Tuke, in 1533, which demonstrates how important this infrastructure was becoming to the process of government and development of trade. Reliability and security from robbers was the key. In 1555, Philip and Mary paid sums from their accounts, for horses to bolster the links between London and Dover's waiting boats. But it was the arrival of Scotland's King James VI, who assumed his cousin Elizabeth Tudor's throne in 1603, that added to the need for a nationwide system of posts. Under Queen Anne, in 1711 an imperial postal service was established to link England, Scotland, Ireland and the British Colonies in North America. The Rowland Hill reforms of the 19th century introduced the uniform penny postage for inland mail, and to this day there is a uniform rate paid inland no matter if it is to cross the street or to reach from Cornwall to Caithness. That restriction on pricing may be under threat as the Post Office considers its ability to retain the diminishing network of local post offices, which still includes the one at Sanquhar.

The main street of Sanquhar has all the shops you would expect to find in a high street – a baker, a newsagent, a super-market, a chemist and a post office. Britain's oldest post office has changed very little since it was first opened 1763. The oldest building that contains a post office is in Painswick, Gloucestershire.

OLDEST BANK

A bold man wrote to Elizabeth I to suggest a banking system for England in November 1581. His name was Christopher Hagenbuck and it is likely that the lending houses of Venice, which were making a tidy sum at that time, had impressed him. The queen was interested and Francis Walsingham wrote a positive reply but nothing seems to have come of the venture. The oldest private bank in Britain is one of the companies that finally did start a lending business in the 17th century and it is remarkable because, since 1953, it is the only remaining private bank still in business. The first mention of these embryo banks can be found in the London Directory of 1677, which describes a number of goldsmiths who were keeping 'running cashes' that were available for loans. In 1665, Richard Hoare was engaged as an apprentice goldsmith to Robert Tempest, who had one such business. One year later the Great Fire of London swept the city but the business survived. Richard was the son of a successful horse dealer, so this was quite a change of direction. It was to be the last big change that the family would make because, in 1673, Richard took over Robert Tempest's business on Cheapside, in the City of London and the family have been bankers ever since. Above the shop was a sign, which was in the shape of a golden bottle and this is still the symbol above the door of Hoare's Bank on Fleet Street. Richard's clients were influential and this must have helped him establish the business. Among them were Queen Catherine of Braganza, the artist Sir Godfrey Kneller and the diarist Samuel Pepys. The business moved to Fleet Street in 1690, and in 1862 the family had saved enough profits from banking to build what is now the oldest example of a purpose-built bank in Britain. It was a bold decision to construct a new building with a banking hall, and room for the staff, which were called 'Gentlemen of the Shop', to live above the premises. There is a special feel about this family business today, which still operates from a single location. It is remarkable too that the business has survived through the economic cycles that felled many of their rivals or saw the merging of others, such as Coutts, Child's and Goslings into larger high street banks. The golden bottle reminds the partners of the brave start made by their ancestor. The longevity of both this symbol and the family banking business give confidence to the rather different cross-section of people and businesses granted the opportunity to open an account.

Hoares, the oldest bank, is based in London's Fleet Street and run by the Partners who all work together in one room. Those seen here are the 10th and 11th generation descendents of Sir Richard Hoare, founder of the bank. The bank's archives have been kept meticulously throughout its history, and are frequently used by researchers and historians today. Since the bank was founded, it has been tradition that one of the Partners has to sleep in rooms over the bank every night.

BUSINESSES

Farthings, groats, shillings, crowns and sovereigns are included in this selection of coins struck by the Royal Mint over the course of its long history. Alongside gold nobles of Edward III are set guineas of George III, Anglo-Saxon silver pennies, modern base metal £2 coins, and the beautiful Petition Crown of Charles II takes its place beside the much-loved Victorian Bun Penny. Since the reign of King Henry VIII, the profiles of the Monarchs have alternated, looking left then right.

OLDEST COMPANY

Jangling in almost every pocket are the coins of the realm: the cash we use to get about. Goods and services have been exchanged for currency since the earliest times and so it is not surprising that, following the chicken and the egg paradox, what must have come first is the company that makes the coins. The Royal Mint has been in production striking the nation's coinage since Alfred the Great was king of England. At that time there were many sources for the coinage and more than seventy mints in London alone. In time these were rationalised into just one supplier and so this is arguably the oldest company in Britain. In 1975 it was established as a Government Trading Fund, so that it could be a free agent and find business beyond these shores. Many other nations commission coins and medals from the Royal Mint though it is still, just as it has almost always been, a department of Government. Once it was answerable to the king, who had a vested interest because the coinage was struck from his own gold. Now it is still answerable to the Executive for the Rightness of the Currency and it does this in an annual test, called the Trial of the Pyx, which takes place annually at the Worshipful Company of Goldsmiths. When the trial is convened the Royal Mint bring their pyx (which are the boxes that contain samples of the coinage) to London from the present site in Llantrisant. It is counted, measured, melted and checked to ensure that the Royal Mint has not short-changed the Government by cheating on the metals used or the sizes struck. It is the only time an object is put on trial in a court of law. Once the trial is complete the report is given to the Master of the Mint, who is also the Chancellor of the Exchequer.

In the latter part of the 12th century, after the dispersed mints had consolidated into a single one, it was co-located with the goldsmiths' quarter in the City of London. However, in the 13th century the operation was taken inside the Tower of London in order to better protect the currency. For 500 years the craftsmen hammered out the coins from precious metals and it was only when the mechanised process of rolling out the coins developed that the secure fortress became too cramped. It

was therefore decided to establish a new purpose-built location on Tower Hill. This way the required protection was still close at hand, while the coinage for Britain and subsequently many of the colonies could be safely made to the required quality and standard of alloy.

The new building on Tower Hill was in operation in 1811, while the wars against Napoleon were in full swing. James Johnson designed the building, which was to have a military guard and look adequately imposing. However, little survived the constant need to improve the machinery and improve production. In the 1950s the decision was taken that the site was no longer adequate and the historic need to keep the Royal Mint in London no longer seemed valid. The search for a suitable site came when the decision to decimalise the country was made. The Royal Mint would not be able to deliver without upsetting its traditional national customers elsewhere, who provided a significant income to the Government. The result was the new site in Wales's Llantrisant. The coins have their history too and have always been marked with the monarch's likeness, just as the coin that Christ showed his followers was marked by Caesar. In these coins the history of the oldest company can be read.

OLDEST PATENT

Henry VI founded two great scholastic institutions that survive today; Kings College is part of Cambridge University and Eton College, which is possibly the most famous British public school. For both of these foundations the king granted funds for fine chapels to be built.

At Eton College, which is located just below the walls of Windsor Castle on the north side of the Thames, the work required stained glass. John of Utyman was given the task of preparing the glass for the windows. He was Flemish but was

encouraged to bring his technique for staining glass into England with the first British Letters Patent, which means letters opened for all to read. The Patent granted John the right to practise his invention free from competition for twenty years from the date of the grant, which was the year 1449. Letters Patent are still the means by which inventors are encouraged today. It was originally the way that the Crown controlled trade, and the protection offered by Letters Patent is as valuable now as it ever was.

OLDEST ROYAL WARRANT HOLDER

Whether it is just commercial snobbery or the reassurance of knowing that the Royal Family chooses to buy from the same shop as you may use, the system of Royal Warrants has been in operation for centuries. Most Royal Courts in Europe ran similar marks of esteem. The firm to hold a Royal Warrant for the longest un-interrupted period is Swaine, Adeney and Brigg, of St James's Street in London. The company supplies whips and gloves to The Queen, umbrellas to the Prince of

Keen horseman always have a collection of crops such as this, purchased from the oldest royal warrant holder, Swaine, Adeney and Brigg.

Wales and it still displays the late Queen Mother's warrant. From the Middle Ages until George III, the monarch was the principal buyer of everything the nation needed, because all revenue in the Treasury was his to spend for the country's good. This meant that from 1155 kings issued Royal Charters or Warrants for the supply of anything from naval ships, to flour for the palace kitchens. The nature of Government has changed radically since then, and so applications to win warrants to build ships go direct to the Ministry of Defence. By comparison, the Royal family's needs have become much more domestic. Since the late 18th century warrant holders have been able to display the Coat of Arms of their patron; something which Queen Victoria developed into an art form. In her heyday most of the shops around Balmoral and Osbourne groaned under great plaster casts of her Royal Arms. Warrant holders today follow tradesmen like Dick Whittington's Mercers Company in 1394; the first printer William Caxton, in 1476; Charles II 'Operator for the Teeth' and, in 1789 while the rest of Europe worried about the French Revolution, the British court issued warrants to a Mole Taker, Rat Catcher and Card Maker.

OLDEST REGALIA MAKERS

The adoption of signs, symbols and badges, as a means of identifying with a belief, organisation or rank, is almost part of human instinct. Metalworkers and enamellers have always been busy supplying the symbols of their day in a form ready for wear since Egyptian times. The products they make are called insignia and are designed to convey a message about the wearer. When insignia are Royal, like the symbols used at a coronation, it is called Regalia. The status quo in almost every country provides the chance for crafts-people to provide the symbols of its institutions. In Britain,

the oldest company that has been committed from the out-set to provide insignia is called Toye, Kenning and Spencer. Based at Bedworth in Warwickshire, the family business was begun in 1685, and a member of the Toye family has always been involved in producing what they call 'fine identity products' for both the Fraternal Societies as well as Civil and Military markets. The principal Fraternal Society that the company produces insignia for is Freemasonry, which often calls its symbols 'Regalia'. Much less popular than it was, this fraternity has a complex structure of rank, which is conveyed in the ceremonial aprons, sashes and jewels that are worn. Masonry has existed in the country for centuries, but this company probably benefited from the union of two large parts of Freemasonry in England in 1717. Nearby, in Birmingham, is the company Firmin Group that was estab-lished to make buttons for the uniforms of the new stand-ing army in 1677. Firmin's is older than Toye, Kenning and Spencer, and it is arguable whether buttons and military badges form insignia or not. The stars, badges and medals of orders of chivalry, like the Order of the Garter, British Empire, or St John of Jerusalem are all called insignia and have been supplied by different companies since metal insignia were first required to identify recipients.

OLDEST BREWERS

In the last decade, Shepherd Neame launched one of Britain's most successful beers, which demonstrates the dynamic creativity of a company that claims to be the oldest brewer in the country. The two parts of the name also reflects the balance in which two separate companies have evolved together in order to survive. Shepherds, the original brewers, depended upon hops farmed by the Neame family on the surrounding countryside. The Neame family claims to have farmed here since the time of the Norman Conquest and, when it seemed that Shepherds faced financial hardship, the Neamses bought the business in order that their own farms would survive.

In the 12th century King Stephen founded a Benedictine Abbey at Faversham, situated on an inlet from the Thames estuary on the north coast of Kent. To this foundation came monks influenced by the monastic philosophy developed in the Normandy Abbey of Cluny. They quickly discovered the benefits from mixing spring water with harvested barley. Over a century after the monastery was dissolved, in 1698, a mayor of Faversham called Richard Marsh established a new brewery close by. Once again, the spring water from an artesian well was captured in the new Court Street location for brewing. The Marsh family business grew successfully and by 1741, when his daughter died, the business was larger than the other 23 in the town. This figure gives an idea of how prolific brewing was – in a nation renowned then, as now, for its thirst for alcohol. A local landlord called Samuel Shepherd bought the brewery and brought his sons into the business. One of them replaced horses in the production process with a steam engine, to move the hops and barrels around. This changed the company name to Faversham Steam Brewery at a time when steam was the height of modern technology. Shepherd Neame now own over 370 public houses dotted around all over south-east England. They have considerable brewing capacity. In addition to brewing their own beer they also brew a range of beers for supermarkets. A number of well-known foreign brands are also made here under licence, which include Swiss, Philippino and Indian lagers.

OLDEST BREWERY

With the dissolution of the monasteries and the consequent cessation of the supply of brewed beer, secular breweries sprang up to meet demand. One commercial brewery still stands where the original started during Elizabeth I's reign. This is now believed to be the oldest brewery in Britain, and is in London's borough of Wandsworth on the southern shore of the River Thames. Today it is called the Ram Brewery because in 1581 Humphrey Langridge started his business brewing here at the sign of the Ram, which had been a well-known drinking establishment since 1533. It was quite a large concern because, whereas most pubs and inns brewed for their own drinkers, the Ram Inn brewed sufficient to supply other locations. It was also a place where travellers could stay and stable their horses, as it was located in one of the villages outside Westminster and

close to a river crossing. The source of fresh water was a vital ingredient, and it was drawn from a well that is still there, although modern demands and requirements mean that this is no longer the source. In due course the horses with their drays drew barrels from the Ram Brewery around the growing city. The other useful route for distributing the beer barrels was the river. The lightermen would take barges up and down the Thames, and barrels would be exported from the Port of London. Today the brewery still occupies some of the original site but, apart from some Victorian equipment and the dray horses, which are still in use, it is run with modern technology.

Jonathan Neame, the fifth generation of the brewing family to run the business, stands at the bar in front of some of the popular beers brewed in Faversham. To keep pubs at the heart of rural communities, some Shepherd Neame pubs also contain post offices.

Belfast's Bushmills distillery has been distilling and maturing single malt whiskey for the last 400 years. It differs from scotch whisky in a number of ways besides its spelling: it is distilled three times and it does not have the distinctive smoky flavour that scotch whisky has.

OLDEST GIN DISTILLERY

It was William III who encouraged spirit stills to be set up all over England. Earlier in the 17th century British soldiers serving abroad in the Thirty Years War had taken what was called 'Dutch Courage'. This was the new drink developed in Holland for medicinal reasons, which was called gin after the juniper berries that were added to distilled grain to mask its taste. The new drink became popular in Britain and began to rival beers in a country with a culture traditionally thirsty for alcohol. In Plymouth, a malting house was established in the old monastery buildings of the Black Friars, close to the harbour in 1697, and a century later Mr Coates established the first gin still. This was the building where the Pilgrim Fathers had spent their last night before sailing to America in 1620: a link that is commemorated on the bottle labels, which show the *Mayflower* ship in which they crossed the Atlantic. Ironically, it was the developing colonies of America's east coast that would increase the demand for what became a large export business for Plymouth's gin. The other boost came from the dangers of malaria in the empire, which the Royal Navy's ships sailed to from Plymouth. Quinine was discovered to be the best preventative against this mosquito-borne disease and a medicinal tonic was prepared, called tonic water. To make its ingestion more pleasurable, gin was added and the 'Gin and Tonic' was born, now drunk worldwide. The Royal Navy popularised a further ingredient, called angostura bitters, and known as Pink Gin. However, it was in New York where gin from Plymouth's still became the most famous base ingredient for the sophisticated café society's growing cocktail industry. Prohibition in America stifled trade for a time but perhaps it will always be the endless need for 'Dutch Courage' in social places that will keep the oldest still at work.

OLDEST DISTILLERY

Scotland is synonymous in many people's minds with whisky, the spirit distilled from cereal grain, using the peaty waters that flow off the rain soaked hills of the Highlands. The first record of a spirit of this type dates back to 1494 in the Scottish Exchequer Rolls, but the oldest distillery in Scotland is the one at Glen Turret, near Crieff that was built in 1775. Originally, whisky was known as *uisge beatha*, the Celtic words for 'water of life'. It is also known as *aquavitae*, which is the drink James IV ordered when he stayed in Inverness during September 1506.

In 1644, the Scottish Parliament saw the opportunity to tax this pleasure and a duty was imposed. Forty-four years later the duty reflected the strength of the spirit and some crofters around the country established illegal stills of their own, whilst avoiding the Red Coats, who patrolled the Highlands looking for wrongdoers. Beneath the peaks of Ben Chonzie and the Achnatree Hill is Lock Turret. From it, to the south-east runs Glen Turret and its burn. The distillery built to benefit from this water in 1775 is named after its source, as the Glenturret Distillery. The malt whisky produced is bottled today in different vintages, up to 25 years old. The bonded warehouses, which are where the spirits mature, turn a different colour because of the effect of evaporating alcohol. This evaporation reduces the liquid and is known as the Angel's Dram: a dram being a small shot of whisky.

Despite Scotland's hold on the image of whisky, the oldest distillery in the British Isles is in Northern Ireland. The Bushmills Distillery received its licence to trade in 1608 from James I, just five years after he took the throne of England and Ireland. It still operates where it always has, in the county of Antrim just a mile from one of the nation's most remarkable settings, the Giant's Causeway. In this part of the kingdom, the passion for the water of life has always been strong. There is a 13th century reference to Uisce Beatha, which became Fuisce, which in turn became whiskey. Perhaps one tragedy from which Bushmills benefited, was the great potato blight in the 1840s. This and other factors caused a mass migration to America. Many of these immigrants became a powerful and successful force in American life and, remembering the land of their birth, they chose Bushmills whiskey, and hence established a steady trade and reputation for this 17th century distillery.

OLDEST LAW FIRM

Lawyers do not always attract notoriety, but Britain's oldest law firm is noted in the *Guinness Book of Records* and dates from the 16th century. England was able to prosper under the Tudors, and with this prosperity developed a greater awareness of land and its value beyond that of feudal dependence. The established method for exchanging or passing on chattels was through wills and other documents. The mid-16th century saw the dissolution of monasteries and with the destruction of these ancient buildings went the dispersal of their learned clerks. It

was therefore necessary to find people that could write and understand the format of words required to achieve the desired result.

In 1570, just such a man founded the oldest law firm. Nicholas Hooper was a curate at Tonbridge Parish Church. This was no easy time for ministers of religion. There was uproar in Europe following Henry VIII's break with Rome, and the country had been torn by the vicissitudes that followed, in the struggle to establish a legal faith that satisfied the nation and its monarch. Nicholas meanwhile busied himself drawing up indentures, wills and charters. In some cases he instructed his young son, John, to witness these. Some of the earliest documents survive in the council archive. The Hooper family evolved the business through the dangers of the Civil War, when Tonbridge was a Parliamentarian stronghold against King Charles. George Hooper was pragmatic enough to do good business from this situation, while his son, the second of four Georges to run the practice, benefited from the opportunities that came with Charles II's Restoration in 1660. After the last Hooper died out, the thread of continuity stitched its way through many different names. In 1946, the first of two large amalgamations took place, when Hooper's company, then called Walker, Freer and Brown, merged with Thomson and Passmore. In 1968 the second occurred — a result of the increasing complexity of law. This gave life to Thomson, Snell and Passmore, which now occupies premises in Tunbridge Wells's Lonsdale Gardens.

Glenturret Distillery is the oldest scotch whisky distillery. Famous Grouse, created by the Gloag family in 1897, is distilled here. Few distilleries remain in private ownership today, and Glenturret was sold to Highland Distillers to pay death duties. It distills little whisky these days, and its main business is as a visitor centre.

OLDEST FORGE

In 1697, the first forge in Worcestershire's town of Lye was built. This is now Britain's oldest forge and is located to the west of Birmingham. It was constructed where a grain mill had stood for at least a century, beside the River Stour. Within the next half century the Industrial Revolution would change the surrounding Black Country, so named because of the soot that poured from the factory chimneys. The forge first produced pig iron, the raw form of iron ingots, which got the name because when the freshly poured liquid metal set, it sounded like suckling piglets. The invention of steam propulsion to drive the vast

hammers increased the output of wrought iron. It was to this developing site that James Folkes came in 1797. He brought his skills as a blacksmith from the Surrey village of Abinger Hammer, where the ancient mill-driven hammer had produced iron since Queen Elizabeth came to the throne in 1558. The mechanisation of Lye and its neighbouring industrial output had stifled the Tudor business and Folkes needed to find new work. He worked at several jobs to improve his prospects, and by 1853 his two sons were able to take over the business – it has been a family concern ever since. The original site of Lye Forge was abandoned only recently, in the year 2000, when a new

site was established at Wednesbury. While the tradition of the original site was lost after a history of 300 years, the business continues as the oldest of its kind in Britain.

OLDEST MANUFACTURING COMPANY

The Great Fire of London in 1666 probably destroyed the original foundry of Britain's oldest manufacturing company. It is believed that, although the Whitechapel Bell Foundry can prove to have been in business since 1570, the work probably started in 1420. Master Founder Robert Chamberlain was casting bells in Whitechapel in the years immediately following Henry V's victory over France at

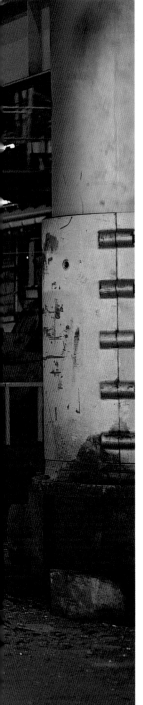

Agincourt. The new foundry was built in 1670, on the site of the Artichoke Coaching Inn – it remains virtually unchanged. The company has never ceased business and it has been responsible for casting some of the most famous bells to sound in the world. Among them, the Liberty Bell for the Assembly of the Province of Pennsylvania and Big Ben, which strikes the hour at the Palace of Westminster.

Thomas Lester cast the Liberty Bell because he was the most accomplished founder in the company at the time. The bell was to have a prophetic inscription from the Bible's Book of Leviticus (25:10) which read 'Proclaim Liberty throughout all the land unto the inhabitants thereof.' The 2,000-pound bell was sailed across to Philadelphia but it cracked on first strike; this is always a danger because the metal must remain brittle to get a free tone. The bell was recast and hung in the State House steeple, where it was hanging while the Declaration of Independence was signed in the rooms below. Britain lost the American Colonies and also, in 1834, the Palace of Westminster was burnt to the ground. The new building was to have a vast clock tower. The Whitechapel Foundry was charged with a commission for bells, including

a large one to mark the hour. Nine feet in diameter and seven and a half feet high, it weighs more than 13 tonnes. It was cast on 10th April 1858 and, just over a year later, on 31st May, the bell was heard for the first time ringing out from the Great Clock. The name 'Big Ben' was inspired by the plump MP called Sir Benjamin Hall, who waffled on for hours in a debate about what the bell should be called and so it was named after him. The foundry was narrowly missed during the Blitz, and it was diverted temporarily to war production during hostilities. Some of the first bells cast after 1945 replaced the City of London's bells destroyed in the fighting. At the entrance of the foundry the vast cross-section used to cast Big Ben still stands.

OLDEST MOTOR MANUFACTURER

At the start of the 20th century in 1901 the oldest British motor manufacturer's story began. In south London two men set up their first engineering workshop. John Portwine was a wealthy butcher and his friend John Weller was an enthusiastic engineer. With the investment of one and the enterprise of the other new ground was broken – they wanted to build motorcars. By 1903, they had something to show the world and wheeled into the British Motor Show two separate vehicles: a two-cylinder car powered to 10 horsepower and a four-cylinder that boasted 20 horsepower. Probably the oldest motor magazine, *Autocar*, was reporting on the event and predicted a good future for the two men. They formed a company the next year called Autocarriers Limited, which in time became just plain AC. Perhaps because John could appreciate a butcher's needs, the first design was a tricar for business, which was then followed by a more 'sociable' version. In 1911, the business moved to Thames Ditton and developed further improvements, but it was not until after the War in the 1920s, when cars still lacked public approval, that the AC brand made its mark in the Surrey town of Brooklands. A racing track was built here, with heavily cambered ends in order that the new speeds could be tested on the relatively small oval track. This is the oldest car racing track in Britain and is about to reopen as a museum run by Daimler Chrysler. In 1922, JA Joyce drove 100 miles in one hour on the track in an AC and later in the decade, Victor Bruce won the Monte Carlo Rally with his six-cylinder AC. In the 1930s, AC's vehicles adopted leaner form and sleek lines – the lasting characteristic of the cars, now that more than a century has passed since the AC company began.

A 43 ton steel ingot is forged by this 4000 tonne computer-controlled press at Wednesbury. The Folkes family has owned this business for 300 years and there are families who have worked in the forge for generations. The company produces forgings for the oil industry, rudder stocks for naval vessels, drive-shafts for frigates, parts for the landing gear for Airbus Industries and recently, a crankshaft for an old Dutch windmill.

OLDEST MOTOR MARQUE

Daimler is almost certainly Britain's oldest motor marque, or make, of motorcar. It resulted from the meeting between Gottlieb Daimler, the engineer, and Frederick Simms. Gottlieb was born in Schorndorf in 1834 and developed his skills as an engineer at Stuttgart Polytechnic. He worked from 1872 with Otto and Eugen Langen on developing the gas engine. In 1885, he developed almost the first-ever roadworthy motorcar and it was a version of this that he brought to an engineering exhibition in 1890. There he met Frederick, who was impressed by Gottlieb's single-cylinder four-stroke engine. There was potential for this in the market and there did not seem to be the support available to do this in Germany, so Frederick encouraged Gottlieb to bring his design to Britain. Three years later, in 1893 the Daimler Motor Syndicate Ltd. was established and patents were safely lodged that May. It was royal support that really got the car business in general, and Daimler in particular, off the ground. Queen Victoria's health was declining, and with her so did many of the strict old-fashioned values that the Victorian social system held dear. The great pioneering rebel who sought the new age was her son, Albert Edward the Prince of Wales. He bought a Daimler car and thus put the seal of distinction on the brand. The company was successful because other aristocrats followed and the new rich that were driving social change, in turn, copied them. Daimler bought space to build a factory in Coventry, where a great deal of other engineering was based. The factory that was established is now the oldest automobile plant in the country.

OLDEST SHIPPING COMPANY

Even before the Vikings landed on its shores, the Isle of Man had a maritime culture. It was imperative for trade with Ireland, England and Scotland and so in both Douglas and Peel, harbours were active with boats. In the early 19th century the oldest shipping company in Britain was established because the people of the island were no longer satisfied with the intermittent service from ships, which came from Belfast, Bristol, Liverpool and down from the Scottish ports.

At a gathering in Douglas during 1829, the decision was taken to fund a steam packet, the name given to a boat driven by a reliable steam propulsion system. The next year, on the 30th June *Mona's Isle*, the new ship arrived in Douglas. It cost £7,250 which was a huge sum but worth it to the islanders that set sail for Liverpool.

The Isle of Man Steam Packet Company was born, and it has continued to provide the island with reliable and regular links to the surrounding countries for more than 175 years. During the First World War one of the company's ships was converted into the first aircraft carrier and another, called the *King Orry*, led the German Fleet into Scapa Flow after the surrender. A short time afterwards, that once glorious fleet, built during the rush to arms by Kaiser William, scuttled itself and still lies on the seabed. In the Second World War the company's ships took part in the frantic bid to save British expeditionary troops from slaughter on the beaches of Dunkirk. On this occasion, one of the first ships to do a clear run to the beach and back was *Mona's Isle*. It has been assessed that 1 in 14 lives that were saved in that military escapade were due to one of the company's ships. Links are still maintained with Liverpool and Heysham in England, Northern and Southern Ireland.

OLDEST BUILDERS

Sometimes it seems impossible to find a good builder these days, or to rely on them. Not so with a company that has been in the building business, providing the highest quality of craftsmanship and reliability, for more than 400 years. This is the reputation of Britain's oldest building company, called R. Durtnell and Sons Limited. The Durtnells were around at the time of the Norman Conquest, but came to prominence when Henry VIII sent his Vicar General to dissolve the monasteries. Robert Darkall (which was the name's spelling at the time) quickly turned his hand to the distribution and sale of the monastic assets in Kent. It turned him a profit and helped his heirs get established; however, it did not do him much good because he ended his life swinging from a gibbet. The story really began in July 1591, when John Durtnell apprenticed himself as a carpenter, which would have involved him in building houses at that time. His father was Rector at Penshurst and the first house he helped to construct was for him, and still stands today with the completion date of 1593. A mixture of good marriages, crafty planning and a dedication to the profession the family knew best, guided them through boom and bust up to the present, when builders have probably never been in such demand. The firm turned its hand to vital war work both at Biggin Hill, where Spitfires that fought the Battle of Britain were stationed, and also building the concrete pill-boxes that would have been the last defences of Britain, had Hitler managed to invade.

The renovation of Old College in Sandhurst's Royal Military Academy was a prestigious contract but even the standing Army has not been around for as long as these builders.

OLDEST FILM STUDIOS

The oldest film studios in Britain are located in London's Ealing, and they are probably also the oldest film studios in the world. A man with enormous ambition and imagination was the inspiration for the tradition of film-making that started here in 1904. It all began when Will Barker bought a house called West Lodge beside Ealing Green, in 1902. Two years later he turned the garden and the area around it into the site for Barker Motion Photography Ltd. Almost immediately, he set about shooting the story of Henry VIII, and he paid Sir Herbert Beerbohm Tree a staggering £1,000 per day to play the leading part. The stage sets from Her Majesty's Theatre were rebuilt in the new studio and he established a new way for distributing a completed film that helped to build a new more successful film industry.

In the 1930s the studios were taken over by Basil Dean, who was a pioneer of talking pictures. This was when the films created at Ealing Studios really became popular. The Ealing comedy format produced during the 1950s celebrated a generation of British humour that was desperately needed after the war years. The subjects of films like *Kind Hearts and Coronets*, *Ladykillers* and *Passport to Pimlico* all played upon divisions in British society and may have done something to help the newly empowered post-war generation to address social issues in a way that only humour can inspire.

Another surge in activity at Ealing came when the BBC bought the studios in 1959 and spent the following two decades making drama series for broadcast. In the year 2000 four ambitious men purchased the studios in order to revive its status and success; they were Uri Frucktmann, John Kao, Harry Handelsman and Barnaby Thompson. Some of the recent films made using the facilities Ealing studios provide include one *Star Wars* episode, *Notting Hill* and *The Importance of Being Earnest*.

OLDEST BELL-HANGERS

It must have caused a great deal of surprise to the locals of The Greyhound in Besseleigh when their innkeeper, Alfred White, started moonlighting as a bell hanger. He was quite an all-rounder. Not only was this sideline going to become the oldest bell-hanging company in Britain, he was also a baker, ran the village shop and provided metalwork from his forge. In his time, Alfred must have been seen as something of a 'Renaissance' man. He had even found time to learn the art of campanology, which is the ringing of bells, when the nearby Appleton Church exchanged its peal of three for a ring of six bells in 1818.

At the age of 24, Alfred began his bell-hanging company and travelled all around Oxfordshire and beyond, with his scaffolds, ropes and frames – to remove, rebuild and replace the equipment in all types of bell tower. He took his sons into the business and called it simply, A. White and Sons. It was not long before churches and cathedrals all over the country hired his skills. Alfred installed new bell oak frames at three Oxford colleges: Merton, Magdalen and Christ Church. He made everything at his workshops, originally at The Greyhound, then at The Three Horse Shoes in Appleton and finally at a workshop in the centre of town. Whites of Appleton became a limited company in 2003.

Durtnells, Britain's oldest building company, uses the most up-to-date building techniques and materials to constuct new class-rooms at Bedales School. Joinery has always been the company's speciality and this is done in Brasted, Kent, on land that has been in the family since 1496. The company is now run by the 12th generation of the Durtnell family.

TAXES

On the Friday after Easter, the Hungerford Court meet in the Town Hall. The Tuttimen go round the town with flower bedecked poles, gathering rewards for services performed over the year. Reluctant kisses are rewarded with oranges and the children scramble for pennies. All this merriment is for the administration of levies over the grazing and fishing rights on land given to the town by John O'Gaunt.

l–r: The Tuttimen, the Town Crier and the Constable in front of the Town Hall

OLDEST TAX

Income tax was introduced when the Crown could no longer pay the costs of the State from its landed possessions. This occurred in the year 1798, when William Pitt the Younger was Prime Minister. Up until this time the Crown Estates, which still technically belong to the Crown but are administered by the Government, were used to provide the money needed to pay for the nation's needs, including defence.

The Napoleonic War was punitively expensive on the country, especially as Napoleon's Continental System was designed to make it impossible for Britain to trade. Although Income Tax was abolished after the defeat of Napoleon in 1815, it returned in 1842 and has so far remained the principal form of direct taxation faced by everyone. However, there were older taxes and it is believed that the first direct taxation at source was in 1512, at the time of Henry VIII's first invasion of France.

The oldest taxes that the nation faced and inflicted on its peasantry, were either feudal dues or the even older Danegeld. Both of these are no longer part of the British tax system, though in a few incidences they remain ceremonially collected. The Danegeld was first levied by the Anglo-Saxon king Ethelred the Unready in the year 991AD. The Danish army defeated Ethelred at the Battle of Maldon and he foolishly embarked upon a policy of buying them off. Even though his country was wealthy, the new Danegeld tax was harsh and inevitably the Danes could not believe their good fortune and kept coming back for more.

In the small Berkshire town of Hungerford there is an annual ceremony at Hocktide, which is the second Tuesday after Easter, when the commoners of the town are expected to pay a levy. It is said that this tradition links back to the Danegeld, which would make it the oldest revenue levied in Britain. The payment is extraordinary. Men must pay a penny and women must give a kiss — it has obviously been hideously distorted into a joyous ritual over the centuries. Perhaps it was maintained due to a unique enduring feudal link to the fishing and grazing that John of Gaunt granted to each house. The influence of this gift is visible from the air —

Hungerford is probably the best surviving example of the way houses once came with narrow strips of allocated land at their rear. These strips can be seen today stretching away from the houses on the High Street. The Hocktide tax is collected by the Tutti Men, who carry decorated poles with an orange on top – many refuse to pay. This invokes another bizarre ritual, which hopefully does not attempt to mimic the Danish habit of dealing with the vanquished. The Tutti Men then set up ladders to break into the houses, where the penny and kiss are forcibly extracted from the non-payers and a glass of whisky is enjoyed.

Hungerford's royal links include an event that changed the nature of the British monarchy. A rose is still given to every new monarch when they visit Hungerford because it was here that the Crown Commissioners offered the Crown to William III. The gift of a rose is the payment of other feudal dues that contend to be the oldest tax. In 1514, Robert Knollys was given a property in Oxfordshire in return for the payment of a Red Rose on Midsummer's Day. He was also fined a Red Rose for building a footbridge across Seething Lane in the City of London, and, in a revived ceremony, the Church Wardens of All Hallows by the Tower pay a rose to the Lord Mayor, even though the offending footbridge has long since disappeared. When Sir William Clopton built the town hall in Hadleigh in 1438, it was agreed that the rent should be one rose a year. The decendents of Sir William died out in England, but a distant cousin in America discovered that the tax had not been paid for 512 years, and arranged for it to be paid plus interest. This should have come to 1,303,364 roses, but they agreed on five, one for each century. A party of 80 Cloptons came to Long Melford Church in 1984 to see the the Mayor of Hadleigh place the roses on on Sir William's tomb, and the payment of the revived tax continues today.

OLDEST INLAND REVENUE TAX

Anyone who has bought his or her own home has been affected by the oldest tax still gathered by the Inland Revenue. Called Stamp Duty, it was a Dutch invention. There had been a competition in the Netherlands in 1624, to find a way to raise needed funds. Seventy years later, in 1694, King William III, who incidentally came from Holland, and his wife, Queen Mary II, introduced the same tax into Britain in order to pay for the war against France. The French were still keen to oust William and Mary so that a Catholic could be put back on the British throne.

Although tax is never popular, this purpose was important to the powerful as the 17th century came to a close. The new tax required documents to be validated with a stamp before they became legally binding and getting that stamp would cost money. When the same tax was imposed on the American Colonies in 1765, the reception was not at all favourable. Colonists agitated against arbitrary rule from London. Their famous rallying cry against the American Stamp Act was 'No taxation without representation'. It was repealed the next year but the damage had been done and, quite possibly, this error proved to be a catalyst for the American War of Independence. In 1797, William Pitt the Younger suddenly almost doubled the tax. In 1840, in a bid to fund the postal system more reliably, the Stamp Duty concept was evolved. Correspondents

Sir William Clopton's effigy lies in Holy Trinity Church in Long Melford. The church also contains fine stained glass windows, one of which was the inspiration for Tenniel's illustration of the Duchess in *Alice in Wonderland*.

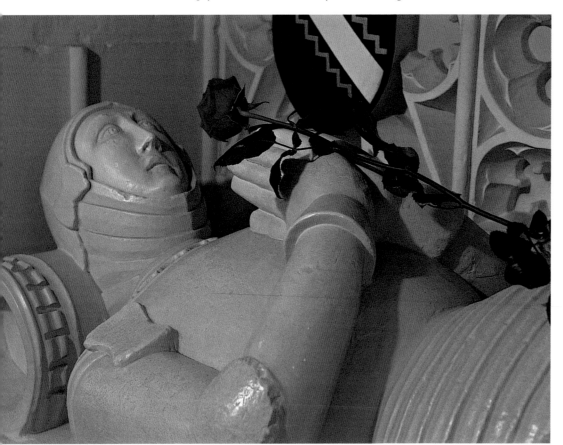

were required to fix the new Penny Black to the letter as a symbol that duty had been paid in advance. This would then be 'stamped'. The Penny Black and all designs that have followed became known as stamps, after the tax.

OLDEST EXCISE DUTY

Each year the Chancellor of the Exchequer delivers his budget to Parliament and a proportion of the country wait with bated breath to see how the changes made to the cost of beer, whisky and cigarettes are going to affect their weekly budget. The tax that is being tweaked is the oldest excise duty in Britain and beer is the oldest commodity on which it is still levied today. The Dutch Republic pioneered excise duty in Holland, where the intent was to tax the commodities at the point of manufacture. The word excise evolves from the Dutch word *exijs*, which means tax. Customs had been levying charges on imports and exports at the ports in England since the Winchester Assize established the precedent in about 1203, during the reign of King John. The new system of excise was introduced to Britain during the 17th century in order to fund the costs of the Civil War, and in 1643 the Long Parliament established the first Board of Excise. At first it was just London and the provinces that were affected with levies on beer, ale, small beer and imported beer. With the Restoration of the monarchy in 1660 the public assumed that the unpopular Board of Excise would be scrapped. On the contrary, it was confirmed by statute because the returned administration discovered the wealth it accrued. The public reaction was very hostile. In 1683, a permanent Board of Excise was established in England and Wales and the system was introduced to Scotland as part of the process of union in 1707. With its two separate histories dating back to the 13th and 17th centuries respectively, HM Customs and Excise is one of the oldest revenue-gathering departments in the country. Every swig of beer you take accrues more of the oldest excise into the Treasury.

OLDEST RATE-PAYER

The tax on tea was slashed in 1784, which made the drink affordable to all people in Britain. Perhaps the most influential advocate for the Commutation Act, which sharply reduced the duties, was Richard Twining, who was highly regarded by the Prime Minister William Pitt. He was an influential tea importer whose family had been in the business since 1706, when Richard's grandfather, Thomas Twining, bought Tom's Coffee House in London's Strand.

Adjacent properties were also bought and in 1717, the teashop opened at 216 Strand.

The property is still the home of Twinings tea and it is believed that this premises is now the oldest payer of rates in the country. Rates were levied on properties by local government when taxation was insufficient to cover their expenditure. Rates tended to be specific; for instance the need to fund the poor in any area would result in the Poor Rate. For the Twining family, such responsibilities were a religious duty. The Twinings adopted the symbol of a Golden Lion and placed it above the threshold of the door because it represented Daniel in the Bible, whose example, piety and innocence enabled him to survive a night in the lions' den. Three years after the Commutation Act, in 1787, the new doorway was unveiled. It shows two Chinese men sitting on either side of the lion, as if to echo Daniel's miraculous survival but, more specifically, to show the source of tea, which was then bought only from China. Below the lion is the name 'Twinings' (without an apostrophe) in black block letters on white. This has remained the logo for the company since 1787 and is therefore believed to be the oldest logo, in continuous use, in the world.

Twinings has no shop front, just a doorway on the Strand in London.

NEWSPAPERS MAGAZINES & PUBLISHERS

OLDEST DAILY NEWSPAPER

The Times is the oldest daily newspaper in Britain and, amongst other news, it reports daily on the financial markets of London that were the ultimate cause of its inception. The insurance market, Lloyds of London, has had turbulent times and broken the financial life of many speculators. It did just that to John Walker in 1781, who was a successful coal merchant in London. John had been a businessman since his father, Richard Walker, died in 1756, and therefore he had enough experience in his early forties to start again. With loans and the help of friends, John bought the patent for logotypes from Henry Johnson – a way of setting printing blocks with whole words or parts thereof, rather than one letter at a time. John developed this process and took a property in London's Blackfriars to establish a printing business, where he initially printed books. On 1st January 1785 he printed his first newspaper, called *The Daily Universal Register*, later on 1st January 1788 (the 980th edition) he changed the title to *The Times*. There had been daily newspapers before, like Edward Mallett's *Daily Courant* in March 1707 and the *Daily Advertiser* in 1754, but only John's paper survives to this day. Business was not easy and John faced potential ruin again over a libel that was printed concerning the Duke of York the following year – the institutions of the day did not welcome their activities being reported and talked about by the paper's readers. John was sentenced to a £50 fine, a term of one year in Newgate Prison and had to stand in the public pillory for an hour. He was liberated and eventually pardoned, only to be sued again by Lord Cowper. By this time he had handed the business to his son and retired to Teddington. He died in 1812, three years before the account of the Battle of Waterloo appeared in his newspaper. The paper is sometimes called the 'London Times' now in order to differentiate it from the *New York Times* and others. However, it predates all other 'Times' newspapers.

OLDEST IRISH NEWSPAPER

In a part of the United Kingdom that has so many difficulties to struggle with, it is interesting that its oldest newspaper, the *Belfast News Letter*, should be described as 'The Pride of Northern Ireland'. Its pages have certainly had some sorry tales to relate about a province caught in the vicissitudes of religious and political struggle. More recently, however, there seems to be more hope in its copy of resolution and peace.

The paper was first published as a weekly paper in 1737. At this time Ireland was one country and ruled

from Dublin. It was a period called the Protestant Ascendancy, when the Irish land settlement that strongly favoured Protestants above Catholics was setting the agenda for the next chapter of discord. In the northern province, called Ulster, Protestants were in the majority as a result of the aggressive settlement policy of the Tudors and Stuarts, which encouraged Scots to settle in land they could seize from Catholic families. The new paper was marked by the peacock symbol on its masthead, which is still used in an evolved form today. It was published by Francis Joy, at a site that is now called

Joy's Entry in Belfast. Perhaps its greatest scoop was intercepting a despatch that came ashore when a ship from America sailed into Londonderry unexpectedly. The news it carried for London was urgent and the journalists of the *News Letter* discovered the facts. On the 23rd August 1776 it published news that King George III still did not know, but that would haunt him for the rest of his long reign. It was through the *Belfast News Letter* that the people of Ireland and then Great Britain came to learn that the American Colonies had declared their independence from the Crown.

Antony Flanaghan sells *The Weekly Newsletter* in front of Belfast City Hall.

OLDEST SCOTTISH NEWSPAPER

Aberdeen is called the Granite City and has a culture to match the sturdy structure of its buildings. On 29th December 1747, just a year after the defeat of Bonnie Prince Charlie at nearby Drumossie Moor, in the Battle of Culloden, the city saw publication of the first *Aberdeen Journal*. At that time, the Scottish Highlands were still suffering from the repression of its clan system by the Hanoverian redcoats, who were fearful of further Jacobite uprisings. The landscape was dotted with the frantic construction of forts in order to provide protection for King George II's status quo. Today, it is the oldest surviving paper in Scotland, though it is now called the *Aberdeen Press and Journal*. It is linked to the equivalent *Inverness Press and Journal* and they provide the principal local newspapers for the disparate communities that populate Britain's most sparsely populated area.

OLDEST SUNDAY NEWSPAPER

The hunger for wealth is the motivation for many things and for WS Bourne, in 1791, it was the inspiration for risking his shirt by establishing Britain's first Sunday newspaper, which is now the oldest. He thought it would deliver him a fortune but in just three years he was a bankrupt, with a debt that exceeded £1,600. Bourne wanted *The Observer* newspaper to be unbiased and free from all party political affiliation but facing this debt required desperate measures, and he turned to the Government for help. The Government rejected Bourne's pragmatic offer of sale because it saw no advantage in a

state-owned Sunday newspaper. The paper that is now owned by the Guardian Media Group sought from the start to be independent, but it has changed greatly in the two centuries of its publication. At times the paper was little more than a sleazy gossip rag; it occasionally fawned to the Government of the day becoming its mouthpiece, but mostly it has been a stout defender of all citizens against the Establishment's vested interest. One bold decision probably did more to build the paper's reputation than any others. It came in 1820 when the paper published all the details of a trial the Government wanted suppressed. This brought to public awareness the details of the Cato Street conspirators who wanted to assassinate the whole Cabinet while they dined, and then take the Mansion House by force and declare a provisional Government. Death was the inevitable sentence but public sympathy demanded that the grim medieval process of drawing and quartering was withheld. Possibly because of *The Observer*'s reports, the conspirators became popular with a population that had little affection for the Cabinet. The man suspected of executing the men was attacked in the street and nearly castrated. *The Observer*'s proprietor, William Clement, ignored injunctions, never appeared in court and refused to pay his £500 fine. Arguably this was a precedent for the freedom of the presses to print at liberty and without censorship by authority.

OLDEST REGIONAL NEWSPAPER

Britain has a regional newspaper that claims to be the oldest surviving regular newspaper in the world. It is the oldest regional newspaper in the country. The story began close to the famous Battle of Worcester where the future of Britain's monarchy hung in the balance, or near the Boscobel Oak to be precise. Charles II hid with Major Careless in an oak tree while Cromwell's victorious troops searched the grounds for the new king. This was certainly a story but it came at a time when freedom of printed expression was heavily suppressed.

In 1690, soon after the reign of James II and with wider freedoms to print, the first imprint of a paper in Worcester appeared. It was erratically printed but the foundations of the paper had been established. Regularity started when, in 1709, Stephen Bryan took over the paper. An apprentice from London, he brought the latest know-how to this regional title, but he had to buy a house in order to qualify as a freeman and therefore qualify as a legitimate printer. He called the paper the *Worcester Post-man*, a title he copied from *The Postman* that he had read in London. With Queen Anne's picture on one side of the title page and a trumpeting post-man astride his horse on the other, the paper was sold throughout the Midlands from Gloucester to Wolverhampton, Warwick and Birmingham. Initially it covered national news with a few advertisements, a trend that would later dominate the regional genre. When Stephen died in 1748, Hervey Berrow became proprietor. A newly revived paper was published on 23rd June that year, just three days after Stephen's burial. Hervey had been educated through his father's links as a man of the cloth at Christ's College Cambridge. Although not a great deal is known of Hervey, the paper suddenly changed its title from the plain-sounding *Worcester Journal* to *Berrow's Worcester Journal* on 11th October 1753.

OLDEST TABLOID

Alfred Harmsworth was so impressed by the papers he found circulating in the United States that he imported the format to the United Kingdom. The American press baron Randolph Hearst pioneered mass media with two titles. The oldest was called the *San Francisco Examiner* and was first published in 1880, while the *Morning Journal* started in 1895. Alfred had edited his school magazine, which included a gossip column; he also wrote for local newspapers whenever he could escape the classroom. In 1896, Alfred launched the *Daily Mail*, which was the first mass circulation newspaper that reflected much of the style he had been interested in at school. The *Daily Mail* changed the style of British reporting and it was soon followed in 1903 by another title that was initially intended for female readers. This was called the *Daily Mirror* and it is regarded as the oldest 'tabloid' newspaper even though the *Daily Mail* was in circulation before.

Stewart Gilbert, the editor of the world's oldest regional newspaper, has a meeting with sub-editors Paul Francis and David Hudson-Wood. The paper has been produced every week for the last 300 years, and back issues in the archives show that what was making headlines then still makes news today.

The *Daily Mail* was originally seen as another in the established stable of titles, whereas the *Daily Mirror* seemed to establish a completely new style of reporting, albeit tested at the *Daily Mail*. In order to sustain these papers and the vast quantity of new and existing titles that Alfred subsequently took into ownership, he bought up large territories in Newfoundland and farmed their forests vigorously for paper. Alfred became Viscount Northcliffe and his brother, Harold Harmsworth, became Viscount Rothermere for transforming the British media.

OLDEST PUBLISHERS

The tradition of English publishing is linked to printing. William Caxton established himself as a printer in 1476, at Westminster, having developed a crude but influential process. The art of impressing words and characters onto paper by means of pressure using ink was revolutionary in every respect and it was to change society. No longer was education to be the privilege of monastic clerks, it would be gradually more available and thereby threaten to affect social thinking and power.

When Henry VIII granted a Charter to Cambridge University 1534 he established a press that, since the first Press book was published in 1584, is not only the oldest press and bookshop in Britain but also the oldest in the world. Being an integral part of the university, scholars would come to the Press to buy their textbooks and there is still a shop there offering the complete range of publications. The reputation of the Cambridge University Press is also unique in Britain and it delivers works of scholarship commercially and as part of a charitable foundation to advance education, research and knowledge everywhere. Among the esoteric publications handled here are exam papers and Bibles, which were controversial during the Reformation, and Cambridge University Press is still one of the few licensed printers of the King James Version. Countless academics have looked to the Cambridge University Press to print their scholarship: notable among them Sir Isaac Newton.

OLDEST MAGAZINE AND PERIODICAL

The glossy society magazine called *Tatler*, which was given a vibrant new look in the last decade, claims to be descended from Britain's oldest magazine. The first *Tatler* was published on 12th April 1709, by the freemason Sir Richard Steele but it only went to 271 issues and ceased after the 2nd January 1711 issue. After a gap of

more than one and a half centuries, *Tatler* was revived in 1901 and, apart from a brief gap in the 1960s, it still survives today – however, these days it concentrates less on aristocratic parties, gossip and peccadilloes than it once did.

The word 'magazine' derives from the Arabic word for a store place, that the French applied to a shop. It was first applied to English periodicals when the *Gentleman's Magazine* began in 1731. The founders described their new organ as 'a monthly collection to treasure up as a magazine' and this word became the common description for periodicals containing fiction. As illustration developed and the printing process enabled the publication of ever more glossy images, the word magazine evokes a whole new meaning. Sir Richard also went on to co-found *The Spectator* on 1st March 1711, with Joseph Addison. They wrote articles under the pseudonym of Isaac Bickerstaff, in order to maintain anonymity and to promote matters of interest to the middle class. The idea was to publish the views of a small club that met frequently in order to provoke the issues they most wanted to publicise. *The Spectator* of today is a revival of the original because the duo published their last edition in 1712, though Joseph revived it temporarily in 1714. The influence of both *Tatler* and *The Spectator* was considerable. They embody an interesting social history that gave a kick-start to journalism and article writing, which became the corner stone of a thriving British obsession.

OLDEST MAGAZINE FOR WOMEN

Ignored and distrusted for centuries in Britain's patriarchal society, the end of the 19th century saw the first flicker of women's rights and growing influence. It was still some time before the effects of the Reform Acts would inevitably embrace women's right to vote into the franchise but, in 1885 Britain's oldest women's weekly magazine was first published. It was the first of its kind and set a gentle style that has been broadly maintained ever since. It is called *The Lady*, which would have seemed fairly innocuous and unthreatening in the 1880s, but it marked a small and significant point in the development of an equal voice in a changing society.

OLDEST PICTURE LIBRARY

With brilliant foresight, Herbert Ingham predicted the public mood when he launched his newspaper on

Saturday 14th May 1842, just a few days after Queen Victoria's fancy dress ball at Buckingham Palace. This was important because his *Illustrated London News* was the first paper to have pictures and then, as now, interest in royalty drove his sales. It is the oldest illustrated paper in Britain but it is also the oldest picture library. This was because the paper was to chart the entire Victorian and Edwardian age, grow to include other magazines and papers and therefore accrue the greatest picture archive in the nation from which images will always be required. Not only did that first publication, of what was called the '*ILN*', show in hastily prepared woodcut drawings the flamboyant palace guests, it also covered subjects like the fire in Hamburg, the war in Afghanistan and Paris fashions.

Despite selling 26,000 copies of the first publication, it was marketing a laxative that established the financial security of the business. By 1856, the circulation had reached 200,000, compared with *The Times*, which was stable at 70,000. This was an incredible success. So was the system of turning drawings into woodcuts, and later the pioneering of photographic illustrations. All the plates and blocks were stored. Ever since 1842, the archive of negatives, prints and drawings has grown. These are a valuable resource, though even in the digital age, the dangers of deterioration, corruption and fire present problems to the curators. However, it is possible that whatever event since the mid-19th century you may need a picture of will be supplied from this collection.

The Illustrated London News picture library has over 2 million engravings, drawings, paintings and photographs covering world events and social history from the archives of a number of 19th and 20th century magazines. Amongst their treasures are paintings done in the trenches at the front during the first World War.

TRAVEL

BOATS

previous pages

The Sweet Track (see page 176) is one of a network of walkways that covered the marshy ground of the Somerset Levels about 3500 years ago. A causeway of oak planks on timber piles, which is not visible here, was discovered in 1970 not far from Glastonbury Tor. A modern reconstruction was made at Shapwick Heath Visitor Centre but the health and safety inspectors closed it for public access.

right

The *Moonbeam*, a Tyne class lifeboat, traditionally the work-horse of the RNLI, is stationed at Montrose in Scotland. A short distance from the shore and harbour's mouth is a shifting sandbank that is extremely hazadous to shipping in rough seas. There has been a lifeboat station here since 1800 to rescue those in peril.

OLDEST LIFEBOAT STATION

Drowning is one of the most dreadful fates: even when safe on land the imagination can provoke a sense of instinctive insecurity and suffocating helplessness. Britain's maritime history is marked by the names of countless souls that have been lost at sea through the inevitable dangers of seafaring. Mariners of the town of Montrose in Scotland were particularly prone to ship-wreck on the Annat Bank in the 18th century when all navigation was under sail. The Annat Bank is a shifting sand bank that sits across the entrance to Montrose Bay. It is shifted by tides and presents a significant obstacle to sail boats battered by an easterly gale. As a result, in 1800, the mariners and trades people came together and bought a lifeboat, which is now the oldest duty lifeboat station in Britain. This set a precedent for others that were paid for by local subscription at different ports around the country.

Twenty-three years after, Montrose had a manned watch at its lifeboat station, Sir William Hillary called the nation to do something about its responsibility to sea-far-ers and the property that was being lost. His paper was published on 28th February 1823 as 'An Appeal to the British Nation, on the humanity and policy of forming a National Institution, for the preservation of lives and property from shipwreck'. A Member of Parliament took up this cause and both support and finances were quickly forthcoming. The Archbishop of Canterbury persuaded the King to be Patron and the new body was given the right to call itself the Royal National Institution for the Preservation of Life from Shipwreck. As a result the foundations for the Royal National Lifeboat Institution were established and this now administers the oldest lifeboat station in Britain in the town of Montrose.

'The Annat Bank was a favourite ship trap and made this a really hazardous area, which was one very good reason for the community to establish the first lifeboat station,' explains John West, who is the Lifeboat Operations Manager at Montrose, 'There were ship-wrecks every time an easterly gale blew up and this is always the time when the seas off Montrose are most dangerous'. The boat that Montrose bought in 1800 was one of the thirty-one specially designed lifeboats built by Henry Greathead from South Shields. Today the station operates two lifeboats; the all-weather Tyne Class lifeboat that responds to calls out at sea and an inshore inflatable boat for rescuing people off the sandbanks, from rocks or wherever the smaller craft is required for access. Montrose is fearfully proud of its lifeboats, as John explains, 'This is a relatively small town, virtually surrounded by water. The sea, trade, fishing and shipping are rooted in the community and therefore the lifeboat station and its history is a focus of collective pride and responsibility today, as it was in 1800'.

OLDEST PADDLE STEAMER

If the fleet of small craft, called the Little Ships, had not played their part in saving the British and allied soldiers from annihilation on the beaches at Dunkirk in 1940, the Second World War would have been brief and Adolf Hitler would have replaced King George VI as Britain's head of state. The bravery came at a cost and the Luftwaffe bore down to blast many of the ships from the water. One of the vessels lost was the paddle steamer called the *Waverley*.

In the aftermath of victory, the decision was taken to build a new *Waverley*. The paddle steamer was built on the River Clyde in 1947 and it was intended as a ferry to run between Craigendorran and Arrochar along the picturesque western coast of Scotland. This business withered but the *Waverley* went on to provide charter and regular trips all around Britain. The famous lines of her design have been well-photographed, possibly more than any other boat. She is now the oldest paddle steamer in service in the country. Generous grants from the Heritage Lottery Fund and Glasgow City Council enabled the operators to restore the *Waverley* to her 1940s elegance. However her

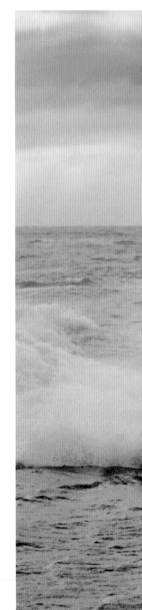

operators, Waverley Excursions Ltd., faced a set-back the following year when the *Waverley* ran aground off Kintyre, leading to a safety review. There is no doubt that this much-loved paddle steamer will survive this set-back and continue to serve the public. It is hoped that this *Waverley* will never have to answer the national call to arms its predecessor faced at the onset of the last World War.

OLDEST CROSS-CHANNEL HARBOUR

This island has been a trading nation for longer than most realise. The oldest harbour in Britain that engaged in trade with the continent is in Poole, and is also the largest natural harbour in the country. It sits protected by a narrow entrance and the hills of the Isle of Purbeck on the south coast. Historians know that Cerdic, the Saxon chief who formed the kingdom of the West Saxons landed somewhere along the southern coast; they also consider that Alfred the Great's embryo navy may have used the harbour.

Recently archaeologists made a find between Green Island and Cleavel Point in one of the many channels that thread about this large enclosed expanse of water. They identified the remains of wooden piles driven into the harbour floor. Their research confirms that these date from about 250 years before Christ and formed the foundation for two jetties from which Iron Age inhabitants traded pottery and shale jewellery with boats that plied the English Channel. Boats would have found their way into this substantial quay through the narrow harbour entrance and across the wide harbour. The two jetties were 160 and 55 meters long and made firm with clay rubble and topped with Purbeck limestone slabs.

ROADS
RAILWAYS
AND
CANALS

OLDEST ROADS
Sweet Track

It was a peat cutting operation near Glastonbury, that brought to light the oldest road in Britain, which is called the Sweet Track. Preserved in layers of peat that had been formed by centuries of flooding over the reeds that grow in the boggy marshes of Somerset, the workmen came upon buried wooden planks. The work stopped and scientists stepped in to investigate. The wood was discovered to be nearly 6,000 years old. In fact a precise date for the oak, ash and lime wood was given as the year 3806BC. Our ancestors had needed to cross from an island in this marsh to the high ground at the side. It was a distance of about two kilometres. To do this they brought wood and shaped it into posts and long planks. At short distances from one another, posts were sunk into a deeper wooden foundation, forming a cross. These were then used as supports for the

long wooden planks that were placed between them in order to provide a walkway that was above the water. Sadly the wetlands are being drained, but in order to preserve the oldest surviving road in Britain and possibly the world, efforts are being taken to keep the timbers submerged.

Ridgeway

Another ancient road is much more accessible. The Ridgeway follows the high ground for 85 miles (137 kilometres) between Avebury in the south, past Uffington, Wallingford and Chinnor to the Ivinghoe Beacon north of Tring. In fact it was part of a much longer and more complex system of roads that crossed the whole country and provided communication for the prehistoric inhabitants of Britain. The Ridgeway follows a chalk ridge along the North West Downs and into the Chilterns, passing the River Thames between the two. Iron Age forts are a

reminder of the importance of this route at that time. The Ridgeway once connected the route from Dorset's coast to the Wash, which was one of the most significant arterial routes in the country. Many of the original pathways have been lost because in 1750 the Enclosure Act brought areas of the country that had not been farmed before, into agriculture. The path had to be bordered with banks and thorn, in order to keep the animals from straying. As a result some of the links that had survived from the time when the Vikings used this route to invade Wessex were lost. However, the Ridgeway also served a purpose in medieval times as a drover's road. Along it from end to end would pass shepherds and herdsmen with their livestock heading for markets. Today it is an escape for those seeking leisure and fitness. It still offers the same advantage for which it was originally selected – dry feet; something our ancestors wanted even more than we might today.

Walkers, cyclists, horses, mortobikes and off-road vehicles all use the 85 miles of track of the Ridgeway, near Marlborough. There are plans to close the road to recreational 4x4s as they do so much damage to the parts of the road that are grass.

Vicars' Close, the oldest street, with Wells Cathedral beyond. Unusually for this day and age, there are no TV aerials or cars in the street.

Yarnton

In the last 10 years another clue to the evolving peoples of Britain has come to light; the oldest metalled road in the country was uncovered near Yarnton near Oxford. The surprise is its presumed age. Experts believe that the 35-metre long causeway dates from the Bronze Age, or possibly from even further back to the Neolithic period and that it linked two settlements. The Bronze Age refers to the period between the Stone and Iron Ages. There are few human remains from the Bronze Age and therefore the road is of greater significance; this is because cremation was the favoured way of body disposal whereas burial had been the Stone Age way. The road is five metres wide and therefore quite a thoroughfare for the time, and it was built using limestone. This also gives an interesting insight to the engineering efforts used at the time because the nearest source of these limestone pebbles is found nearly five miles from the site. Wooden posts suggest that a rail existed in order to help those crossing and the survival of this wood provides the best means of dating the structure accurately.

OLDEST STREET

Wells is in Somerset and the magnificent setting of its cathedral church and surrounding close are unsurpassed elsewhere. There is a real sense of history around the original wells from which the settlements here have always taken life. Bronze Age evidence and the remains of the early minster to St Andrew were the foundations of worship for the great cathedral church that stands here now. The Bishop of Bath and Wells had his palace through an archway and beside a pond that always seems to have swans swimming its boundaries.

One of these bishops was called Ralph of Shrewsbury, who the Canons were in such a hurry to install in 1329 that they never consulted the Pope. Ralph had to pay a penance whilst the second stage of building the cathedral church was under way. This may have delayed his ambition to found a Vicars' College in 1348. Vicars held ordinary ecclesiastical jurisdiction and would have been junior to the canons (the word comes from the appointment given to subordinate officials to the praetorian prefects in Rome).

These Vicars needed lodgings and therefore a purpose-built street of houses was constructed. Gardens were added in 1420 but otherwise the street, with its chapel at one end and hall at the other, is much as it was originally intended. The tall chimneys stand like an avenue of trees along the route that generations of the Vicar's Choral – which they became known as for singing the services – would pass from their homes and cross the bridge into the cathedral church for the many liturgical rites of the day.

OLDEST ROAD IN WALES

From Bishop's Castle in Shropshire an ancient walkway heads west across the Marches and into Wales. It is called the Kerry Ridgeway and it is the oldest road in Wales, dating back to before the Iron and Dark Ages. It is one of the few ancient tracks that have been discovered, and was probably used by the first humans to live on these islands. Along its route are hints to the civilisations that dominated this landscape. It passes by Caer Din Fort, where Bronze Age tools were discovered and which is probably either a late prehistoric earthwork or an Iron Age stronghold. The existence of the Bishop's Castle, which was originally one of the largest motte and bailey wooden castles built by the Normans shows how significant the Kerry Ridgeway must have been. William the Conqueror quickly realised how vulnerable he was to the west, and the Bishop of Hereford was responsible for keeping the Welsh from crossing into England. Centuries before, King Offa had created a massive ditch to divide Wales from his part of England; this was Offa's Dyke, and it is particularly visible from this ancient walkway. The Ridgeway became a drovers' road when times were amicable between the two countries, enabling the cattle bred in Wales to be herded by their farmers to the markets of middle England. Today, like so many other spectacular historic routes, it is the fiefdom of the walker.

OLDEST ROUNDABOUT

The Great Fire in Chicago of 1871, had an enormous effect on the 21-year-old Ebenezer Howard, who was born the son of a shopkeeper in London and would create the first British roundabout. Ebenezer had emigrated to become a farmer but this failed, and he found himself in the city soon after the plans to rebuild Chicago began. He worked with stenographers drafting the revival of the city and learnt how planning issues were addressed. When he returned to London, he worked as an official Parliamentary reporter, at a time when worries about the effects of urbanisation united all political parties.

The oldest roundabout in Britain came into being as a result of the next event in Ebenezer's life. He read a futuristic book by Edward Bellamy, an American novelist, that described Boston in the year 2000. The Utopian dream it depicted inspired him to build a garden city that combined both city and countryside, encouraging a co-location of skills and culture. Ebenezer wrote his own book, called *Tomorrow a Peaceful Path to Real Reform* and it laid out a blueprint for the perfect garden city. The chance to put this idea into practice came in Letchworth, just north of London in the county of Hertfordshire. The design of the town was based upon a series of six avenues radiating from a central park, with circular roads connecting the residential, office and farmland areas. The plan provoked the need for an arrangement where those six routes converged. The solution was a roundabout along with the corresponding rules on how horse-drawn vehicles would give way to each other in order to avoid chaos. The plan in Letchworth was also put into practice near Moscow, Tokyo and Paris. The roundabout, as a solution to converging roads, is now common for drivers around the world, although, ironically, there is reputedly only one roundabout in America.

Six roads meet at the oldest roundabout that is situated on the edge of Letchworth, the oldest garden city, built in 1903.

OLDEST TRAFFIC ISLAND

A passing comment from one of the trading families of London's St James's Street has caught the attention of this book but remains unproved. Simon Berry of the wine merchant Berry Bros. says the traffic island that runs through the centre of St James's Street is the oldest in Britain. The street was one of the most significant to develop in London because of the Court, which moved to St James's Palace with the monarch after fire destroyed Whitehall Palace. The presence of the most powerful and wealthy men in the land led to the establishment of businesses, coffee houses and gentlemen's clubs, which competed to gain their custom. Women did not much frequent this male bastion. It was a place of masculine gossip, politics, barbers, shoe shops, hatters and other male accoutrements. The street was always wide by conventional standards in the 16th century, in order that the Clock Tower of St James's Palace could dominate the scene. As a result of the hub that the principal royal residence provoked, the street was always full of

You need a safe haven to cross busy St. James' Street. The building of this traffic island is mentioned in the records of Berry Bros, the oldest wine merchants (see page 143), which is just opposite.

horses and carriages. The incidence of accidents caused by horse- drawn vehicles in towns was always very high. This wide avenue was a dangerous thoroughfare to cross and therefore the supposition that this would be the natural birthplace for a safe haven in the middle of the street would be logical. It is possible to make out the existence of some sort of traffic island on Richard Horwood's map of London, which was prepared at the start of the 19th century but there is no clear reference in the map made by John Rocque of the same area in the first half of the 18th century. The 'keep left' traffic rule that ordered St James's Street, until it became part of the oneway system, was established when it was imposed nationally in 1835. However, the oldest use of the keep left rule was on London Bridge, where it was first imposed in 1756. Scottish towns were the next to introduce the rule in 1772 but from 1835, traffic islands became relatively common.

OLDEST INDEPENDENT RAILWAY

Slate was the reason for a railway to be built in Wales's mountainous Snowdonia region. The railway was originally constructed in order to move the valuable commodity from Blaenau Ffestiniog to the sea, because relying on horses and carts across the rugged roads was time-consuming, expensive and dangerous. The Rheilffordd Ffestiniog Railway is the oldest independent railway company in Britain and in the world. It became possible in 1811, after William Maddox built a cob across the River Glaslyn's estuary, this created a natural harbour at one end called Port Madoc. James Spooner was invited to survey the land and plan a route for the rails of a horse tramway to pass. In this landscape the task was considerable, but James managed to achieve a route that dropped at a consistent and steady gradient from the top to the shoreline. This enabled the loaded bogeys to descend to the west by gravity, and then to be hauled back empty to the pit by horses. The gauge of the rails is just 23 inches wide, it is 14 miles long and there are 700 feet of height between one end and the other. Construction began in 1832, soon after the Act of Parliament granting it the go-ahead was signed. It opened in 1836, and the significance of the engineering feat was quickly communicated around the world. As steam locomotion became popular the line acquired its first locomotive in 1863; this replaced the horses and increased speed. Business expanded and so the railway introduced a passenger service, which enabled workers from the mine to travel to work rather than camp at the mines. In 1869, the

first of Robert Fairlie's double bogie locomotives went into service; these looked as if the train was pulling in opposite directions. Within a year, railway experts from around the world charged with developing comprehensive railway systems, came to see the success at Ffestiniog. It was forced out of business after the Second World War but enthusiasts have revived the track and it is now a tourist attraction.

OLDEST PUBLIC RAILWAY

Another railway was constructed in the early 1820s, in order for the coal of Darlington's mines to reach the port at Stockton-on-Tees. This is not only the oldest railway to be used by steam locomotives, it is also considered to be the world's first modern railway. Much of it is still in operation today, though with all the constituent parts replaced. It was designed as a wagon way for horses to pull coal. This was commonplace and just another evolution of the wooden-railed tramways that first appeared in the

mineral districts of Newcastle during the 16th century. Edward Pease, a wealthy wool merchant, put up the money and while the work was being done the engineer, George Stevenson, persuaded the managers to let him trial his steam locomotive. In 1814, George had designed his first locomotive, called *Blucher* – possibly in salute to the Prussian general who came to Wellington's aid at Waterloo the following year. He had also designed his own line between Hetton and Sunderland, which was the first to have no animals, just engines. Permission was granted and so George had the chance for his trials. Ignatius Bonomi was the architect of the Stockton-Darlington line and he made allowance for the possibilities of greater weights in his calculations, especially for the first bridge that he constructed. The Stocton-Darlington line opened to the public on 27th September 1825, and George's locomotive, called Locomotion No 1, pulled open wagons with 600 passengers. It took two hours to cover 12 miles.

The Ffestiniog Railway runs through Snowdonia National Park. Nowadays, the trains carry passengers and railway enthusiasts but not long ago this was an industrial area employing thousands of people to produce roofing slates. The last slate train ran in 1964, but there are plans to re-open several more of the old slate lines.

The Laigh Milton Viaduct, the oldest railway bridge, is now part of a footpath. The railings have been added to meet 21st century health and safety requirements.

OLDEST INTERCITY RAILWAY

The attention of Parliament was fixed upon the development of railways during George IV's reign. In 1826, parliament approved the plan to build a line between the growing industrial cities of Liverpool and Manchester. George Stephenson and Joseph Locke designed the 35-mile-long route, which is still operational today and is the oldest inter-city railway line in Britain.

Some of the distance was across boggy ground, in particular Chat Moss, which was almost five miles across. The solution they reached in overcoming the problem remains solid today, even though modern trains vastly exceed the weights envisaged at construction. In 1829, the directors of the new line prepared for completion. They wanted the best locomotive for the task and ran a competition. Having designed the railway and ensured that the gradients were at a minimum, George Stephenson tendered a locomotive design of his own, which he called the *Rocket*. The competition was held at Rainhill and the *Rocket* managed a speed of 30 miles per hour, which no rival could match. At the opening of the Liverpool to Manchester Railway, on 15th September 1830, there was considerable excitement. The Prime Minister, who was then the Duke of Wellington, attended. However, a tragedy occurred when William Huskisson, who was Member of

Parliament for Liverpool, was knocked over and killed by the *Rocket*. It was the first fatality on an intercity line.

OLDEST RAILWAY BRIDGE

Coal was vital to the industrial output of a country at war. Scotland was perhaps never more united in the British union than it was when facing the enemy in Napoleonic France at the start of the 19th century. In order to shift the coal mined around Kilmarnock to the port at Troon, so it could be carried north into Glasgow, an efficient railway was needed. The Third Duke of Portland, who had been Prime Minister twice, put up money to build the line; however, he was dead by the time the project was completed.

Part of the plan required a bridge to span the River Irvine at Gatehead. This bridge still carries the railway and is therefore the oldest still operating in Britain. It is called the Laigh Milton Viaduct and apart from the metal railings added by the requirements of more modern health and safety requirements, it is much as it was when the first coal passed across its spans in 1811. The line was originally served by horse-drawn wagons that carried the coal. However, as the technology developed, locomotives replaced the animals and the Kilmarnock to Troon Line became Scotland's first public railway. The influence the railway had on the region was immense. It attracted heavy industry, not least the manufacture of locomotives. It was in Kilmarnock that Andrew Barclay built the first locomotive in 1859, and his success was followed when both Grant Ritchie and Co. and also Dick Kerr and Co. were established as engine builders in the town.

OLDEST TRAIN

Winding along the narrow gauge Ffestiniog Railway in Wales's Snowdonia is Britain's oldest locomotive that still pulls trains on the line for which it was originally built. It is probably also the oldest regularly working steam locomotive in the world. It is called *Prince* and like all engines, it has a character. In 1863 Albert Edward, Prince of Wales, married Alexandra of Denmark. That same year the first steam engines were commissioned for the Ffestiniog railway from George England and Co. of Hatcham and two of these were called *Princess* and *Prince*. They were the first made for a narrow gauge railway but the oldest of these to survive in working order is *Prince*, the Old Gent, which bears a plate on the front with the

words, 'The Talking Train' in English and Welsh. When the line closed in 1946, *Prince* was in the works being fitted with a brand new boiler. The railway could only be scrapped by an act of parliament, so it and the surviving locos survived intact until they could be rescued. Thus, when the line was reopened by volunteers in 1955, it was natural to pick *Prince* as the first engine to be restored. Albert Edward became Edward VII and his great great grandson, Prince Charles, drove the locomotive *Prince* in 2003, at the opening of the Welsh Highland Railway, which has given the Old Gent a new lease of life.

OLDEST TRAM

The Isle of Man has the oldest tram system in service in the British Isles, and it still operates 'Tram Car No 1', which was built for the opening of the network on 7th September 1893. The trams are known as streetcars and once provided a vital transport link for travellers on the east side of the island. In the 1950s there was a big reduction in use of the system which sparked a debate about what cuts to make in the service. The Government of the Isle of Man is independent from Westminster, and it decided to take over the operation of the streetcars in order to keep them running. However, this was not a sustainable option and in September 1975 the decision was taken to close the whole line. As often occurs when this sort of decision is made, there was a strong public reaction and enthusiasts stepped forward to help make the operation of the tram a going concern. The rails were restored and the trams given a polish, and in 1977 the revived system went into service, principally as a tourist attraction. The island also has the oldest horse-drawn trams in the British Isles. The first ever horse-drawn trams appeared in New York City in 1832.

below left
Rob Coulson drives *Prince* or 'The Old Gent' in the Boston Lodge Works of the Ffestiniog Railway Company where the engine has been since 1863. Behind are the slate wagons, each one containing £2000 worth of roofing slate.

below
In 1893, three electric trams were built for the Manx Railway Company. No. 1 and No. 2 are still working, but No. 3 was lost in a fire. The line runs daily from Easter to October, going to Douglas, Ramsey and Laxey.

OLDEST TRAMWAY TUNNEL

Some sections of the Peak Forest Tramway, in Derbyshire, are still used as bridleways and footpaths. It finally closed in 1926, after operating for 130 years. Unfortunately parts of the old tramway were bought into private ownership, which means it is not possible now to walk the whole route. The Stodhart Tunnel, which is about half way between the Dove Holes limestone quarries and the Bugsworth Canal Basin, is thought to be the oldest tramway tunnel in Britain. It is now on Derbyshire County Council's buildings at most risk list because they list it as the oldest 'railway' tunnel in the county.

The first part of the tramway, which included Stodhart Tunnel, was constructed between 1794 and 1796 in order to transport limestone dug from the quarries in Dove Holes Dale to the canal system. The line, its bridges and tunnel were constructed by Benjamin Outram and Thomas Brown, two engineers working for the company who had rejected the original plan of building a canal from the quarries to the great canal.

It is a pity that the cast iron rails have all disappeared from where they were set. Their special design was the opposite from that used by the British national rail system. The latter has simple flat rails that the train and carriages adhere to through flanged wheels, with a rim to guide the

bogey on the inside of each wheel. The tramway had flat wheels that were guided by flanged rails. This was because when the wagons reached the mine they were rolled from the track along the ground and needed flat wheels.

OLDEST CABLE TRAMWAY

The Bradford Trolleybus Association trundled to the rescue when the nearby Shipley Glen Tramway faced ruin. With their enthusiasm and voluntary support Britain's oldest cable tramway was saved.

Sam Wilson originally had the idea to build it, in order to provide a leisure attraction for the hard-working folk of the Leeds and Bradford area of West Yorkshire. Sam was an engineer who believed that he could open up Shipley Glen to the public. In addition to opening his tramway in 1895, he also launched a toboggan run, but this was closed immediately after an accident in 1900. Lastly, Sam was a pioneer of cinema for the area – he tried to launch a Bioscope show in the Saltaire Institute, and when he found this impossible he established a tent outside a local hotel for people to come and view entertainments.

However, it was back to the tramway that Sam returned because this was what gave him the greatest pleasure. He had initially installed a suction gas system to drive the two twin trams on adjacent lines, which had a small gauge of

An early-morning sculler on the Exeter Ship Canal near the double locks, with the Cathedral in the background. The canal is unique in that it has a tow path on both sides. The last commercial sea-going vessel used the canal to reach the city basin in the late 1960's and it is now mostly used by rowing clubs and canoeists.

just 20 inches. The incline was manageable and at its steepest the gradient reached 1 in 7. The power system was changed first to town gas, then oil during the First World War, and finally it was converted to electricity in 1928. The oldest cable tramway continues to provide access to the Children's Funfair and Pleasure Ground at the top of the glen, due to the hard work of the voluntary helpers.

OLDEST CANAL

It was in 1539 that Henry VIII's Parliament passed an Act that gave permission for a canal to be constructed beside the River Exe, and thus make access to the ancient quays of Exeter navigable again. This is now the oldest canal in Britain, though other more basic canals predate it that were constructed in Roman times – such as the one near Sedgefield, which was a series of man-made lakes linking the Rivers of Wear and Tees. Work finally began in 1563; by then, the lock technology that would make canals viable had been developed in Europe during the 14th and 15th centuries, with Leonardo da Vinci credited for a series of six locks that united the canals of Milan in Italy.

Exeter had always been important. The network of roads in the area still follows ancient routes planned by the Britons, which can be identified on a current map. From the vast estuary of the River Exe there was no great distance to open between the sea and Exeter's Roman quay. However, during the Middle Ages shoals and weirs impeded navigation, because it was permitted for feudal superiors to block the waterways that they controlled. The worst culprit was Countess Isabella de Fortibus, who built up weirs in the 13th century deliberately, in order to stop boats reaching Exeter and to boost trade in her town at Topsham. The first leg of the canal stretched from Exeter to the Countess's weir, which was the tidal point of the estuary. This was fed with water from another, constructed by John Trew in 1566 for £225. In 1698, William Bayley deepened the canal to 14 feet in order that sea-going vessels could reach the city, but the next year he disappeared leaving the canal unusable. It was reconstructed in 1701, and a further stretch of two miles was opened in 1824.

OLDEST SUSPENSION BRIDGE

Spanning obstacles, like rivers or deep cuttings, had always involved the construction of traditional stone bridges, which supported a platform that was lifted up from the ground. However, this changed when the concept of suspending a simple platform by means of strong cables from

sturdy stanchions was developed. The oldest suspension bridge in Britain built in this way is probably the Wynch Bridge over the River Tees, which was first built in 1704 by lead miners in order to enable them to get from Newbiggin to the Holwick estate where they lived. It crosses perhaps one of the most picturesque stretches of the river, as it descends from the Pennines, which is called Low Force.

Tragedy struck at the start of the 19th century when the original bridge, which was then a century old, collapsed killing eleven people. It was not until 1830 that the present bridge was repaired using strong cables to act as support on the stanchions. Suspension bridge technology has become the principal method to span great distances, where the traditional stone or brick bridges cannot compete. The enormous number of walkers that come to view both Low Force and the more magnificent set of waterfalls further upstream, called High Force, use Wynch Bridge as a means of access. It also links with the Pennine Way, one of Britain's oldest and most popular walks.

This suspension bridge, built in 1830, replaced the original which crashed into the River Tees at Low Force. The bridge is used by walkers to reach the high moors of the Pennnine Way.

OLDEST IRON BRIDGE

Close to the town of Coalbrookdale in Shropshire is a bridge that was built out of iron in 1779. It was an incredible feat that instantly brought visitors from around the country to marvel at what could be done with cast iron. Hitherto the spans of a bridge had been opaque and stone but here was a structure carrying great weight that was partially transparent. So impressed were these people by what they saw that the place where this innovative river crossing was built became known as Ironbridge. It is the oldest iron bridge in Britain and it stands as a remarkable memorial to a period of the country's history and therefore it became known as the 'Stonehenge of the Industrial Revolution'. A crossing was needed because this part of England was rich with seams of coal that lay just beneath the surface. This valuable commodity was dug up and transported for export. The River Severn, which winds south through England to the Bristol Channel, presented an obstacle to this and there were no other crossings for some distance. The narrow gorge presented the possibility and the Shrewsbury architect, Thomas Farnolls Pritchard, suggested a bridge made from iron. An Act of Parliament was passed in March 1776 that granted leave to build and secured the viability of the project by making it unlawful to

offer a ferry service nearby. The raw materials were at hand and it is believed that the furnace at nearby Brosley provided most of the cast iron pieces. In order to make the joints strong, carpenters' skills were used and dovetail joints were cast into the molten metal under the direction of Abraham Darby. Unfortunately in 1789 the vast stone abutments started to crack and the bridge has required constant refurbishment ever since. However, the iron bridge served its purpose, and it stands as a memorial to a bold endeavour, with all the elegance of a Cathedral Church.

OLDEST BRIDGE WITH HOUSES

The London Bridge that was covered in houses has long since disappeared. It was the first in a number that once spanned the rivers of Britain. Today the oldest bridge with houses is in Lincoln and it crosses the River Witham.

The trend in bridge houses in London was the result of a call from the church for funds to build bridges. It became common practice for pious gifts to be made 'to God and the Bridge'. William II issued a call for money to rebuild the wooden bridge across the Thames in London in 1097. In 1176, Peter de Colechurch began building the first stone crossing. He was a priest and one of the Brethren of London Bridge. The structure had 19 arches and took more than 30 years to complete but it lasted nearly six centuries. Above the arches rose shops and houses, which accrued considerable revenue for the City of London – it was administered from an office in a building aptly named Bridge House. This is still one of the charities that dispenses funds on behalf of the City authorities. Sixteen years before Peter began to span the Thames, a bridge was built across the River Witham at Lincoln. When it was built in 1160 there was no plan for a house to rise above the single spanning arch of 22 feet.

It is called the High Bridge, or Glory Hole, though it has also had the misfortune of being known as the Murder Hole. Boats came to bring fresh catches from the sea and the area around the bridge became a market and focus of trading. The River Witham connected Lincoln with the sea just as the Foss Dyke, which had been cleared by Henry I, provided the city with a navigable inland link for further trading. The half-timbered houses that now sit above the High Bridge were built in 1540 and were plastered over by the Victorians. The bridge was restored at the start of the 20th century and much of the original buildings are visible once again.

OLDEST DAM

There was money to be had in coal mining. One of the lairds in Clackmannanshire who had a lot to gain was Sir John Erskine, the 6th Earl of Mar. He was a political vacillator who started as a Whig but kept changing sides and was known as 'Bobbing Joan'. He inherited the estate from his father in 1689 and sought to benefit from the minerals beneath its soil. However, he had a problem because there was bad flooding in his coalmines at Sauchie. In order to remove the water he needed power and so he directed the building of the oldest dam in Britain that is still in use.

John wanted to create a reservoir that would provide him with the necessary head of water needed to deliver power that would drive pumps and empty the mines. It was a bold project. To start with a dam had to be built, which was done by constructing a significant earthwork that incorporated a series of sluices. These delivered water from a height and at a speed sufficient to drive the wheels that generated the required power. The next challenge facing John was bringing water to the Gartmorn Dam. He built what is called a lade, which is a small canal that carried water drawn from the Black Devon and carried across

The building on High Bridge in Lincoln has been used for many purposes but both floors are now a café. The rear view is known as 'The Glory Hole'.

country. The water flowed from the dam and its overflow into the Brothie Burn and flowed towards the town of Alloa. The project was completed with total success in 1713 but the following year John was distracted from his estates by the death of Queen Anne and the invitation by Parliament to the Protestant Hanoverian Prince George to take the throne. Like many of his countrymen, John resented the incomer and set his allegiance to James VIII, otherwise known as the Old Pretender. John led the Jacobite Rebellion in 1715 but was defeated at Sherriffmuir a short distance from the dam. Rejected and without land John was exiled and died in Aix-la-Chapelle. The dam, lade and the abundant water supply was a lasting boon for Alloa.

OLDEST VIADUCT

The Nine Arches viaduct spans the Sankey Valley in a testament to patience, obstinacy and ingenuity. The Liverpool to Manchester railway now seems to be a natural step in the evolution of transport; however, when George Stephenson was appointed chief engineer of the project in 1826, he faced the inevitable opposition of Luddites. A number of objections were raised against the plan, and none more so than by the Sankey Brook Navigation Company. The Sankey Valley is 14 miles east of Liverpool and runs north-east from the course of the River Mersey. Through it the navigation company had cut a canal, called the Sankey Navigation that connected St Helens Coalfield with the Mersey and the port at Liverpool. The new railway had to cross the valley and the canal, but the navigation company insisted on a 60-foot clearance, which put an enormous logistical burden on the plan. The solution was a bend in both the railway and the Sankey Navigation, in order to reduce the acute angle between them both. It was necessary to build an enormous embankment, which required more than a hundred thousand tonnes of moss, marl and brushwood to be shifted into position by hand and simple tools. At the same time the foundations were dug deep into the valley floor. A vast hammer was brought in to drive the timber piles into the stratum, which took immense skill and patience to get right. Great sandstone slabs were quarried nearby and set on the piles as foundations for the wide brick piers, which were then built up to the required height. There are nine spans at 50 feet intervals carrying two rail tracks on a platform that is 25 feet wide. The canal was re-cut in order for its barges and boats to pass unimpeded beneath the great structure, a tradition followed by many other railway lines that would later negotiate the mountainous terrain of

Scotland and Wales. The solution found at Sankey was also exported to railroad building projects around the world, including the imperial outpost of India.

OLDEST AIRPORT

The home of the British Army has been at Aldershot since Victorian times. In 1905, the Royal Engineers needed a clear site where they could make and launch balloons. They chose a field just outside Farnborough, near to Aldershot, for the factory and cleared an airfield, which is Britain's oldest. Much of the military development of balloons and aeroplanes that took place on Farnborough's Aerodrome would be put to the test in France. This was where the Western Front's worst fighting took place and the developments from Farnborough were pitted against the Germany's air force and the ace flying of Baron von Richthofen. Unfortunately, within a generation of winning the First World War the old combatants were at war again and the developments of Farnborough were deployed to protect the nation during the Battle of Britain. Right up to 1991, when the Ministry of Defence declared that Farnborough was of no further use, it has been the location for some of the most important developments in British aeronautics, both civil and military. It is still a busy airport and also the scene of the annual Farnborough Air Show.

OLDEST AIRPORT TERMINAL

Three south coast towns decided in 1930 to pool their assets and build a terminal for the new airport at Shoreham. Work began on the art deco building in 1934 and the next year, on July 13th, Olley Air Services took over running the aerodrome and established a service for passengers, which went from Croydon in south London, stopped at Shoreham before crossing the Channel to France's Deauville airport. Little has changed since and the building is much as it was when opened by the Mayors of Hove, Worthing and Shoreham. Quickly other companies began to run services from the airport to the Channel Islands and France. Before the war, planes could not cover the distances we are used to now and therefore the facilities in terminal buildings needed to be comfortable, stylish and convenient. Looking at Shoreham today, it is difficult to realise how important it was as a stopover on the long journey to Paris. However, as its whispering gallery and spectacular window above the entrance show, the terminal building was intended to be a testament to pre-war travelling glamour. It is Britain's oldest terminal building.

Below the Stampe SV4C biplane is Shoreham Airport which has the oldest airport terminal and grass runway still in use. During World War II, air-sea rescue planes were based here. Now scheduled flights to the Channel Islands and Europe operate from Shoreham, as well as a number of flying schools.

HERITAGE

MILITARY

OLDEST COMMISSIONED WARSHIP

The greatest moment for HMS *Victory* came at the Battle
of Trafalgar, on 21st October 1805; this was after she had
already been commissioned for 27 years – she is now the
oldest warship in Britain. The first timbers were laid down
for her keel in 1759 and the plan was that she would be a
First Rate, which was the largest of warships designed for
major fleet sea battles. It took six years to build the ship,
which would displace 3,500 tonnes, was 226.6 feet long
and had a beam of just over 51 feet. *Victory* was launched in
1765 but it was not for another thirteen years that she was
commissioned into service with the Royal Navy. During
this time her timbers weathered and seasoned,
and much of this aged oak still forms part of her structure
today. There were 104 guns positioned on three decks
and the forecastle, which ranged in calibre from 12 up to
32 pounders. As Lord Nelson's flagship during that crucial
Battle of Trafalgar, her three masts carried perhaps the most
historic message that any commander has ever given before
battle, 'England expects that every man will do his duty'.
The defeat of the French and Spanish fleets halted
Napoleon's plans for invading Britain but the hero, Horatio
Nelson, was felled by a sniper's bullet. The dead admiral
was pickled in brandy and brought home to a hero's funeral
in London. He was buried directly beneath the dome of
St Paul's Cathedral in a tomb built by Cardinal Wolsey. His
memory lives in the Royal Navy, which he established as
the unbeatable ruler of the waves.

When the First Rate wooden warships were superseded by ironclads and steam propulsion, *Victory* was too
valuable to the Navy's psyche to be broken up. Instead,
she was kept in Portsmouth harbour and eventually taken
into dry dock for permanent preservation. *Victory* has
worn the colours of commissioned service since 1778,
which is now the White Ensign. The Royal Navy's ships
may decline in number with every defence review but the
Victory is too valuable for the nation to lose: its gun decks
echo with history both of Trafalgar's fame and the brutality of life for the ordinary seaman.

Victory was taken out of action in 1812, after 47 years
of action, at precisely the same age as Nelson at the time
of his death. In 1889, she became Flagship of the Second
Sea Lord, Commander in Chief Naval Home Command
and she remains his Flagship to this day. The Second Sea
Lord regularly hosts dinners in Nelson's Great Cabin and
Victory attracts around 360,000 visitors each year.

OLDEST REGIMENT

Immediately north of the City of London is Armoury
House. Its entrance is a pastiche castellated gate that opens
onto a large playing field surrounded by a skyline of city
office blocks. To this place come volunteers from those

offices to exchange their pinstripe suits for military fatigues. This is the barracks of Britain's oldest regiment, the Honorable Artillery Company. Henry VIII granted them the Charter of Incorporation in 1537 and instructed his new corps to develop their skills at the long bow, the crossbow and hand guns to 'better increase the Defence of this our Realm'. First called the Overseers of the Fraternity or the Guild of St George, their name evolved to be the Gentlemen of the Artillery Gardens, and then the Artillery Company. Finally, in 1860, Queen Victoria confirmed the prefix 'Honourable' that had been informally adopted in 1685. It was Henry's daughter, Elizabeth, who deployed them for the first time in defence of a threatened realm in 1588, when the militia marched to Tilbury and camped there in case the Spanish Armada attempted to land their ships along the Thames. Luckily, however, the Spanish ships suffered storms in the English Channel and the military threat of the fleet was dispersed . Today, the volunteers do not just practice military skills, they deploy on active service to such war zones as Iraq, Bosnia and Afghanistan, returning months later to return to their desks with a different perspective on the job at hand.

OLDEST REGIMENT OF THE LINE

The individual identity of Britain's oldest regiment is about
to be subsumed into the new Royal Regiment of Scotland.
In a pragmatic move towards force rationalisation by the
Government, the history of the Royal Scots that goes back
to 1633 will not be lost, but it will be merged with others
into the collective history of Britain's newest regiment. In
the Army, age is synonymous with seniority and therefore
the Royal Scots, known as the 'First of Foot' because they
are the oldest infantry unit, was always the senior regiment;
though the regiments of the Household Division, who are
the monarch's own troops, take technical precedence.

The Royal Scots were formed in 1633, to serve in
France under Sir John Hepburn. He recruited experienced mercenaries that had fought for the Puritan ideal
in the Thirty Years War under Gustavus Adolphus of
Sweden. The regiment was absent from Britain during the
Civil War and returned in 1661 to form the new Regular
Army, after the disbandment of Cromwell's troops. In
1680, the regiment won its first Battle Honour defending
the dowry of the king's Portuguese wife in Tangiers and
was rewarded with the title, 'The Royal Regiment of
Foot'. Perhaps the most affectionate title is the informal
one used by soldiers, who call the regiment, 'Pontius
Pilate's Body Guard'. This is because some claim that
Scots were serving in the Roman Legion that occupied
Judea at the time of Jesus Christ's crucifixion. It is not

likely that this could ever be proved, but the antiquity of
the regiment is not doubted and, like all military units,
its age is no barrier to its performance on military operations today. The Royal Scots approach amalgamation
determined to maintain the traditions of service that
were most recently demonstrated in Iraq and Bosnia.

OLDEST BATTLE HONOUR

For a military unit sent out to fight there can be no better
reward than a Battle Honour granted by the monarch. It
marks the courage of all ranks and remains with the corps
for ever. Depending on regimental traditions, Battle
Honours are displayed on flags, called Colours or
Standards, on cap badges and cast into the guns. The oldest
is borne on the standard of one of the Queen's Body
Guards. Henry VIII appointed what he called 'Gentlemen of
Noble Blod' to act as his close protection soon after coming
to the throne in 1509. Just four years later they went to
France to fight Louis XII at the Battle of the Spurs, near a
town called Guinegatte. The name Guinegatte and the date
of 1513, is embroidered into the silk Standard that is low-
ered to the Sovereign every time Parliament is opened. The
Honourable Corps of Gentlemen at Arms, as they are now
called, predated the regular Standing Army that Charles II
established in 1661, after the Restoration. That same year
the king married Catherine of Braganza and part of her
dowry was the distant town of Tangier, on the north coast

HONI·SOIT·[QUI·MAL·Y·P]ENSE.

PRINCESS OF WALES'S

QUEEN'S & ROYAL HAMPSHIRE'S

TANGIER 1662-80

GIBRALTAR 1704-5

...ILLIES

MALPLAQUET

LOUISBURG

of Africa opposite Gibraltar. Trouble at this remote outpost led Charles II to send a number of the new regiments to protect Tangier. This led to the Battle Honour, 'Tangier 1662' which is the oldest one still carried by units of the Regular Army today.

OLDEST MILITARY SYMBOL

The heraldic representation of the Paschal Lamb carrying a banner with St George's Cross is thought to be the oldest symbol to have been carried by military units into modern times. Christian soldiers have always sought the reassurance of God's support when they take up arms. It particularly took hold in Christian Europe when Pope Urban II preached the Crusade at Claremont in 1098. In calling on all Christians to take up arms to free Jerusalem, the Church legitimised military force, changing the peaceful image of Christianity for generations. The Paschal Lamb symbolises Jesus Christ. In the Bible's Gospel of St John, Christ is described as the 'Lamb of God that takes away all the sins of the world'. The word, 'Paschal' comes from the Jewish feast of Passover, when it is said that God spared the Israelites. Christ's Last Supper with his disciples is seen as a second Passover and hence the Paschal Lamb symbolises both the innocence and strength of God in his sacrificial son Jesus Christ. The power of this symbol to Christians was why the Knights Templar took it as their badge during the Crusades. Since 1241, the Paschal Lamb with its English banner of St George appeared on Templar seals. It became a popular symbol of Christ for the English. Hence, when the standing Army was established in 1661 the badge was adopted as an identity by some units. In particular the Tangier Regiment, which became the Queen's Royal West Surrey Regiment. Under the leadership of their commander, Colonel Percy Kirke, the regiment performed with abject cruelty in Tangier and later at the Battle of Sedgemoor in 1685. Ironically the Colonel's soldiers were called Kirke's Lambs. In recent times amalgamations have removed the Paschal Lamb from the semiotics of the Army but it appears on war memorials throughout England.

A fully-laid army mess table is a wonderful sight when all the silver is on display. The Queen's Royal West Surrey Regiment's centre piece – the badge of the regiment – is the Paschal Lamb. There are many old pubs on the route to Dover called The Lamb and Flag – a reminder of the days of the crusades.

OLDEST BODYGUARD

At every significant royal ceremony in England the Queen is attended by the Yeomen of the Guard, who dress in Tudor scarlet livery, with lace ruffs at the neck and wide-brimmed black hats. They form the oldest military corps in Britain, having been formed by Henry VII after the Battle of Bosworth Field in 1485. Quite possibly they are also the oldest military unit in the world. No longer a fighting force, as such, the Yeomen are recruited as an honour from former senior Non Commissioned Officers in the Royal Marines, Army and Royal Air Force.

The term Yeomen comes from a feudal social order that has long since disappeared. It defined a soldier that was junior to an esquire, who in turn was aspiring to be a knight. The first ceremony they attended was the coronation of Henry VII, on 30th October 1485, when Cardinal Bourchier was Archbishop of Canterbury. Charles II established the Regular Army in 1661, and formally recognised the Yeomen of the Guard as part of the nation's fighting force. It was as close protection for Henry VIII that they travelled with him to the Field of the Cloth of Gold, near Calais in France. The meeting between the ambitious Tudor and the capable King François of France was a significant diplomatic event. Every year the Yeomen guard the Garden Parties at Buckingham Palace and recently one of them leapt into action and vaulted the barrier to stop a protester reaching the Queen.

OLDEST MILITARY DRESS

The oldest military dress still in regular use is the tabard worn by heralds. It evolved from the simple russet garment worn by peasants in medieval times and is referred to in the prologue to Chaucer's *Canterbury Tales*. Knights adapted it in the 12th century to wear over their armour, in order to display their heraldic identity, which was embroidered into the cloth. As a result, personal armorial bearings are still called Coats of Arms today. The same unique heraldic design was painted or fixed to the knight's battle shield. Together, the tabard and shield ensured that followers could identify their knight in the chaos of battle. The king passed old or spare tabards to his heralds. This enabled them to be identified and to benefit from the special agreements that all armies observed, concerning the free passage of heralds across the battlefield. Wearing the royal tabard also made it clear under whose authority the heralds worked. Today's heralds in England and Scotland wear tabards made of silk and velvet according to their rank. They are decorated with

the monarch's quarterly Coat of Arms. In England the first and fourth quarters show England's three gold lions on a red background, which was first worn by Richard the Lionheart in 1195; the second shows the red lion rampant on a gold field for Scotland and the third quarter has Ireland's gold harp on blue. The Scottish heralds have Scotland's lion in the first and fourth quarter, with England's lions in the third, thus giving precedence to Scotland. The medieval tabard may now be a decorative garment almost totally unrelated to the military use of its origin. However, as the most historic dress to survive, it provides a direct link to the medieval period and the Age of Chivalry.

OLDEST MILITARY UNIFORM

When Henry VII dressed his new close protection corps, called the Yeomen of the Guard, in his royal scarlet livery he was establishing the first military uniform. The uniform they wear today has hardly changed. Hitherto, military forces had worn all manner of outfits and identified themselves with badges. In the Civil War, which Henry's victory at Bosworth Field in 1485 had ended, the opposing sides were identified with red and

white roses. Soldiers fighting for England would typically wear the red cross of St George and the heraldic badge of their feudal superior. This informality lasted until the start of the Civil War in 1642. The Parliamentarians recognised that their combatants looked identical to the Royalists and therefore a uniform was designed for Cromwell's New Model Army. The Commonwealth did not last and nor did the first field uniform. However, when Charles II was restored to the throne in 1660, he took no time in establishing the country's first Standing Army. The lesson had been learnt and uniforms were ordered. The royal livery of scarlet became the principal theme for the English military uniform and the country's soldiery were called Red Coats as a result. The only uniform to survive until today is the one still worn by the musicians in the Household Cavalry Mounted Band. Apart from the dark blue velvet jockey cap, which was introduced in the 19th century, the Gold Coats are still made to the original design, making it the oldest uniform still worn in the Regular Army. The king wanted the mounted band of his Life Guards to look magnificent. However he did not have the money to pay for the thick

On major state occasions, there are many uniforms on show and the oldest is that of the Heralds, seen here walking down the hill to attend the Garter Service in St George's Chapel, Windsor. The tabard evolves from the garment worn by knights over their armour, which was called a coat of arms.

gold braids and velvet. The City of London offered to
pay. No one had forgotten the City's part in Charles I's
downfall and so this gesture may have been a peace
offering. In return, the king granted the Lord Mayor of
London special permission to have the band wear State
Dress for the City's ceremonies as well.

OLDEST WAR MEMORIAL

War memorials mark villages, towns and cities in Britain,
providing a focus for the ceremonies
of Remembrance, one of the most
respected annual events that the
nation marks. Most date from the
tragic slaughter of the First World
War and carry names of families that
still live in the area. To this roll call
were added names of brothers,
sisters and children that fell soon
after, fighting the Second World War.

A few memorials survive that mark
earlier battles against France or in the
struggle to build and hold an empire.
But it seems that the oldest war
memorial is probably the window of a
parish church in Lancashire. In the
heart of the Midlands, just to the
north of Rochdale is the small village

of Middleton. From here a knight led his followers to
defend Henry VIII's England against an attack by the largest
army any Scottish king had taken to battle. It was 1513,
and the war was going badly for the English, who had
already lost four castles to James IV of Scots. It was
opportunism by James, who was married to Henry's sister
Margaret Tudor. James hoped to mediate between France
and his English brother-in-law but Henry was on the
Continent locked in warfare with the French. With Henry

away James took his chance and struck. The call to arms reached Middleton. Sir Richard Assheton responded and rode to the north with his archers, who had probably trained in the lee of St Leonard's 12th century parish church. On a wild afternoon in September 1513 he placed them on Flodden Field facing the Scots army. By the end of the day, England was victorious and the king of Scots lay dead, surrounded by the finest of his country's knights, felled by English arrows. Richard Assheton did not bring all of his archers home – their names are recorded in the stained glass of a window in the church, which portrays them kneeling there, dressed for battle and carrying their quivers and long bows. Henry VIII returned to England from his disappointing campaign to be presented with James IV's blood-soaked tunic by his wife Catherine of Aragon. In the headlines of history, this touching memorial is a reminder of the cost to small villages of the feud between England and Scotland.

OLDEST ORDER OF CHIVALRY

It is an attractive myth that Edward III was so angered by his Court when they laughed at Joan of Salisbury losing her garter on the dance floor that he picked it up, placed it

around the leg of his son, the Black Prince, and uttered the words, *'honi soit qui may y pense'* ('shame to those who think evil of it'). Whatever the truth may be, the Garter became the symbol of the order of knights that the king mustered around him in 1348, at the onset of the Hundred Years War with France. The Most Noble Order of the Garter is Britain's oldest order of chivalry and is regarded as the oldest continuous order in the world. King Edward was inspired by stories of Arthur and his Round Table. He had been born at Windsor and sought to establish there a spiritual home for the bravest knights in England. This was pragmatic because through giving the honour he also hoped to secure their loyalty. Each knight was required to take an oath in the name of God, which was something all men regarded with awe in the Middle Ages because they believed they would go to Hell if they broke the promise. The Garter is blue because this was the livery colour of French kings. Edward had defeated France at Crecy and Calais, and therefore claimed the French throne as his own. The French Coat of Arms, showing golden fleurs de lys on a dark blue background was 'quartered' with England's three gold lions on red. Around this Edward placed the buckled blue Garter, just as it appears today on the Royal

The oldest order of chivalry has evolved since it was founded by Edward III and is the sole gift of the sovereign. Here, the Queen and Prince Philip are driven back to Windsor Castle after the Garter Service in St. George's Chapel at Windsor. The Queen wears the Garter Star on her left side. All other companions wear the Badge of the Order.

Arms. Subsequent claims that Joan of Salisbury was a witch supposedly led this Christian order to take steps to protect itself from any attendant evil. The Tudors developed the order into a diplomatic tool but all political bias was finally removed when Churchill gave the right to select knights to George VI. Elizabeth II opened the order to women.

OLDEST MILITARY CEREMONY

Every evening at 10 o'clock the gates into the Tower of London are shut. This procedure is as important symbolically today as it was when the first military piquet was posted in the 11th century, in order to protect the principal bastion of royal power in the City of London. Although the Ceremony of the Keys is now an event of pageantry, it is the continuing daily observance of the oldest continuous military ritual in Britain and probably the world.

It is inconceivable that when William the Conqueror took hold of London he did not post a guard over the fortress that stood there. This would have been strengthened when Gundulf started to construct the White Tower in 1078. It still occupies the central part of the Tower of London, with its four corners topped by heraldic weather vanes. The vital sacrament of unction was so important during coronation that new monarchs sealed themselves in the Tower until all the preparations had been made at Westminster Abbey. Until the sacramental oil was administered, the monarch did not have a full grasp on power. Once anointed, God-fearing subjects did not dare to commit the terrible sin of killing a king. In 1327, Edward III moved the symbols of coronation to the Tower. They are called the Royal Regalia and consist of the vessels used for anointing, the orb, sceptres, swords and crowns. The symbolism of these objects to the state was considerable, which meant that the military guard was never relaxed. It was only in Charles II's reign that Colonel Blood attempted to rob the Tower of its Regalia and nearly succeeded.

The military guard carry out the Ceremony of the Keys every night with the Yeoman Gaoler to ensure that the gates are firmly bolted and the keys, which are called Queen Elizabeth's Keys, are handed to the Resident Governor for safekeeping. The tradition is logical and necessary and was not even interrupted at the height of the London Blitz.

OLDEST POLICE FORCE

A society is judged by its respect for the law and the maintenance of the social contract. With this in mind, it is surprising that the police force we have come to know and expect today, protecting our liberties, is a relatively modern invention.

In medieval times, order was imposed upon the people through the feudal system. At the top was the king who had his Lord High Constable to direct the army in war and to impose royal discipline throughout the country. At the bottom, each of the most lowly manorial lords also had constables of their own, to perform similar responsibilities at the local level. This is why the most junior police officer was given the rank of constable when Sir Robert Peel established the Police Force in 1829, to continue the links with an appointment that everyone recognised and respected. One of the reasons that the country needed an established police force at this time was because the feudal structure was in decline and the Industrial Revolution had attracted enormous migration into the cities. As a result, crime rates soared, and some wealthy people were compelled to establish their own squads of vigilantes to ensure security. In 1812, the first of many Parliamentary committees was established to look into a policing system – but by 1818 Lord George Cavendish could not wait. He was the third son of the fourth Duke of Devonshire and he had built an arcade of shops leading off London's Piccadilly. In order to secure the site and clear undesirable people from the area, George recruited his own security force. He looked to his old regiment, the 10th Hussars and recruited his Beadles. When what became known as the Burlington Arcade was opened in 1819, the laws of the Regency were in force and they still are.

It was not only land that needed policing. The River Thames was also dangerous as thieves ambushed merchant ships arriving at London, stealing their cargoes. In 1798, the first Chief Constable of the river and fifty petty constables formed the Marine Police Establishment, now part of the Metropolitan Police.

OLDEST GRANT OF ARMS

Heraldry is the oldest, most exclusive and decorative form of regulated personal identity in western culture. It emerged out of the need to identify knights wearing armour at tournaments and during battle. In order to regulate the system and emblems used to make each Coat of Arms different a special language developed, called blazoning. This became recognised throughout Europe and Heralds were required to regulate the science, ensure that everyone used what they were entitled to and that no new design was drawn up that looked like an existing format.

The Beadles are responsible for keeping order in Burlington Arcade, off London's Piccadilly. No running, whistling or singing has been tolerated since 1819, when they took charge so that Lady Cavendish and her friends could shop unmolested.

The way Arms were granted is through a document called a Grant of Arms. This defines the arms both through blazon and illustration. It also explains exactly who is the rightful recipient and it is engrossed with the signature and seal of the authority making the Grant.

The oldest record of a Coat of Arms in Britain dates to 1127, when Henry I of England hung a shield around the neck of his new son-in-law, Geoffrey Count of Anjou, as part of making him a knight during his marriage to his daughter, Matilda. The Worshipful Company of Drapers in the City of London holds the oldest extant Grant of Arms. In 1435, Henry VI granted powers to the company in a Charter, which gave it influence over the entire draper's craft. The Master petitioned the first Garter King of Arms, who had been appointed as the king's senior officer of Arms, for the Drapers Company to have its own Grant of Arms. William Bruges had been appointed Garter in 1415, the year of Agincourt. The Drapers Grant was engrossed on 10th March 1438.

OLDEST FUNCTIONING STATE INSTITUTION

Leadership has always been the single most natural guide to man. The monarchy has provided an evolving form of leadership since the first post-Roman king, or chief, called Vortigern in the 5th century. It is the oldest functioning state institution and was the catalyst for all the others.

In earlier times, tribal chiefs were selected by dint of their physical strength alone. This was a prerequisite in the Dark Ages, when the British Isles was made up of many separate fiefdoms that were often locked in territorial warfare. The next factor for selection was heredity. The early kings of the Heptarchy, which divided England into seven or more separate kingdoms, claimed legitimacy for consideration by proving descent from the Norse God-king called Woden. But the choice of the great men that gathered to select a ruler was still based on strength. Christianity replaced pagan legitimacy with the sacrament of unction and the missionaries recognised the importance to their plans by affirming heredity as a Godly selection.

When the country united to form England, a single monarch was chosen to hold sway. The one selected was descended from Cerdic, the first ruler of the West Saxons, who had landed on the south coast in the year 495AD. As proof of heredity, Elizabeth II can trace her lineage from Cerdic. She also counts the ancient king of the Britons,

known in nursery rhymes as Old King Cole, as one of her forebears. Others include the first monarch of a united Scotland, called Kenneth MacAlpin, many high kings of Ireland and Llewelyn the Prince of Wales. Heredity and the need to assure stability led monarchs to legislate in favour of their eldest sons succeeding, thus removing a struggle among siblings in order to capture both crown and unction first – a struggle that often plunged the country into the mayhem of interregnum.

However, the tradition of election was never completely dispensed with. Those who gather to elect in modern times are the successors of the ancient Saxon council called the Witanemegot. They are not so much free to choose as necessary to affirm the true successor according to law. The gathering, now called the Accession Council, last met the day after George VI died in February 1952 – an age of deference enriched by the figurehead of leadership provided by the king and queen. The council affirmed the new Queen, Elizabeth II, who was struggling to return from her safari trip to Africa.

Monarchy is less popular in the modern world where the individual seems to need little, let alone a national figurehead. However, the institution of monarchy that is both hereditary and constitutional, having all power and yet arguably none, still holds the majority of support. The process of government is still carried out through the person of the Sovereign and the institution of the crown. However, since the Bill of Rights in 1689 the Crown and its powers have been subject to the will of Parliament. Parliament is therefore the strongest national institution but the monarchy that gave it life is the oldest.

OLDEST ALLIANCE

It may well be something to do with the Port wine that is passed around the best tables in Britain that still keeps the old friendship alive in the 21st century – the nation has always kept true to the alliance that England signed with Portugal in 1373. It is the oldest extant Treaty in Britain and probably in the world. In many ways the two countries felt similar. They stood at the western perimeter of Europe at a time when the Atlantic was believed to be the edge of the world, short of the dragons that were believed to occupy the unknown beyond the seas.

It started with a call for help from King Ferdinand of Portugal, who had bid for the vacant throne of Castile, in Spain, but had been rejected by the Castilian nobles who

backed one of his rivals, Henry of Trastamara. Ferdinand allied himself with the Moslem Moors in order to invade Castile, but Pope Gregory XI, who had just been elected to the exiled Papacy in Avignon, intervened in the situation and suggested that Ferdinand should marry Henry's daughter. This would create an alliance and solve the dispute. Ferdinand, however, preferred his Portuguese mistress, and this infuriated Henry who then invaded and surrounded Lisbon. Ferdinand then called on England's John of Gaunt for help. John was another claimant to the Castilian throne, through his wife Constance, and he was well-connected because he was the son of Edward III. John left his daughter, Philippa of Lancaster, in Lisbon to marry the future king Joao of Portugal, and this helped to secure both the Treaty and also led to a line of successful Portuguese monarchs that guided their country into the golden age of discovery. Perhaps one of the greatest luminaries of this period of exploration was the 4th son of Joao and Philippa, who was called Henry the Navigator. The alliance between England and Portugal was confirmed in 1386, when the Treaty of Windsor was signed between Richard II of England and the Portuguese royal House of Aviz.

OLDEST STATUTE

British law claims great antiquity and rests upon legally enforceable documents that have been made by the sovereign power, called statutes. Since its development, Parliament, in concert with the sovereign, has developed legislation, in the form of statutes, which guides the courts. The judiciary must then interpret this legislation when cases are brought to court and these decisions add to the wealth of precedent that forms the law of the land.

Almost every statute that has been issued since records began can be found in the archives of the Houses of Parliament. Henry III signed the oldest of these statutes at the town of Merton in 1235. It was traditional for statutes to take the name of the place where they were signed and engrossed. Thus the Statutes of Merton were made by Henry 23 years before Baronial discontent and Civil War led to the first English Parliament (from the French word for discourse).

The Statute of Merton was principally about land. It gave lords the right to take wasteland into ownership but it also established the rights of ordinary people over shared spaces, called commons. Most villages and towns still have commons today as a result of this statute. Other

The beautiful gothic monastery in Batalha in Portugal is the site of the tomb of King Joao I of Portugal and his wife, Queen Philippa, daughter of England's Prince John of Gaunt. Their union was the basis of England's oldest alliance, which was signed in 1373.

topics covered by the 1235 statue were 'Special Barstardy', 'Damages on Writ of Dower' and 'Trespassers in Parks'. However, all of this statute has now been superseded by subsequent legislation. The oldest statute that is still extant in Britain is the Distress Act, which was part of the Statutes of Marlborough signed in 1267.

The Magna Carta is older than both the Statutes of Merton and Marlborough but it takes a later date. This is because even though King John signed Magna Carta at Runneymede in 1215, its statuary power was revoked when the Pope annulled its effect, which would have been upon the wishes of the king and therefore a sovereign act. The Magna Carta was resurrected by Edward I in 1297, when it was confirmed again in statute. This confirmation of 1297 is technically referred to as the *confirmatio cartarum* and various provisions of many articles remain part of the law today.

OLDEST LIVERY COMPANY

The City of London maintains a traditional system of livery companies that still grows to embrace new trades, like the Worshipful Company of Tax Advisors, which was approved in 2005. There are now 107 livery companies in London but the oldest of these, which is the oldest in Britain, is the Worshipful Company of Weavers.

From the very beginning as western economies developed, Europe built a trading system based on livery companies. In each country the respective head of state granted charters with responsibilities, influence and powers to these companies in order to regulate trade. But in 1789, the French Revolution overthrew the French system and in that nation's reorganisation, Napoleon Bonaparte abolished the liveries. In their place he established the Code Napoleon as a template for all trade, finance and administration. The reach of the French Grand Army carried with it this Code and as a result it is almost impossible to find guilds and liveries anywhere but in Britain.

The Weavers existed in 1130 but the first Royal Charter came from Henry II in 1155. The preamble makes reference to the Guild serving Henry I, his grandfather. The powers granted were sweeping and involved the maintenance of a monopoly, the right to punish wrongdoers and the responsibility to maintain standards. This monopoly would reach its full extent when England became the dominant influence in the textile industry between the 14th and 17th centuries. Two major waves of immigration challenged the Weavers' hold. The first was

Edward III's invitation to Flemish weavers, who set up in opposition. This destabilised the Weavers Company and led to the establishment of two further companies to share the business. The second came in the 17th and 18th centuries when the Huguenot weavers presented another threat. In each case the threat was resolved with unity and the company moved on. Much of the company's work today is in inspiring and developing the industry but it no longer enjoys the powers Henry II gave. It also distributes charitable funds. Surprisingly for the most senior livery in London, it has no Hall – after a series of misfortunes the site of the last Hall was sold off in 1962.

OLDEST EMBASSY

The international diplomatic corps probably developed from the highly effective system run from Rome by the Papal Curia, which had sent legates to all the European Royal Courts in order to keep an eye on the Church's interests. The Catholic Nunciate might have been Britain's oldest embassy had it not been for the break with Rome.

Following the example of Rome, the countries that divided the Italian peninsular during the middle ages developed a pragmatic system for diplomacy in order to co-habit during the 15th century. Perhaps the most effective of these was the wealthy Venetian republic, which had first established rules for embassies in the 13th century. Missions were sent out to England but no evidence for a formal and permanent representative can be found until 1496, soon after Henry VII took the throne, when two merchants were appointed by Venice to be sub-ambassadors in London.

The oldest embassy in London appears to be the Spanish Ambassador to the Court of St James. Doctor Roderigo Gondesalvi de Puebla arrived in England as the first Spanish ambassador in 1487. He had come to find out about the new Tudor monarch who had marched from Wales to seize the Plantagenet throne two years before. Not long after, Ferdinand of Aragon established his daughter Catherine as the first female diplomatic representative. She had married Henry VII's son, Prince Arthur, but when he died switched to become the younger son, Prince Henry's, consort. The conflict of interest she must have had as dutiful daughter and wife may have taught her the diplomatic skills to last as long as she did in a son-less marriage with Henry VIII. Nowadays, ambassadors complain that Governments all too frequently sideline the diplomatic route favouring the speed of e-mails to get answers to international questions.

Peter Afia wears the robes of the Upper Bailiff of the Worshipful Company of Weavers, in the textile warehouse of the business started by his father. The oldest livery company was formed in 1130, and its Royal Charter was granted in 1155. 'Weave with Trust' is their motto.

SYMBOLS AND STATUES

opposite

The Master of Lauderdale, Viscount Maitland, the Hereditary Bearer of the National Flag of Scotland, stands on Salisbury Crags above the Palace of Holyroodhouse in Edinburgh.

below right

The red triangle used by Bass on its beer products is the oldest trade mark. It may have originated in the late 18th century on casks sent to Russia. A bottle of Bass appears in Manet's 'A Bar at the Folies-Bergere' and the beer is still exported worldwide.

OLDEST FLAG

The Union Flag dates from 1801, when the third Act of Union brought Ireland into the United Kingdom of England and Scotland. The second Act of Union in 1707 had united England with Scotland, and the first united the Principality of Wales into England, in 1535. It is the combination of three crosses, which represent the patron saints of each kingdom. The oldest of these flags is Scotland's white cross of St Andrew on a light blue background. St Andrew was one of Christ's disciples, the brother of St Peter. It is believed that he was crucified by order of the Roman Governor of Patrae in Achaia, during the time of Emperor Nero; possibly on 30th November in the year 60AD. He was bound, not nailed, to a decussate cross, in order to increase his suffering. A missionary, called St Rule, brought some relics of St Andrew to Scotland. He landed on the east coast and the place has been called St Andrews ever since. The saint was buried in Italy at the church of Amalfi but this landfall of the saint's bones impressed the newly converted Christians among the Pictish and Scottish people.

In 832, not long before Scotland became united, Angus MacFergus, the High King of Alba, faced the Northumbrian army at Athelstanford in Lothian. As he prayed, so the story goes, St Andrew appeared to him in a vision. The next morning, above the battlefield, clouds formed in the shape of a great white decussate cross against the blue sky. This gave the troops courage and rallied them to victory. The blue flag with its white saltire cross became the identity of

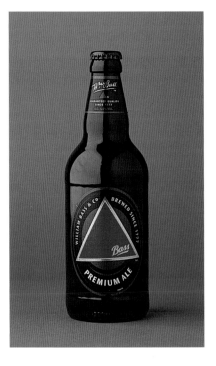

Scotland, which makes it the oldest by far. England's red cross of St George has been used since the 12th century, but it was in the 14th century that Edward III adopted the saint as England's patron.

In order to combine the red cross of England in 1707 with the flag of Scotland, the blue had to be darker. The union with Ireland in 1801, presented heralds with a further problem because St Patrick was not identified by a symbolic cross. One was invented. Inspiration came from the FitzGerald family Coat of Arms. One of Ireland's oldest Norman families, the red saltire on white would fit perfectly into the existing design. However, in order not to extinguish Scotland's position in the union, a compromise was reached. In the 'hoist' or senior side of the flag, the white cross would appear uppermost, whereas in the 'fly' the red of Ireland would take precedence. The Union Flag is often called the 'Union Jack', however, this name should only be used if the flag flies from the Jack Mast, which is the one at the front, or bow, of a Royal Navy warship.

OLDEST TRADE MARK

Somewhere in the rusting hold of the SS *Titanic* will be crates of Bass Pale Ale that were loaded onto the superliner before its fateful trip to New York. Bass beer has been an established product since 1777, when William Bass started brewing in Burton-upon-Trent and marked his bottles and barrels with a red triangle. It was even rumoured that Napoleon intended to build a brewery in France soon after defeating Britain and that Buffalo Bill served it to his visitors. With such a history and reputation there is little surprise that the red triangle symbol, which is on every bottle of Bass Pale Ale, is the oldest trade mark in Britain and probably the world. This is empiric because a Bass employee went to great lengths to make it so. He slept on the street outside the Registrar's office on New Year's Eve in order to be the first to register when trade mark registration began on 1st January 1876. The previous year, the Trading Registration Act had been passed through Parliament, during Benjamin Disraeli's second administration. The Act was intended

The Black Watch, wearing Government No. 1 Tartan, the oldest formal tartan, on parade at Fort George near Inverness. The Scottish regiments are to be amalgamated and which tartan they will use has yet to be decided. However, the Black Watch tartan will still be the background of their rank slides and will be used for the bags of the pipes.

to control the use of specific marks on products to protect both the customer and the trader from fraud. At the same time, the Bass employee registered a red diamond, which has been used on other brews. The simplicity of the red triangle set above the Bass logo has been protected ever since and is recognised around the world. The beer even almost reached the South Pole with Sir Ernest Shackleton's expedition of 1914–1916.

OLDEST FORMAL TARTAN

In August 1822, George IV visited Scotland, the first monarch to do so for nearly 200 years. Just forty years before this, tartan, which had been illegal since 1747, was legalised once more. This royal visit awoke an enthusiasm for not only tartan itself but also for the symbolic power of association that tartan provided with clans, and a history that had all but disappeared in the reforms that followed the Jacobite rebellion. The architect of this revival was the romantic historian Sir Walter Scott. Tartans themselves had gained recognisable form only in the 18th century. Jamie Scarlet, the authority on tartans, explains this evolution, 'Tartan was first a cloth, it then developed a pattern and then this became a meaningful pattern'. These patterns evolved when it was required that the independent companies of the Government army should devise some uniformity in their plaid. The clans of the 45 Rebellion followed this lead for their regiments. 'There are some very old fragments of Fraser of Altyre', says Jamie Scarlet, 'but perhaps the Mackintosh could be argued as the oldest because many tartans evolved from this design'. Some argue that the Black Watch tartan, still worn by the Scottish regiment of that name, is the oldest. This was one of the earlier Government tartans that survived when tartan was outlawed after the battle of Culloden. It may well have evolved from a much older sett.

OLDEST EFFIGY

Queen Elizabeth II has one of the most recognised faces in the world today. Like her forebears, she has been promoted on coinage, also on postage stamps but most effectively in the endless media coverage and public interest that follows the nature of a monarch's position. Medieval rulers were hardly recognised by those they ruled and we can only guess what the Norman kings looked like. However, when Edward III died at Sheen in 1377, a likeness was made directly from his corpse that is now the oldest effigy in Britain. At a cost of twenty-two

pounds four shillings and eleven pence, according to the king's Wardrobe Account, Stephen Hadley was commissioned to make 'an image in the likeness of the king'. He was given just 24 hours to achieve this, in Westminster, on the day before the funeral. This cannot have been a peaceful time to work, whilst the monks made funeral preparations, and knights that fought for Edward at Crecy and Calais in 1346 visited to view the great ruler of the Age of Chivalry. The image, which is just one and a half inches short of six foot in length, would have rested on the royal coffin during the obsequies. It was crafted from hollowed-out walnut. Recent research has identified evidence of plaster around the face, which suggests that the image was made from a death mask moulded directly from Edward's face. Close inspection of the mouth shows a drop on one side, which could be evidence of the stroke that killed the 64-year-old monarch. His tomb is close to the sacred site of Edward the Confessor's shrine, behind the High Altar in the abbey. It is surmounted by a bronze effigy, which is similar to the walnut one but with stylised hair, beard and with all the royal regalia. The walnut effigy looks bare today because the hair has long disappeared. Water damage caused during the Second World War deteriorated the effigy. As it dried some of the paint that illuminated the face peeled and chipped away. The effigy is kept at Westminster Abbey, along with others crafted from the corpses of monarchs brought there for burial. There is no better place to see the faces that created the history of England and directly influenced the lives of most British ancestors.

OLDEST BRONZE STATUE

On the 30th January every year a band of committed monarchists gather in Trafalgar Square at the foot of the oldest bronze statue in Britain to remember a royal martyr. Not only is the statue of Charles I remarkable because of its age, it is also significant because of where it is placed and why. It was the first equestrian statue of a king and it symbolically linked his status with the majesty of Roman emperors. It was cast in 1633 by the French sculptor, Hubert le Sueur, for the Earl of Portland's garden in Roehampton. After the execution of Charles on 30th January 1649, the statue was sold to St Paul's Church, in Covent Garden. In the following year there was an outcry against royal memorials and this statue was given to a brazier in Holborn, called John Rivett, who was instructed to melt it down. Rivett did no such thing – he buried it in his garden and pretended that the bronze trinkets he sold to Parliamentarians or distraught Royalists came from the statue. The same outcry caused the destruction of the medieval memorial, called Charing Cross, which Edward I had built where the statue now stands. It was one of 12 crosses marking the stages in the funeral procession, in 1290, of his queen Eleanor, who was brought from Nottinghamshire for burial in Westminster. The memorial standing today outside Charing Cross railway station is a copy. After the Restoration, the statue was dug up and bought by Charles II. The king pardoned all but the men who actually tried and sentenced his father. They were put on trial, sentenced and executed on the old site of Charing Cross. It was therefore an act of deliberate irony when, in 1675, Charles II placed his father's statue on this spot. It replaced a lost royal memorial, marked a victory over adversity and gave Charles I a heroic view down Whitehall to the place he met his own execution. His martyrdom is annually honoured at this place, from which all distances to London are measured.

OLDEST LEAD STATUE

Britain's oldest lead statue stands between Parliament House and St Giles' Kirk, in Edinburgh. The site was originally meant to have a statue of Oliver Cromwell, the Lord Protector who established union between Scotland and England during the Commonwealth. However, the manner in which this was achieved did not please all Scots. The execution of Charles I in 1649 horrified Scotland. Even those most committed to the king's downfall baulked at regicide. He was a Stuart and a Scot, after all, and the idea of such a violent end to God's anointed was unsettling. Immediately the Scots proclaimed his son Charles II as king. But Cromwell wooed back support by offering a solution to the long battle of Christian presbyters who wanted a Church free of bishops chosen by the king. However, having made promises to gain support, Cromwell broke them and he then squashed all resistance to him and support of the king with violent military rule in Scotland. As the Commonwealth lost credibility, the exiled Charles II in turn hinted at freedoms for the Scottish presbyters in order to gain support. But this too was soon forgotten soon after he reclaimed his throne in 1660. The planned statue for Cromwell was cancelled. In its place, Edinburgh erected the first lead statue to their absentee monarch in 1685, the year Charles II died and his Catholic brother became James VII. The statue is known in the city as 'Two-faced Charlie',

either because of the second face shown on his armour buckle or because of the way he lied to gain support from Scottish presbyters. The union Cromwell established with England dissolved with Charles II, only to be reinstated in 1707 by Queen Anne, the last Stuart monarch. Now that desire for the end of union is alive once more.

OLDEST ALUMINIUM STATUE

There is an old wives' tale that if you walk around the statue at Piccadilly Circus, affectionately referred to as 'Eros', the god of love, lust and sex, then you will be rewarded during the night that follows. This is hardly an edifying reflection on the high-minded purpose for the memorial. It was erected to mark the philanthropic life of Anthony Cooper, the 7th Earl of Shaftesbury, who was a champion of factory reform in the 19th century. He was largely responsible for three Factory Acts between 1847 and 1859, the Coal Mines Act of 1842 and the Lunacy Act in 1845. He also championed the work of Florence Nightingale and strived for the welfare of children in poverty. In 1893, his memorial was placed in the middle

Eros, surely one of the most photographed statues in the world, stands in Piccadilly Circus, London.

of Piccadilly Circus. Sir Alfred Gilbert was commissioned to fashion the design and he cast it in aluminium, which had been done only once before. He modelled the Angel of Christian Charity. But a naked statue was revolutionary in Victorian London and the excited public re-named him Eros. The statue was originally in the middle of the Circus with the angel aiming his bow to the north, up Shaftesbury Avenue. However, during the Second World War it was removed for safety. After hostilities, the entire memorial was moved from the centre to the southern side of the Circus. Then Eros was put back but was mistakenly placed

pointing the wrong way. More insult was to come; in 1994 a drunk clambered up and bent the figure.

The Science Museum in London has on loan the oldest aluminium cast statue in the world from the Aluminium Federation, one of its sponsors. The statue is affectionately known as 'Diane' in the Louvre, named after the original 2.25m marble statue, Diane de Gabies. It is thought that the aluminium version, which stands at a third of the original's height, dates back to between 1858 and 1860 and, therefore, predates Eros by over 30 years. This also makes it one of the oldest pieces of aluminium in existence.

OLDEST STONE STATUE

Geologists regard chalk as a stone. Therefore the very rare and tremendously rough human forms carved from chalk in Neolithic times represent the oldest stone statues in Britain. Dating them is almost impossible and some academics who cover this period question the provenance of a few examples that have come to light.

The oldest of these chalk statues may have come from Grimes Caves in Norfolk, which was a series of flint mines for the nation's earliest settlers. The statue is now in the British Museum and called the Chalk Goddess. It is rotund and crudely made but not unlike smaller examples of a similar kind that had been discovered at the prehistoric site at Maiden Castle in Devonshire. The archaeologist, Leslie Armstrong, discovered the Chalk Goddess in 1939, but some think that it was made by his workforce to trick their master. While it is possible to date stone it is not easy to assess when it was worked into a certain shape. The oldest stone statue may yet need some further developments in science for proof to be empiric. Iron Age or Roman statues, which once stood as deities and celebrations of great people, are now in museums or yet to be discovered.

OLDEST HERALDIC BEAST

Heraldry is the oldest, most exclusive and decorative form of regulated personal identity in western culture. It is everywhere: on school buildings, council offices, great castles and forms the letterhead of most institutions. The science of heraldry evolved slowly as it became necessary to identify knights when they were obscured by armour. Naturally, the strongest and most influential warriors sought to be identified with powerful beasts. The first of these was the lion and therefore it is the oldest heraldic beast. When Henry I of England created Geoffrey of Anjou a knight, in 1128 at Rouen, the monarch placed a shield around his neck with six golden lions. This is the oldest reference to heraldry that survives and it defines the use of lions. Geoffrey married Matilda of England and their son became Henry II. Lions had been used as symbols of power in the Roman Empire and had been used in the semiotics of all the ancient civilisations. As the beast of preference, it was adopted by most European royal states. Richard the Lionheart first adopted England's three golden lions on a red background for his Coat of Arms in 1195. Scotland's king William the Lion reigned from 1165 until 1214, and it is assumed that he first adopted the golden shield with a red lion rampant, which means rearing up on its hind legs. The Princes of Wales had lions as did the Princes of Leon. Today the Danish and Norwegian monarchs have lions. Nowadays, requests for lions in Coats of Arms are invariably turned down because there are no original ways to display the beast that have not been used already.

The lion at Hampton Court. The entrance to Cardinal Wolsey's Palace is flanked by 10 heraldic creatures. They carry the shields of the Royal Houses of Britain and are known as 'The Queen's Beasts'.

REFERENCE

PLACE
LOCATOR

Use this map and the key on the following pages
to explore Britain's cultural heritage.

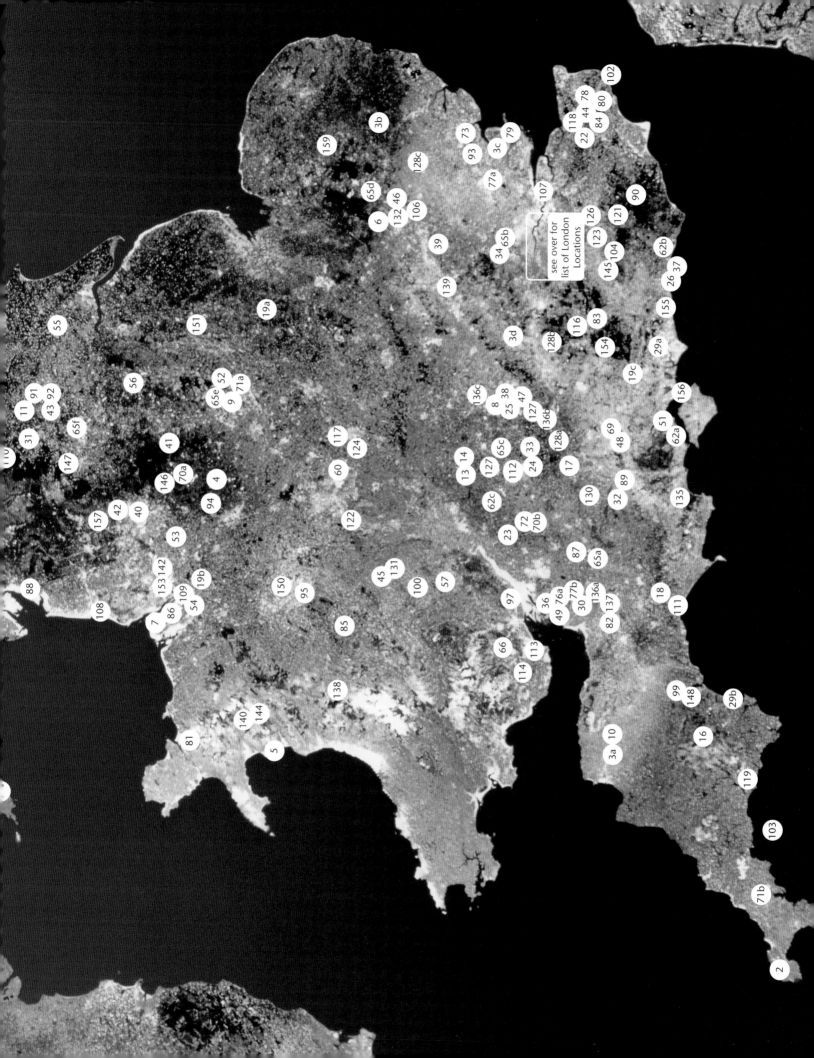

see over for list of London Locations

KEY

NATURE

LANDSCAPE

ANIMALS

TREES

SOCIETY

PEOPLE

ARTS

CHARITIES

EDUCATION

SPORT

PUBS AND INNS

FAIRS

BUILDINGS

PEOPLE AND BUILDINGS

STRUCTURES

COMMERCE

SHOPS

BUSINESSES

pages 214 and 215 The Caledonian Forest between Glen Affric and Loch Beinn a' Mheadhoin (see page 34).

INDEX

ACKNOWLEDGEMENTS

JULIAN CALDER: This book would not have been possible without the help of all the people who contributed and who understood it takes time to make a picture. As a photographer, you always hope people will say 'Yes, I think we can arrange that.' It often requires extra work from those involved and I am very grateful.

My thanks to everyone (in the order in which they appear in the book): The Forestry Commission; The National Trust; Dr. Mark Horton, Archeology Dept. Bristol University; John MacLennan at the Stornoway Harbour Commission; Richard O'Brien at Birkenhead Park; Louise Allen at the Oxford Botanical Gardens; Sue and Nigel Cowgill of the Cleveland Bay Society; Alex Anderson, the Achnalloich Herd, Oban; Jim and Alan Henson at the Cotswold Farm Park; Pat Meecham of the Welsh Terrier Owners' Society; John Stokes of the Tree Council; Farmer Richard Blanchard; Nicholas Burton; Simon and Joan Fawcus; Sarah Willams at Lambeth Palace; Dr Emma-Jane Lamont, Curator of the National Fruit Collection; The Livingstone Family of Lismore; Professor Daniel Bradley at Trinity College Dublin; Colm Rooney, historian of the de Ros family; Nicholas Bates at St Alban's Cathedral; Clare Drakley and Jane Pritchard of the Rambert Dance Company; Margaret Reid at Dulwich Picture Library; Colonel Malcolm Torrent of the Royal Artillery Band; Mrs S.M. Meikle and the pupils of King's School Canterbury; Alastair Land and the pupils of Winchester College; Graham Hart of Southampton Bowling Club; Fran Cotton of Blackheath Rugby Club; Verity Green at Chester Races; Bridget Till of the Sinington Hunt; Tony Cuthbert and Ken Davy of Notts County Football Club; Andrew McKechanie member of the Musselborough Golf Club; Kathryn Morrison and Andrew Davison of English Heritage; David Stapleton at the George Inn; Jonathan Montagu–Pollock of Wadworth Brewery; Mike McCarthy in Scarborough; Trudi Williamson, Managing Director of Isle of Man Newspapers; David Howard of Isle of Man Transport; Lt. General Michael Willocks KCB, Gentleman Usher of the Black Rod; Hedley Duncan Yeoman Usher; The Rev. Robert Dixon in Etchingham; Henry Button of the Tercentenarian Club; Joan Ringrose of Durtnell and Sons; Kieth and Gloria Tordoff the Sweetshop Pateley Bridge; The Balson family in Bridport; Robert Reavley in Burford; The Lobb family in St. James's; Joanna Broughton at Trufitt and Hill; Simon Hoare, Hoares Bank; Dr. Kevin Clancy and Graham Dyer at the Royal Mint; Jonathan Neame of Shepherd Neame; P.V. Mitchell and Megan Anderson of Somers Forge Ltd; John Roots in Hungerford; John Schofield at English Heritage; Barry Cox and John West of the RNLI; Paul Lewin at Ffestiniog Railway; Captain Mark Little of Fast Helicopters; Mike Chapman of the Real Flying Company in Shoreham; Dr. David Allan FSA; Kate Patfield at HM Navel Base Portsmouth; Lieutenant Commander Frank Nowosielski of HMS Victory; Major Erica Bridge RA; Captain Adam Rout PWRR; The Rev. Canon Nick Feist of Middleton Church; Captain Neil Tomlin, The Black Watch; Jamie Scarlet MBE.

Thanks, of course, to everyone who appears in the pictures and to Ken Sethi and Joe Thomas at Genesis for photo preparation; my assistants – Paul Gregory and Sarah Bailey; to Louise Millar and Duncan Soar for helping with the research; to Austin Taylor for making the book look so good and to John Mitchinson and Michael Dover for commissioning it; to Charles Harington, Britain's oldest living General, for his help, encouragement and enthusiasm and lastly my biggest thanks go to Clare, Sam and Rory without whose help, understanding and support, it would not be possible to do these type of projects.

ALASTAIR BRUCE: It would not have been possible to complete the research required for this book without the support of many people. Firstly, a large number of the people directly associated with the oldest things in this collection and, secondly, the authorities in so many areas of British life that gave provenance to the assessment as to which was the oldest in each category – no matter what we looked at there was generally an association, club or expert prepared to affirm which was the oldest of the old. Most of these names have been highlighted in Julian's list. As far as researching the information in order to write the book, I would like to thank the librarians and staff at the London Library, the British Library, the Guildhall Library in the City of London, Winchester County Library and the Imperial War Museum. In addition, I would like to thank my colleagues, the heralds, at the College of Arms in London for their encouragement; the people I work with at Sky News (especially for the research help given by Maggie Cammiss and the team in the News Library); the officers in the Media Operations Group (Volunteers), which is the Territorial Army unit it is my privilege to command – many have given me assistance in some form or other while I struggled to meet my deadline. I am grateful for the patience that Robin Douglas-Withers, Julie Delf and Anna Cheifetz at Cassell Illustrated, especially when Pope John Paul II died, causing my delivery of text to be interrupted by broadcasting events in Rome for Sky News. Above all I would like to thank Stephen Knott for his support with my research and extend love and thanks to all my family, particularly my parents Henry and Vernon, who are my best critics, for their endless support. Finally, well done Julian for having the idea in the first place.

First published in Great Britain in 2005
by Cassell Illustrated,
a division of Octopus Publishing Group Limited,
2–4 Heron Quays, London E14 4JP

Photography and captions copyright
© Julian Calder 2005, with the exception of
the satellite image on pages 216–217 which is reproduced by permission of Maptec International
Ltd/Science Photo Library
Text copyright © Alastair Bruce 2005
Design copyright © Cassell Illustrated 2005

A CIP catalogue record for this book is available from the British Library.

Managing Editor: Anna Cheifetz
Editor: Robin Douglas-Withers
Copy Editor: Julie Delf
Designer: Austin Taylor

ISBN 1 84403 080 6
EAN 9781844030804

Printed in China

OLDEST ROCK FORMATION • OLDEST LAND MANAGEMENT • OLDEST HED
PARKLAND • OLDEST NATURE RESERVE • OLDEST MUNICIPAL PARK • OLDEST BO
ROYAL PARK • OLDEST NATIVE • OLDEST BREED OF HORSE • OLDEST HERD OF C
OLDEST PIG BREED • OLDEST SHEEP BREED • OLDEST DOG BREED • OLDEST C
OLDEST OAK • OLDEST YEW • OLDEST DOUGLAS FIR • OLDEST APPLE TREE • OLD
• OLDEST ELM TREES • OLDEST MULBERRY • OLDEST ARBORETUM • OLDEST VIN
EVIDENCE • OLDEST SCOTTISH CLAN • OLDEST BURIAL GROUND • OLDEST VIS
SAINT • OLDEST DANCE COMPANY • OLDEST MUSIC HALL • OLDEST THEATRE •
OLDEST ORGAN • OLDEST BRASS BAND • OLDEST HYMN • OLDEST ENGLISH LAN
SOCIETY • OLDEST CHORAL SOCIETY • OLDEST HUMAN RIGHTS ORGANISA
CONVENT • OLDEST SCHOOL • OLDEST GRAMMAR SCHOOL • OLDEST CAMBRI
GIRLS SCHOOL • OLDEST SPORTING CLUB • OLDEST SPORTING TROPHY • OLDE
GROUND • OLDEST FOOTBALL CLUB • OLDEST FOOTBALL GROUND • OLDEST RA
• OLDEST POLO RACE OLDEST FOXHOUND PACK • OLDEST GOLF CLUB • OLD
SWIMMING POOL • OLDEST SWIMMING CLUB • OLDEST YACHT CLUB • OLDEST H
• OLDEST INN IN SCOTLAND • OLDEST PUB SIGN • OLDEST HOTEL • OLDEST FAIR
OLDEST COLONY • OLDEST BUILDINGS • OLDEST PARLIAMENT • OLDEST INHAE
OLDEST SAXON CHURCH • OLDEST ROMAN CHURCH • OLDEST DIOCESE • OLDE
ROYAL • OLDEST COUNCIL HOUSE • OLDEST PUBLIC LIBRARY • OLDEST BATHS •
BOX • OLDEST BRASS WEATHER VANE • OLDEST CLOCK • OLDEST PUBLIC LAW
OLDEST WOODEN BUILDING • OLDEST WOODEN-FRAMED BUILDING • OLDEST
CASTLE • OLDEST FORTIFICATION • OLDEST MUNICIPAL BUILDING • OLDEST S
OLDEST LIGHTHOUSE AT SEA • OLDEST CASTLE • OLDEST DOOR • OLDEST IR
BUTCHERS • OLDEST CHEESE SHOP • OLDEST WINE MERCHANT • OLDEST CHEM
MAKER • OLDEST BOOKSHOP • OLDEST RECORD SHOP • OLDEST BARBERS' OL
OLDEST COMPANY • OLDEST PATENT • OLDEST ROYAL WARRANT HOLDERS
DISTILLERY • OLDEST DISTILLERY • OLDEST LAWYERS • OLDEST FORGE • OLDEST
BUILDERS • OLDEST SHIPPING COMPANY • OLDEST FILM STUDIOS • OLDEST IN
RATE PAYER • OLDEST NEWSPAPER • OLDEST SUNDAY NEWSPAPER • OLDEST REC
OLDEST MAGAZINE FOR WOMEN • OLDEST LIFEBOAT STATION • OLDEST PA
OLDEST STREET • OLDEST ROAD IN WALES • OLDEST ROUNDABOUT • OL
• OLDEST PUBLIC RAILWAY • OLDEST INTERCITY RAILWAY • OLDEST RAILWAY
CABLE TRAMWAY • OLDEST CANAL • OLDEST SUSPENSION BRIDGE • OLDEST
VIADUCT • OLDEST AIRPORT • OLDEST AIRPORT TERMINAL • OLDEST CO
OLDEST BATTLE HONOUR • OLDEST MILITARY SYMBOL • OLDEST BODYG
MEMORIAL • OLDEST ORDER OF CHIVALRY • OLDEST MILITARY CEREMONY
• OLDEST ALLIANCE • OLDEST STATUTE • OLDEST LIVERY COMPANY • OLDE
• OLDEST BRONZE STATUE • OLDEST EFFIGY • OLDEST LEAD STATUE • OL